Ten Questions to Ask before Accepting a Job Offer with Stock Options

- One big catch-all question: How many shares, what is the strike price, and what is the vesting schedule?
- What kind of stock options — incentive, nonqualified, or a combination of both?
- Can I please see a copy of the stock option agreement that I'll be asked to sign?
- Can I also please see a copy of the company's stock option plan document?
- Have there been any changes in your company's stock option plan in the past 12 to 18 months?
- (If you're considering a pre-IPO company) What is the currently planned date or time frame for an IPO?
- What percentage of the company's total ownership do the shares on my stock option represent?
- When can I next anticipate receiving another stock option grant, and under what circumstances? (An annual grant? When I'm promoted? As a bonus? Merit-based?)
- (If you're considering a company that is already publicly traded) What has been the stability of employees who have big stock option gains — have most stayed or moved on?
- Are there any tax implications right now for my stock option grant?

Stock Options Web Sites You Must Visit

- MyStockOptions.com
- MyOptionValue.com
- StockOptionsCentral.com
- www.Stock-Options.com
- MyInternetOptions.com
- www.nceo.org

Stock Options For Dummies®

Cheat Sheet

Signs the Value of Your Stock Options Could be in Trouble

- A revolving door management team
- A disinterested friends-and-investors dominated Board of Directors
- A big jump in employee turnover rates
- Rose-colored glasses syndrome
- High levels of customer dissatisfaction
- Poor internal systems and infrastructure
- Inconsistent communication from management
- Open talk among employees about leaving
- A general sense of panic

Signs the Value of Your Stock Options Could Grow

- A steadily growing company
- A highly-qualified and motivated management team
- An active and interested Board of Directors
- Low employee turnover rates
- Market-leading products or services
- Returning, happy customers
- Solid, functional infrastructure
- Empowered employees
- Thorough training programs for new employees

Wiley, the Wiley Publishing logo, For Dummies, the Dummies Man logo, the For Dummies Bestselling Book Series logo and related trade dress are trademarks or registered trademarks of John Wiley & Sons, Inc. and/or its affiliates in the United States and other countries and may not be used without written permission. All other trademarks are the property of their respective owners. Wiley Publishing, Inc., is not associated with any product or vendor mentioned in this book.

For Dummies: Bestselling Book Series for Beginners

Stock Options
FOR
DUMMIES®

by Alan Simon

Wiley Publishing, Inc.

Stock Options For Dummies®

Published by
Wiley Publishing, Inc.
111 River St.
Hoboken, NJ 07030
www.wiley.com

For general information on our other products and services or to obtain technical support, please contact our Customer Care Department within the U.S. at 800-762-2974, outside the U.S. at 317-572-3993, or fax 317-572-4002.

Wiley also publishes its books in a variety of electronic formats. Some content that appears in print may not be available in electronic books.

Library of Congress Control Number: 00-112156

ISBN: 0-7645-5364-X

Manufactured in the United States of America

10 9 8 7 6 5 4

1B/QX/QV/QR/IN

About the Author

Alan Simon is a computer consultant, author of 26 books (including *Data Warehousing For Dummies*), and farmer. He has held a number of executive positions in technology consulting firms, and has been a computer professional since the late 1970's. His extensive experiences with his own stock options — sometimes painful experiences — have provided him with an objective, no-hype perspective of stock options that he imparts in this book.

Alan lives on a farm in Northeastern Pennsylvania.

Author's Acknowledgments

I'd like to thank the editors with whom I worked on this project including Jonathan Malysiak, Keith Peterson, and Suzanne Thomas for their valuable assistance with this book. I would also like to thank Matt Wagner of Waterside Productions. Jay Klapper, Keren Hamel, and Scott Temares provided valuable assistance with stock option anecdotes and experiences. I would also like to thank Bruce Brumberg of MyStockOptions.com; Wade Williams of MyOptionValue.com; Thomas Grady of StockOptionsCentral.com; and Dale Krieger of Stock-Options.com.

Publisher's Acknowledgments

We're proud of this book; please send us your comments through our Dummies online registration form located at www.dummies.com/register/.

Some of the people who helped bring this book to market include the following:

Acquisitions, Editorial, and Media Development

Project Editor: Keith Peterson

Acquisitions Editors: Mark Butler, Jon Malysiak

Copy Editor: Suzanne Thomas

Acquisitions Coordinator: Lauren Cundiff

Technical Editor: Sandra Sussman

Editorial Manager: Pam Mourouzis

Editorial Assistant: Carol Strickland

Cover Image: © Scott Barow/Imagestate 2005

Composition

Project Coordinator: Dale White

Layout and Graphics: Joe Bucki, Heather Pope, Jeremey Unger

Proofreaders: David Faust, TECHBOOKS Production Services

Indexer: TECHBOOKS Production Services

Publishing and Editorial for Consumer Dummies

   Diane Graves Steele, Vice President and Publisher, Consumer Dummies

   Joyce Pepple, Acquisitions Director, Consumer Dummies

   Kristin A. Cocks, Product Development Director, Consumer Dummies

   Michael Spring, Vice President and Publisher, Travel

   Brice Gosnell, Associate Publisher, Travel

   Suzanne Jannetta, Editorial Director, Travel

Publishing for Technology Dummies

   Andy Cummings, Vice President and Publisher, Dummies Technology/General User

Composition Services

   Gerry Fahey, Vice President of Production Services

   Debbie Stailey, Director of Composition Services

◆

The publisher would like to give special thanks to Patrick J. McGovern, without whom this book would not have been possible.

◆

Contents at a Glance

Introduction 1

Part 1: The Fundmentals of Stock Options 9
Chapter 1: Stock Options: What You Need to Know Right Off the Bat 11
Chapter 2: Taking Your Chances: Getting Rich or Going Broke................................27
Chapter 3: Knowing What Kind of Stock Option Situation Is Best for You...............43
Chapter 4: The Big Guys and The Big Picture..57

Part 11: Details, Details: What You Must Know about Your Stock Options 71
Chapter 5: Deciphering the Legal Language of Stock Option Agreements 73
Chapter 6: Exercising Your Stock Options 93
Chapter 7: Differentiating Pre-IPO and Post-IPO Stock Options 105
Chapter 8: No Trading Allowed! Lockups and Blackout Periods 119
Chapter 9: Finding Stock Option Information Online 125

Part 111: Money! 131
Chapter 10: Determining What Your Stock Options Are Really Worth 133
Chapter 11: Stock Options and Your Overall Portfolio..147

Part 1V: Pay Up! Taxes and Stock Options 163
Chapter 12: Understanding the Basics of Taxes and Stock Options........................165
Chapter 13: Nonqualified Stock Options and Taxes..177
Chapter 14: Incentive Stock Options and Taxes 199

Part V: Changes and Special Circumstances................217
Chapter 15: The Alternative Minimum Tax and Stock Options 219
Chapter 16: Acquiring or Being Acquired: Dealing with Corporate Change...........225
Chapter 17: Trying to Predict What Will Happen to Your Stock Options................239
Chapter 18: Leaving Your Job: What Happens to Your Stock Options? 251

Part VI: The Part of Tens 267

Chapter 19: Special Stock Option Circumstances 269
Chapter 20: Ten Signs That Your Stock Options Will Be Worth a Lot! 285
Chapter 21: Ten Signs That Your Stock Options Will Probably Be *Worthless!* 291
Chapter 22: Ten Things to Look for in Your Stock Option Agreement 297

Index 301

Cartoons at a Glance

By Rich Tennant

"I read about investing in a company called UniHandle Ohio, but I'm uneasy about a stock that's listed on the NASDAQ as UhOh."

page 71

PHIL HARRISON VISITS HIS TAX ATTORNEY

"The new tax law goes on to say that '...all taxpayers shall be exempt from these extra charges except...', and this is the part that bothers me Phil, '...except for Phillip Harrison of 120 Colby Ave, Patterson, New Jersey."

page 163

"And just how long did you think you could keep that pot o'gold at the end of the rainbow a secret from us, Mr. O'Shea?"

page 267

"Perhaps you'd like to buy these magic beans, or this charm that will give you good luck, or this stock that promises a 200% return on your investment in less than 18 months."

page 9

"SELL."

page 131

"I've never been good at this part of the job which is why I've asked 'Buddy' to join us. As you know, business has been bad lately, and well, Buddy has some bad news for you..."

page 217

Cartoon Information:
Fax: 978-546-7747
E-Mail: richtennant@the5thwave.com
World Wide Web: www.the5thwave.com

Table of Contents

Introduction 1

Why I Wrote This Book: The Lessons of 1999 and 2000 1
Who Needs to Read This Book? 3
How to Use This Book 3
How This Book Is Organized..4
    Part I: The Fundamentals of Stock Options......................4
    Part II: Details, Details: What You Must Know
      About Your Stock Options 5
    Part III: Money! 5
    Part IV: Pay Up! Taxes and Stock Options......................6
    Part V: Changes and Special Circumstances 6
    Part VI: The Part of Tens....................................6
Icons Used in This Book...7

Part 1: The Fundmentals of Stock Options 9

Chapter 1: Stock Options: What You Need to Know Right Off the Bat 11

Understanding Stock Option Basics 11
    Knowing what stock options are.................................12
    Knowing how stock options work 13
Exercising Your Stock Option(s) 15
Understanding the Right Nature of Your Stock Options 19
Comparing Stock Options to Actual Shares of Stock...............20
Granting Stock Options: Why Do Companies Do It? 21
    Hard work equals great rewards................................21
    Building (or trying to build) a stable workforce..............22
    "Diverting" cash from salaries to other uses 23
Comparing the Two Main Types of Stock Options 24

Chapter 2: Taking Your Chances: Getting Rich or Going Broke 27

Making Lots of Money: The Upside to Stock Options 28
When Good Options Go Bad..30
    The sad story of underwater stock options.....................31
    Is getting in early the secret?...............................32
Stock Options as Golden Handcuffs 34
    What are golden handcuffs?....................................34
    Conspiracy theory 35
    Why stock options go underwater 37
Reading the Oxygen Meter on Your Underwater Stock Options......38
    Real companies versus fad companies 39
    Realizing failure isn't just a fad 40

Chapter 3: Knowing What Kind of Stock Option Situation Is Best for You 43

Assessing Your Attitude: Entrepreneur, Investor, or Working Stiff? 43
    The entrepreneurial approach to stock options...................................44
    Stock options as an investment vehicle..47
    Job security and a steady paycheck — but with a "kicker" 48
Considering Your Personal Situation..49
The Two Different Types of Employment Situations 50
    High-risk, high-reward situations 50
    Risk-managed situations 50
Putting It All Together 51
Determining the Best Situation for You...52
    The risk-reward balance and your share of the ownership pie 52
    Considering the external environment
      and your personal qualifications 53

Chapter 4: The Big Guys and The Big Picture 57

Recognizing the Big Guys? 57
    Board members..59
    Identifying the big guys and watching their moves 60
Understanding Other Big Guy Investment Vehicles 60
    Restricted stock 61
    Warrants 62
    Convertible debt 62
Knowing How Much of Your Company the Big Guys Own...........................63
    The earliest stages of startup...63
    After the first few rounds of investment..64
    After going public 65
    The Fortune 500 stage 66
The "Friends and Family" Stock Program 67

Part II: Details, Details: What You Must Know about Your Stock Options 71

Chapter 5: Deciphering the Legal Language of Stock Option Agreements 73

Knowing What an Employee Stock Option Agreement Is 73
Figuring Out What Kind of Stock Option(s) You Have: ISO or NQSO 74
Trudging Through the Details of Your Stock Option Agreements 75
    The date of the agreement..76
    The number of shares 77
    What kind of stock 78
    The strike price 79
    The vesting schedule..80
    Split adjustment clause..82
Knowing When Your Option Is Exercisable 84
    Exercising your stock options...84
    Conditions of employment 85

Termination provisions 86
Change of control clauses 87
Blackout periods 88
Replacement clause...88
Restrictions on rights...89
References to your employment agreement 90
The rest of the legal language 91
Signature blocks..92

Chapter 6: Exercising Your Stock Options 93
The Four Reasons to Exercise Stock Options............................93
"Show me the money" 93
"Save the money!"...94
Diversification 94
Tax reasons 95
Procrastinators, Beware! Getting All of Your Paperwork in Order 95
The Mechanics of Exercising Stock Options 96
Be sure to write (or call) 97
What do you get when you exercise?...97
Reading the tax forms when they arrive.....................................98
Exercising Pre-IPO Stock Options 99
How Much Money Do You Need to Come Up With? 99
The cashless exercise...100
Paying for stock with real money 101

Chapter 7: Differentiating Pre-IPO and Post-IPO Stock Options . . . 105
What Is an IPO?..105
IPO basics 106
How about your stock options?..107
Receiving Pre-IPO Stock Options 109
Pre-IPO option pricing...109
What can you do with your stock options before
   your company goes public?...109
What happens to your pre-IPO options when
   your company goes public?...110
What happens to your pre-IPO options if
   your company doesn't go public?..111
Receiving Options When Your Company Is Already Publicly Traded........114
Riding the waves: How your stock options are affected
   by normal peaks and valleys in your company's stock 115
The danger point: Joining a company right after
   a post-IPO stock price runup..116

Chapter 8: No Trading Allowed! Lockups and Blackout Periods 119
Understanding Post-IPO Lockups 119
Getting Through Blackout Periods 121
What is a blackout period? 121
Who is subject to a blackout period?..122
What is your blackout period strategy?.......................................122

Chapter 9: Finding Stock Option Information Online 125

myStockOptions.com 125
MyOptionValue.com 126
StockOptionsCentral.com 127
www.stock-options.com 127
MyInternetOptions.com 128
The National Center for Employee Ownership (NCEO) 128
EDGAR? Who's That? 129

Part III: Money! *131*

Chapter 10: Determining What Your
Stock Options Are Really Worth. 133

Valuing Stock Options...134
    Knowing your options' value: Why it's important 135
    Getting complicated: The Black Scholes Model........................135
The Value of Your Stock Options at Grant Time...........................136
Determining What Your Stock Options Are Worth Now...............138
What Your Stock Options Should Be Worth 139
Determining What Your Stock Options Might Be Worth in the Future.........142

Chapter 11: Stock Options and Your Overall Portfolio 147

Counting the Baskets..147
Understanding the Principles of Personal Financial Planning 149
Considering Your Equity (Stock) Holdings 150
Investing in Your Employer...151
    Buying additional stock in your company................................151
    Your company's Employee Stock Purchase Plan (ESPP) 153
You're Wealthy! But Is Your Wealth Real or Only on Paper?........157
    Two different kinds of paper wealth...157
    Protecting (or trying to protect) your unvested stock profits 160
Sector Exposure 161

Part IV: Pay Up! Taxes and Stock Options *163*

Chapter 12: Understanding the Basics
of Taxes and Stock Options 165

Deciding How Much You Want to Worry about a Tax Strategy
    for Your Stock Options 165
Warnings and Possible Surprises Waiting for You 167
    Tax laws change frequently 167
    Owing taxes even if you haven't received any cash.................168

Key Tax Concepts...168
    Ordinary income...169
    Short-term capital gains...169
    Long-term capital gains..169
    Alternative minimum tax (AMT)....................................170
State Tax Considerations and Michael Jordan?.....................171
International Tax Considerations...173
    Canada...174
    England (U.K.) 175
    Ireland 175
    France..176

Chapter 13: Nonqualified Stock Options and Taxes 177
What Is a Nonqualified Stock Option (NQSO)?.......................177
Understanding the Basics: NQSOs and Taxes 178
    Grant-time tax consequences.......................................178
    Exercise-time tax implications when you hold your shares.............179
    Exercise-time tax implications when you do a cashless exercise 182
    Calculating taxes when you sell shares you acquire
        from exercising NQSOs...184
Complicating the Situation 186
    Why you might owe taxes at grant time 186
    Exercising and no taxes: Delayed income recognition.......187
Understanding the Section 83(b) Election...............................187
    Section 83(b) basics 188
    Section 83(b) risks 189
    Section 83(b) mechanics..189
Tax Withholding and Exercising NQSOs................................190
NQSOs and Your Tax Forms..191
    Your W-2 (and your pay stubs) 191
    Form 1040..191
    Schedule D 192
Timing Troubles: When Should You Exercise NQSOs?...........193
    As soon as possible 193
    As late as possible 194
    At regular intervals 195
    One more consideration 195
Another Key Decision: Which Option(s) Should You Exercise?...................195

Chapter 14: Incentive Stock Options and Taxes 199
What Is an Incentive Stock Option (ISO)?..............................199
Talking Taxes and ISOs: The Basics 200
    Grant-time tax consequences.......................................200
    Exercise-time tax consequences...................................201
    Tax consequences when you sell ISO shares 201
    Pleasant disposition or nasty disposition? 202

Disqualifying Disposition of an ISO...202
    Scenario #1: You make money on the deal 203
    Scenario #2: You lose money on the deal 206
    More about disqualifying dispositions..............................206
Nondisqualifying Disposition of an ISO.....................................207
    Alternative minimum tax (AMT) considerations
        and exercising your ISOs: A preview 207
The Stock Option Titanic Scenario 211
Beware the Wash Sale Rules! 214
Can Section 83(b) Help with the AMT Situation?......................216

Part V: Changes and Special Circumstances 217

Chapter 15: The Alternative Minimum Tax and Stock Options 219

Understanding the AMT 220
Calculating AMT 220
    AMT rates...220
    AMT exemptions 220
    AMT deductions..221
    Combining the basic calculations and rates 221
Getting Some of Your AMT Payments Back 222
State Taxes and AMT Considerations..223

Chapter 16: Acquiring or Being Acquired: Dealing with Corporate Change 225

Understanding Why Companies Sell Out 225
    Seeking growth 226
    Time to do something else 226
    Receiving an unsolicited offer 227
    Selling out was the plan all along..227
Dissecting the Deal 227
    Acquisitions...227
    Mergers...229
    Divestitures..229
    Additional outside investment 230
    Cash versus stock deals...230
Private and Public Companies: The Mix-and-Match Combinations 233
    Public company acquired by another public company.....................233
    Private company acquired by a public company 234
    Private company acquired by another private company.....................234
    Public company acquired by a private company 235
What Happens to Your Options After a Change of Control?.....................235
    The exchange rate means you get a new number of shares 235
    Accelerated vesting (maybe) 236
    Post-acquisition lockups...236
    Sweetening the pot (or the golden goodbye).....................237

Understanding the Tax Implications of a Change of Control.......................238
A Final Word: It's a Whole New Ballgame After a Change of Control...........238

Chapter 17: Trying to Predict What Will Happen to Your Stock Options 239

Looking at What's Going on Inside Your Company.......................................240
    The retention and turnover picture 240
    What's the latest buzz on the company's sales picture? 242
    Watching the big guys and their (legal) insider trading activity 243
    Is company management out of touch with the real world?..............244
    Cronyism 245
What's Going on Outside Your Company? 246
    It's the economy, stupid!......................................246
    Is your company in the buggy whip industry?............................247
    What the professionals are saying about your company 249
    What the amateurs are saying about your company
      (and whether it matters what they're saying)...............................250

Chapter 18: Leaving Your Job: What Happens to Your Stock Options? 251

Does the Reason You're Leaving Matter?....................................252
Tick, Tock, Tick, Tock . . . The Clock Is Running 252
Should You Sign a Termination Agreement?....................................254
Exercising Stock Options After You've Already Left.............................255
Read Your Stock Option Agreements Now!...................................255
What Happens to Pre-IPO Options If You Leave?...............................256
What About Underwater Stock Options?......................................256
Read Your Overall Employment Agreement 257
Beware the Dreaded Clawback Provision!....................................258
How Does Your Soon-to-be-Former Stock Option Package
    Affect Your New Job's Compensation? 261
Special Job Change Circumstances and What Happens to
    Your Stock Options 262
    Switching to part-time employment status 263
    Switching to contractor status...263
    Taking a leave of absence 264
Get the Lawyers! Lost Stock Options and Lawsuits............................265

Part VI: The Part of Tens................................267

Chapter 19: Special Stock Option Circumstances............... 269

Understanding the Three R's: Repricing, Reissue, and Reload Options 269
    Repriced options...270
    Reissued options...274
    Reload Options...277
Using Stock Options as Currency...281

Chapter 20: Ten Signs That Your Stock Options Will Be Worth *a Lot*! 285

A Steadily Growing Company 285
A Stable and Highly Qualified Management Team 286
A Very Active Board of Directors 286
Relatively Low Turnover Among Employees...................................287
Market-leading Products or Services 287
Returning Customers..288
Good Internal Systems and Infrastructure....................................288
Employee Empowerment 288
Thorough New-Employee Training Programs 289

Chapter 21: Ten Signs That Your Stock Options Will Probably Be *Worthless*! 291

The Serial-Entrepreneur Management Team 291
A Disinterested Friends and Investors–Dominated Board of Directors.......292
A Revolving Door of Managers 292
Last One Out, Please Turn Out the Lights!....................................293
Rose-Colored Glasses Syndrome...293
High Levels of Customer Dissatisfaction 294
Poor Internal Systems and Infrastructure.....................................294
Open Talk Among Employees About Leaving..................................294
Inconsistent Internal Communications from Management 295
A Sense of Panic 295

Chapter 22: Ten Things to Look for in Your Stock Option Agreement 297

What Kind of Options Are You Receiving? 297
Are the Dates Consistent and Logical?...298
Are There Inconsistencies in Details? 298
Is There a Clawback Provision?...298
Is There a Provision for a Change of Control? 299
Are the Expiration and Cancellation Details Clear?.........................299
Are There References to the Company's Stock Option Plan?...............299
What Is the Effect of a Stock Split?..300
What Can You Do and Not Do with Pre-IPO Options? 300
Are There Differences Among Stock Option Agreement Documents? 300

Index *301*

Introduction

*E*ven though an estimated 12 million U.S. employees have stock options as a key component of their respective compensation packages, many of those people understand only the most basic aspects of their stock options.

This lack of stock option knowledge, however, is understandable when you realize how most companies handle the granting of stock options to their employees. When a job offer is extended, a representative from the HR (Human Resources) department will usually follow up the salary offer with a bland, imprecise statement, something along the lines of "oh, yeah, you also get 5,000 stock options."

But no mention of the vesting schedule for those shares, no mention of how the strike price for those 5,000 shares will be set, and usually no mention of what kind of stock option grant you will receive — an incentive stock option (ISO) grant or a nonqualified stock option (NQSO) grant, each with different tax consequences. (If this book is your first exposure to the world of stock options, don't worry about the terminology in the preceding paragraph: I cover those terms along with other stock option basics in Chapter 1.)

Why I Wrote This Book: The Lessons of 1999 and 2000

I wrote *Stock Options For Dummies* for several reasons:

- ✔ To demystify the complex terminology, rules, and tax consequences of stock options

- ✔ To provide readers with a realistic picture of what to expect from their respective stock options

- ✔ To help readers get beyond the "you'll certainly get rich!" pitch from less-than-candid prospective employers, and to evaluate stock options as part of an overall compensation picture

You can look at the years 1999 and 2000 to see stock options in a realistic light. For most of the 1990s, having a stock option package was like having a license to print money — very often, lots of money. The stock option phenomenon reached its crest in 1999 as technology stocks and Internet-related stocks in particular zoomed beyond any realistic measures of the underlying values of the companies themselves. The "first day pop" (the day a company went public) became sort of a contest by 1999: Could the company's stock price go up 300 percent the first trading day? 400 percent? Even more?

But the boom was fun while it lasted, and many employees of those companies became wealthy — perhaps even extremely wealthy — primarily on the soaring value of their stock options. The primary concern of many option holders during the late 1990s was how to minimize taxes on the spectacular gains on those options. But the spectacular gains were never in question: They would happen, and quickly!

Alas, when technology stocks — and, again, Internet stocks in particular — crashed during 2000, many of those stock option millionaires or billionaires watched as their wealth shrank or even vanished. In some cases, the plummeting in the value of any given individual's stock options couldn't be prevented, given the rules of stock options with regard to when an option holder is — and isn't — to cash in on paper gains. In other cases, though, the "now you have it, now you don't" magic trick that caused hundreds of billions of dollars in stock option paper wealth to vanish could have been prevented, at least in part.

How? If a stock option holder had followed some of the basic principles of investing and managing a portfolio, then that person may have realized that the company's stock had gone way too high, way too fast. Therefore, that person would have "taken some of the money off the table" by cashing in some of those shares of stock and redeploying the proceeds into other investments. Alas, for so many option holders (just like many technology stock investors in general), greed and unrealistic expectations became the order of the day, and the price was eventually and painfully paid when stock prices went into a tailspin.

But did the stock market of 2000 signal the end of stock options as a key component of employees' compensation packages? Reading some of the press stories near the end of the year, you might think so. "Employees leave behind worthless stock options, seek higher salaries" was the prevalent theme of so many news stories during the fall of 2000, so you might be tempted to think of stock options as little more than a passing fad whose best days were in the past.

I disagree. The stock option genie is out of the bottle, and even those whose dreams of stock option-fueled wealth and early retirement didn't pan out have had a taste of aspiring to more than just a salary from their respective jobs. I believe that stock options are here to stay, but many people will (hopefully) be much more realistic and much smarter about their options packages in the days ahead.

And that's where *Stock Options For Dummies* comes in: to provide that "big picture view" of stock options that takes into consideration not only the basics such as vesting schedules and tax laws, but also the following:

- ✔ How to read your stock option agreement paperwork and look for traps

- ✔ How to figure out if the company making you the job offer with the stock options is a "real" company with solid prospects or just a fly-by-night, get-rich-quick scheme for venture capitalists and its founders — but not for you and your coworkers

- ✔ Understanding the consequences to your stock options of leaving your job, having the company sold, or some other significant change

- ✔ Where to find up-to-date information, group discussion, and assistance on the Internet about critical stock options issues

Who Needs to Read This Book?

Stock Options For Dummies is intended for anyone who has a current stock option package, whether it's doing well or not; anyone who is considering a job with a stock option package and needs to watch out for traps, make sure he's being treated fairly, understand what he's getting into; and finally, anyone who wants a no-hype, realistic discussion about stock options: the good, the bad, and the ugly.

How to Use This Book

Stock Options For Dummies is written in easily understood language from cover to cover, with liberal use of examples. Some of the topics covered are very basic — the stock options basics covered in Chapter 1, for example — while other material, such as the chapters on stock option taxation, is more advanced.

Some readers for whom stock options is a brand new topic (that is, readers who have never had a job with stock options) would be best served by first reading the book cover to cover, and then using the book as a reference for specific topics that come up in the future (for example, finding out an employer is being acquired by another company, and wanting to figure out what will happen to existing stock options).

Other readers with a bit more exposure may want to selectively read certain chapters, and either skip or skim others. I recommend at least skimming every chapter, even if you currently have stock options or have held options in the past and understand the basics pretty well. Most chapters contain not only the basic information about that chapter's subject but also anecdotes and "gotchas" that you may not have come across — yet!

Many of the chapters have a number of cross-references to other chapters — more than you would find in a typical . . . *For Dummies* book. The reason is that so many stock options topics are interrelated, and I wanted to be as thorough as possible within any given chapter to point you to another chapter (or two or three chapters) where you will find related information about a specific example or anecdote.

How This Book Is Organized

Stock Options For Dummies is organized into six parts. The chapters within each part cover specific topics in detail, as described in the following sections.

Part 1: The Fundamentals of Stock Options

The chapters in Part I cover the fundamentals and are particularly appropriate for readers who are newcomers to the world of stock options. (But I recommend even experienced option holders skim the chapters to pick up a tidbit or two with which they aren't familiar or haven't yet come across.)

Chapter 1 covers the stock option basics that you must understand to make informed decisions about accepting a job and an accompanying stock options packages. Vesting, strike prices, how you might make money on your options: It's all in there. Chapter 2 takes an honest, no-hype, no-holds-barred look at "the good, the bad, and the ugly" sides of stock options. Stock options aren't a license to print money, nor are they some type of evil incarnate tool. Stock options are simply a financial instrument that can greatly benefit those who own them, but by no means are those benefits guaranteed.

Building on the basics in the first two chapters, Chapter 3 helps you develop your philosophy about stock options. Should you look at stock options as an entrepreneur might, or are stock options simply a bonus that supplements your salary? You need to match your philosophy to the right stock option situation: the type of company, the type of stock option package you receive, and the amount of risk you're willing to accept.

Finally, Chapter 4 takes a look at the big guys and their stock options, as well as other equity-based instruments they usually have at their disposal. Maybe you're a big guy yourself, or hope to be one day. Make sure that you're being treated fairly, on par with the other big guys at your company, by being as informed as possible.

Part II: Details, Details: What You Must Know About Your Stock Options

The Part II chapters add nuts and bolts onto the basics and philosophical aspects of Part I. Chapter 5 helps you understand the language in your stock option agreement — a legally binding agreement — and where to watch out for hidden traps. Chapter 6 steps you through the process of exercising your stock options, and what happens if you immediately sell the shares you acquire from the exercise versus what happens if you hold on to those shares.

Chapter 7 discusses the differences between stock options in pre-IPO companies and those companies that have already gone public, and what happens to your stock options along the way. Chapter 8 discusses two key restrictions — blackout periods and lockup periods — that govern when you can and can't exercise options and sell shares. Finally, Chapter 9 take you into the Internet and a guided tour of online resources where you can find the latest and greatest about stock options, applicable tax laws, and related material.

Part III: Money!

The two chapters in Part III help you gain a realistic sense of the value of your stock options on their own and in the context of your overall portfolio. Chapter 10 discusses stock option valuation, including different approaches of varying complexity you can use, while Chapter 11 helps you figure out how to balance your stock options and other investments you have in your employer (such as actual shares of stock you hold) with your other investments and your personal and family needs.

Part IV: Pay Up! Taxes and Stock Options

Taxes and stock options can be very complicated, and some of the most serious mistakes people make with their stock options include not understanding the tax consequences of their actions such as exercising and selling shares. Chapter 12 presents the basics of taxes and stock options, providing the foundation for the subsequent chapters in Part IV. Chapter 13 covers taxes on nonqualified stock options (NQSOs), while Chapter 14 discusses taxes on incentive stock options (ISOs). Finally, Chapter 15 takes a brief look at the alternative minimum tax (AMT).

Part V: Changes and Special Circumstances

As time marches on, you may very well find your job and your stock options affected by various circumstances. Chapter 16 discusses what happens to your stock options if your company is acquired. Chapter 17 helps you pick up hints and clues about what might happen to your stock options in the future — will they soar in value, or plummet into nothingness? Chapter 18 discusses what happens to your options when you leave your job — different situations will likely apply whether you are laid off, resign, retire, become disabled, or die while still an employee. Finally, Chapter 19 discusses various types of special circumstances that may change key aspects of your stock options — for example, changes to the strike price, if the options are repriced.

Part VI: The Part of Tens

Each Part of Tens chapter presents ten elements about a key stock option topic. Chapters 20 and 21 give you lists of items that may foretell whether your stock options will be worth a lot or may become worthless, respectively. Chapter 22 ties in with the material in Chapter 5, and warns you about ten key things to look for in your stock option agreements before you sign them.

Icons Used in This Book

As with all . . . *For Dummies* books, the text is annotated with icons to call your attention to various points I make (or try to make!) about stock options.

When you see the Tip icon, the accompanying material is some action you should consider taking.

The Warning icon is exactly that: a warning of some dire consqeuence that might occur should you make the wrong move with your stock options.

When you see the Technical Stuff icon, the accompanying material falls into that category of "thanks, but that's more than I really needed to know." You can certainly get the gist of any chapter's contents by skipping over the Technical Stuff material, but if you want to get under the hood for that chapter's topic, a few moments spent with the Technical Stuff material will help you thoroughly understand that topic.

The Remember icon calls your attention to a point that was made earlier in the chapter or in an earlier chapter, or highlights a key point or two that you should remember.

Part I
The Fundmentals of Stock Options

The 5th Wave   By Rich Tennant

"Perhaps you'd like to buy these magic beans, or this charm that will give you good luck, or this stock that promises a 200% return on your investment in less than 18 months."

In this part . . .

This part explains the basics of stock options: how they work, how you *might* make a lot of money, and — sorry to say — how your stock options might turn out to be little more than a "wouldn't it have been nice" fantasy. You'll see how to match different types of employment situations and stock option packages to your own circumstances and tolerance for risk to help maximize your chances for stock option profits. You'll also get a look at the types of stock option packages the "big guys" in your company — like the CEO and the Board of Directors — have.

Chapter 1

Stock Options: What You Need to Know Right Off the Bat

. . . .

In This Chapter

▶ Knowing the basics of stock options

▶ Figuring out why companies give employees stock options

▶ Knowing what happens when you receive stock options

▶ Understanding the two main kinds of stock options

. . . .

How's this for a new show hosted by Regis Philbin: "Who Wants to Be a Stock Options Millionaire?"

Forget about athletes, actors, and musicians. Throughout the 1990s, the world watched entrepreneurs like Bill Gates (co-founder of Microsoft) and Larry Ellison (founder of Oracle) become billionaires, largely because of their holdings in the companies they founded. Many people were even more enthralled by the legions of plain old regular employees like the "Dellionaires" — workers at Dell Computer who became millionaires from the spectacular rise in their company's stock throughout the decade — whose good fortunes convinced so many others that employment-driven wealth was just around the corner and achievable by almost everyone!

Just because you go to work for a company that gives you stock options doesn't mean you'll automatically become wealthy — but it *might* happen. This chapter explains how stock options work, why your employer might give you stock options, and how you *might* profit from those options.

Understanding Stock Option Basics

Stock options are actually very complex: You'll face many challenges ranging from managing your personal financial portfolio, to taxes, to trying to determine whether or not you should remain at a company where you hold stock options. Don't worry. I address all of these issues in subsequent chapters throughout this book and make the whole process a lot less intimidating. For now, however, just concentrate on understanding the most basic aspects of stock options, as I discuss in this section.

Knowing what stock options are

A *stock option* is the right to purchase a specified number of shares of a company's stock at some point in the future at a contractually specified price — rather than whatever the stock price will be on that future date. And, if the fates smile upon you, that contractually specified price will be lower — hopefully *much* lower — than the market price for the stock on that future date, meaning instant profit for you.

For example, suppose that you begin a new job at GreatPlaceToWork.com as a software developer. In addition to your starting annual salary of $50,000, you also receive a *stock option grant*, which is a legal agreement between you and your employer. This particular stock option grant gives you the right to purchase 10,000 shares of GreatPlaceToWork.com stock at the price of $3 per share.

At some point in the future — say, in five years — GreatPlaceToWork.com has done fantastically well, and the stock price is $103 per share. Because of your stock option grant, you could buy 10,000 shares of GreatPlaceToWork.com stock at only $3 per share, turn right around and sell those 10,000 shares for $103 each, and make a gross pre-tax profit of $100 per share — or $1 million!

You can substitute the term *employee stock options* for the more generic phrase *stock options* for almost all of the discussion throughout this chapter and this entire book. You will almost always find yourself holding stock options as a result of being employed at a company that has a policy of issuing stock options to its employees, including you.

I will specifically note when I am referring to stock options issued to individuals who aren't actually employees of a company. For example, Chapter 4 discusses stock options owned by investors and members of your employer's Board of Directors — people who may not actually be employees, even though they are associated with your company. And in Chapter 19, I'll discuss the now-passé phenomenon of using stock options as a form of currency in exchange for advertising services, consulting work, or leasing office space. For the most part, stock options held by non-employees work the same as employee stock options that you and your fellow workers hold. So while it's safe to think of the terms *employee stock options* and *stock options* as interchangeable, I'll explicitly call your attention to any differences.

TECHNICAL STUFF

Other types of stock options

Stock options issued to employees, Board of Director members, and others with some sort of relationship to a company are *not* the same as *publicly traded stock options,* which you may have heard about or have had some experience with. You can find publicly traded stock options along with the stock price listings in *The Wall Street Journal* or the financial pages of a major newspaper like *The New York Times.*

There are two types of publicly traded stock options:

- *Call options* (or *calls*) allow the holder to purchase shares of stock at a predetermined price, even if the current market price of the stock is higher than that predetermined price.

- *Put options* (or *puts*) allow the holder to *sell* (rather than buy) shares of stock at a predetermined price, even if that price is higher than the current market price of a stock.

Call options work much the same way as employee-oriented stock options, with one major distinction between the two. Calls — like puts — are *publicly* traded, meaning that anyone can buy or sell them. In contrast, employee-oriented stock options are usually *not* marketable, meaning that you're contractually forbidden from selling your stock options to someone, nor can you purchase someone else's stock options.

Calls and puts are a complex enough subject, so all you need to remember is that the types of stock options we discuss in this book are *not* the same as publicly traded stock options. So when you hear phrases such as "covered calls," "straddles," and "naked puts" (don't ask!) in reference to stock options, then it's the publicly traded stock options — not the subject of this book — that someone is talking about.

Knowing how stock options work

This section discusses the basics of how stock options work and what happens when you receive stock options.

As we previously mentioned, when your employer gives you stock options, you formally receive a legal document called a *stock option grant.* The stock option grant contains several very important details about the stock options, including:

- **The strike price.** The price at which you can purchase shares is known as the strike price of your options. No matter how high your company's stock price goes from that day forward, you will always be guaranteed the right to purchase shares of stock at the strike price specified in your stock option grant. (In the GreatPlaceToWork.com example earlier in this chapter, the strike price specified in the stock option grant is $3 per share.) Sometimes, a stock option grant will use more generic language such as *option price* or *exercise price*, but the street slang is "strike price." Note that in your stock option agreements, you'll usually find the term *option price* or *exercise price* rather than *strike price*, but in job offer letters and informal communication with a prospective employer, you'll more commonly see the *strike price* term used.

✔ **Number of shares.** Sure, it would be great if you could turn around and say, "Ok, I want to purchase 1 million shares — no, make that 2 million shares — at my strike price," after your company's stock triples or quadruples in price. Unfortunately, stock options don't work that way. Your stock option grant tells you the maximum number of shares you can purchase. (In the GreatPlaceToWork.com example from earlier in this chapter, the maximum number of shares specified is 10,000.)

✔ **The vesting schedule.** Suppose that you start working at GreatPlaceToWork.com, receive your stock option grant for 10,000 shares at a strike price of $3.00, and three months later the company's stock price goes up to $13 per share. Could you immediately buy 10,000 shares at $3 each and sell them for a profit of $10 each ($13 minus $3), pocketing a quick $100,000? Most likely not, because of the *vesting schedule* specified in your stock option grant.

The term *vesting* is a commonly used term in finance and business. In the case of stock options, the vesting schedule specifies a period of time over which the shares of stock represented by the option grant actually become available to so that you can exercise your options (see "Exercising Your Stock Option(s)" later in this chapter for more information). A common vesting schedule for stock options is four-year *cliff vesting*, meaning that the number of shares specified in your agreement become available to you in equal increments, spread out over four years. So in the GreatPlaceTo Work.com example, the 10,000 shares would vest as follows:

- 2,500 shares (25 percent) would vest exactly one year after the date of the stock option grant.

- Another 2,500 shares (25 percent) would vest exactly two years after the date of the stock option grant, meaning that halfway through the four years, 50 percent of your stock option grant has vested.

- Another 2,500 shares (25 percent) would vest exactly three years after the date of the stock option grant — meaning that 75 percent of your grant is now vested.

- The final 2,500 shares (25 percent) would vest exactly four years after the date of the stock option grant, completing the four-year vesting period.

You might come across other vesting schedules, such as three-year vesting or perhaps a variation on the four-year vesting previously described, in which after the first 25 percent of your stock option grant vests on the one-year anniversary, the remaining 75 percent vests in equal monthly increments over the remaining three years rather than on successive anniversary dates. In Chapter 5, we talk more about vesting schedules.

✔ **Expiration date.** Stock option grants don't last forever, unfortunately. Typically, the grant expires ten years after the date of the stock option grant.

✔ **Details, details, details.** The strike price, number of shares, vesting schedule, and expiration date are the most basic details that describe your potential gains from your stock options and the time frame in which those gains might occur. However, like most legal documents, stock option grants contain many more details that cover just about any situation that might occur during the course of your employment, and how your stock options are affected. These details include:

- What happens if you resign or are fired from your job?

- What happens if your company is bought by another company?

- What happens if you violate the terms of your employment agreement (for example, you fail to keep company secrets confidential)?

- What are some conditions under which your stock options might be taken away from you, such as if you quit and go to work for a competitor?

In Chapter 5, we take an indepth look at all of the details and associated legal language you'll likely come across in a stock option grant.

Exercising Your Stock Option (s)

When you decide to *exercise* a stock option, you make some type of formal declaration *as specified in your stock option grant* that you want to purchase a given number of shares at the strike price of those shares. For example, assume that you've been working at GreatPlaceToWork.com for over four years, and the stock option grant for 10,000 shares you received when you were hired is now completely vested. Your stock option grant may specify that you exercise stock options by contacting a specific financial institution with which your employer has set up a stock option execution program.

You likely will have some other supplemental material that guides you through all of the logistics of exercising stock options, such as paperwork you need to fill out and have on file and the telephone number to call to exercise options. So make sure that long before you even consider exercising your stock options, you have filled out all appropriate paperwork (either on

Traversing the terminology

Chances are, when you find yourself talking with people with stock options, you might hear the following:

"I have 20,000 stock options."

"Yeah? Well, I have 50,000 stock options myself."

"I only have 10,000 stock options now because I just started my job, but next year I should get another 10,000 stock options."

Actually, people who phrase the details of their respective stock options this way are incorrectly describing what they have received from their respective companies. If you were to look at the wording in the typical stock option grant, you'll probably find something like:

"GreatPlaceToWork.com ("The Company") grants to Alan Simon ("The Grantee") the Option to purchase Ten Thousand (10,000) shares of common stock of the Company at an option price of $3 per share."

In reality, the legal agreement that gives you the right to purchase (in this example) 10,000 shares is a *single* stock option. You don't have 10,000 stock options; you *do* have one stock option to purchase 10,000 shares. I realize this might

sound like little more than an exercise in semantics, but consider the following situation.

You go to work for GreatPlaceToWork.com and you are granted an option to purchase 10,000 shares at the strike price of $3 per share. Now, one year later when your annual performance review comes around, you are given a second stock option grant of 5,000 shares — this time at a strike price of $4 per share. You don't have 15,000 stock options; you *do* have two stock options (more precisely, two stock option grants) for a total of 15,000 shares of stock. Each of the two stock option grants is covered by a separate legal agreement. Usually, the majority of each of those legal agreements will be the same, except for the key details we mentioned earlier: strike price, number of shares, vesting schedule (the actual dates at which portions of the option grant become vested), and the actual expiration date of each respective grant.

In the real world, you're more likely to say, "I have 15,000 stock options," rather than the more wordy, "I have stock option grants for 15,000 shares." As long as you understand that the latter is the correct terminology, and the former phrase is a kind of stock option slang, your word choice really doesn't matter.

paper or online, however your employer lets you fill out the necessary forms) and are absolutely clear who to call or what procedures to follow when exercising time comes.

If you look at any stock option grant you receive (and we mention more about the legal language of stock options in Chapter 5), the portion that describes how you exercise stock options may say something like, "The Grantee may exercise part or all of the vested and exercisable option." Translation: Only those shares that have vested can be exercised, no matter how much your company's stock price has gone up and how badly you want to tap into those waiting-to-be-taken profits.

You will most likely hear someone say — or use the phrasing yourself — "I am exercising my stock options" (plural), regardless of whether shares from one or more stock option grants are involved. That's why the heading for this section uses the phrase "stock option(s)" indicating that a decision to exercise could involve shares from a single stock option grant or more than one grant.

If you have received more than one stock option grant — say, one for 10,000 shares when you were hired, another six months later for 3,000 shares as part of an annual bonus, and a third grant six months later (one year after you were hired) for 5,000 shares as part of your annual performance review — then at some point in the future, you may exercise portions of all three option grants at the same time, subject to how many shares you have vested at that point. For example, Table 1-1 shows the details behind the three stock option grants we describe previously.

Table 1-1	Your Three Stock Option Grants from GreatPlaceToWork.com		
Date of Grant Schedule	*# Shares*	*Strike Price*	*Vesting*
May 15, 2001 (25%/year)	10,000	$3.00	4 years
December 15, 2001 (25%/year)	3,000	$3.50	4 years
May 15, 2002 (25%/year)	5,000	$4.00	4 years

Suppose that today's date is January 5, 2004, your company's stock price is $10.00, and you want to (remember the wording from your stock option grant) "exercise part or all of the vested and exercisable option." None of your three option grants has totally vested, so you are exercising part of each of three grants — the vested part of each. Half of your first grant has now vested, because today is more than two years but less than three years from the date of that grant. Likewise, half of your second grant has vested because today's date is more than two years (by less than a month) from the date of that grant. Only ¼ of your third grant has vested, because today's date is more than one year but less than two years from the date of that grant.

So your grant total: 5,000 vested and exercisable shares from your first grant, plus 1,500 vested and exercisable shares from your second grant, plus 1,250 vested and exercisable shares from your third grant, for a total of 7,750 shares.

You may want to exercise your options from all three grants at once, meaning that you will buy:

- ✔ 5,000 shares at $3 per share (total: $15,000)
- ✔ 1,500 shares at $3.50 per share (total: $5,250)
- ✔ 1,250 shares at $4 per share (total: $5,000)

For this example, we assume you immediately sell all of your shares at the market price of $10.00, meaning that you will have paid $25,250 ($15,000 + $5,250 + $5,000) for 7,750 shares that you then sell for $77,500, giving you a pre-tax profit of $52,250.

Suppose, though, that you wanted to only exercise options on 3,000 shares and immediately sell those shares for the instant profit? You could do any of the following:

- ✔ Exercise an option on 3,000 of the 5,000 vested shares from your first stock option grant
- ✔ Exercise an option on 1,000 vested shares from each of your three grants
- ✔ Exercise an option on 2,000 vested shares from your first grant and 1,000 vested shares from your second grant

Or you could try another one of the thousands of options exercising combinations available to you. For example, you could exercise an option on 999 shares from the first option grant + 1001 shares from second option grant + 1000 shares from the third option grant, or 998 shares from the first option grant + 1000 shares from the second option grant + 1002 shares from the third option grant, and so on. Because the strike prices of each of the three grants are different, the amount you pay for the 3,000 shares of stock will be different in each one of the possible combinations available to you. In Chapter 6, we discuss exercising stock options in detail, including the many decisions you need to make when doing so.

You should remember two key points. First, you exercise stock options according to the official and legal procedures specified in your stock option grant(s). Second, you need to be very explicit about exactly how you want to exercise stock options when the time comes, including (when you have received more than one stock option grant) which grant(s) you are exercising at that time, and how many shares from each you are purchasing.

Understanding the Right Nature of Your Stock Options

A stock option grant gives you the right to purchase the number of shares specified in the grant, according to constraints such as the vesting schedule. However, a stock option grant doesn't create an obligation for you to purchase those shares, either at some specified time in the future or at all!

The timing by which you exercise a stock option, either a portion at a time as the option vests or in its entirety at some future date, is totally within your control. Much of the material in this book is intended to help you make an informed decision about when to exercise your stock options and under what circumstances. This book also helps you decide what to do with the shares you buy (sell them immediately or hold them until some future date) after you exercise an option and purchase shares.

However, *you* make those decisions, not your company's management, your stock broker, your financial advisor, or your company's Board of Directors. If you perform the level of analysis that you should and decide that you should exercise options on all of your vested shares tomorrow and sell those shares immediately, then you should do exactly that. On the other hand, if your analysis tells you that you should hold off on exercising options on any shares for at least three more years, then that's the course of action (or, in this case, inaction) you should take.

You may even find that you may never exercise any of your options, even though over the years you may have been granted options on 50,000 shares, 60,000 shares, or even more. In Chapter 2, we look at the financial downside of stock options, specifically what happens when your company's stock price drops below the strike price of your stock options and your options become worthless.

If stock options were an *obligation* to purchase shares at the strike price rather than a right — to do so, then someone could actually force you to purchase a large number of shares at a price that would force you to sell for an automatic loss. Or, at the very least, you could be forced to purchase shares of your company's stock for far more than you would pay by buying shares on the stock market. Fortunately, "stock options" is a self-describing term: You have the *option* to purchase stock, but nobody can actually force you to purchase shares if doing so would be against your own best financial interests.

Comparing Stock Options to Actual Shares of Stock

Say that two college friends — Steve and Kathy — go to work for a consulting company on the same day. Steve takes a job as a recruiter, while Kathy goes to work as a technology consultant. Assume that the company's current policy is that stock options are granted only to employees in certain job functions, such as consulting. However, employees in positions such as recruiting and other Human Resources job functions don't currently receive stock options.

Kathy receives options on 3,000 shares, priced at $3 per share (the company's current stock price on the NASDAQ). Steve, however, doesn't receive stock options but still has good feelings about his new employer, so he scrapes together $9,000 and buys 3,000 shares of stock on the same day that Kathy receives her stock option grant.

True or false: Kathy and Steve have the same equity (ownership) position in their employer: 3,000 shares of stock worth.

Answer: False! Steve *does* have an ownership position in the company because he actually purchased stock that he now owns. True, Steve's ownership position is very small — if the company has 50,000,000 shares of stock outstanding, then Steve's ownership position is only .006 percent. However, at that moment Steve still owns .006 percent more than Kathy does! Why? Because *stock options are not the same as stock.*

In every stock option agreement, you will find a clause called "No Shareholder Rights" (or a similar term) that explicitly states that until actual shares of stock have been issued as a result of part or all of a stock option being exercised, no rights or privileges of a shareholder exist for the option holder. So, for example, Steve can vote his 3,000 shares on all matters brought before the company's stockholders, such as electing members of the Board of Directors, or approving or disapproving motions such as anti-takeover measures. True, Steve's 3,000 shares aren't likely to have any significant weight by themselves when 49,997,000 other shares are out there, and most of them are concentrated in the hands of "The Big Guys" (see Chapter 4). But in the spirit of democracy, at least Steve has a legal right to vote on company matters along with every other stockholder.

Kathy, on the other hand, has no shareholder rights. She will have none until she either exercises her option to purchase shares, purchases shares of the company's stock through some other vehicle, such as an Employee Stock Purchase Plan (ESPP — see Chapter 11), or buys shares of the company's stock through the stock market, just as Steve did.

If Kathy exercises part or all of her stock option but immediately sells those shares for an instant profit, she does *not* have any shareholder rights. Technically, for a very brief instant between the time she receives the shares and the time they're sold, she does own shares of stock and has shareholder rights. But if her intention is to use her stock options as a vehicle for instant profit rather than to buy and retain shares of the company's stock in the future at a discount, then her shareholder rights evaporate as quickly as she can say "show me the money."

Granting Stock Options: Why Do Companies Do It?

Traditionally, workers in the United States and throughout most of the world have spent their careers under an umbrella of "management versus labor," or "us versus them." Until very recently, it was difficult to find many companies that encouraged its employees to "think and act like owners" — much less encourage its employees to actually *be* owners of the company. Employers use stock options for several purposes, including:

- Enabling employees to share in the company's growth and success as owners (or potential owners) in exchange for working hard

- Trying to build and retain a stable workforce in very competitive labor markets and during good economic times

- "Diverting" cash away from salaries and benefits toward other operational uses, and making up the difference to employees through potentially huge gains from their stock options

Hard work equals great rewards

Many companies issue stock options to their employees to encourage them to "go the extra mile" in their jobs — through extra long hours, extensive travel, and generally devoting a good portion of their lives to their company. The equation of "hard work equals great rewards" doesn't always hold true, but most employers agree that if a company's entire workforce works very hard — and very smart — that the chances for success are greatly increased.

But how can those employees be motivated to give so much of their lives to their jobs? In many cases, the answer is money. True, not everyone's primary workplace motivation is financial gain, but many people *will* make a lot of personal sacrifices for their job if they see the potential for high financial reward.

Companies could, of course, handle the reward portion of the equation through very high salaries and even higher bonuses. Some companies do operate on that model. However, other companies keep salaries and bonuses for their employees at ordinary levels and instead rely on stock options as the primary vehicle for granting great rewards. (We discuss more about overall compensation and how stock options figure into the picture in Chapter 9.)

Therefore, the "hard work equals great rewards" equation is actually a bit more complicated — something like "hard work equals company success equals great rewards." Still sounds about the same, right? Not quite!

A company that uses high salaries and bonuses as its means of rewarding employees has direct control over the reward side of the equation. If the company does well, then the profits can be distributed according to a preset schedule of salary increases and bonuses. Not so with a stock option-based model, however. Why? Because increases in the value of employee stock options is tied to increases in the company's stock price, and the company does *not* have direct control and influence over its stock price. Even if the company is doing very well and is very profitable, its stock price could still be depressed if the stock market as a whole is in a slump, or for other reasons that we discuss in Chapter 10. So with stock options, the equation is more like "hard work equals company success equals great rewards, but only if the investing public really likes the company's stock." That warning aside, the motivation for issuing stock options is still "to encourage employees to work hard to make the company successful."

Building (or trying to build) a stable workforce

The days of people going to work for a company right out of college and staying there until retirement are just about gone. Every so often, I run into someone who has been with the same employer for 15 or 20 years, but for the most part, people jump around from company to company these days with increasing frequency.

The more a company's workforce changes and the less stable its workforce is, the less likely it is to gain and hold business momentum in whatever it does – build computer or communications hardware products, provide consulting services to others, manufacture and package toys, or whatever. But how can a company encourage you that the grass really isn't greener on the other side and that staying with the company can have long-term benefits not only for the company but for you as well?

One way to encourage employee retention is through the use of stock options. The multi-year vesting schedule associated with most stock option grants (discussed earlier in this chapter) means that if you leave to go to a new job, any gains from unvested shares will be lost. Therefore, companies want you to consider staying put so that you can gain access to more money as your shares vest.

By periodically issuing new stock option grants to you, your company can always ensure that some targeted number of unvested shares is "on the table" and would be lost if you resign and take a new job. For example, when all of your initial shares have vested, you have no unvested shares left and (the theory goes) no incentive to keep working for the company. But if the company keeps granting you new options (say once a year as part of your annual review), you will never get to the point where all shares on all option grants have vested. Therefore, you would always be "leaving money on the table" if you were to leave (assuming, of course, that the company's stock price is higher than the strike price of unvested shares you're holding). In Chapter 2, we discuss the "mixed blessing" of stock options as golden handcuffs — locking you into a job you don't really like because if you leave, you'll be leaving behind lots and lots of money.

"Diverting" cash from salaries to other uses

The Great Internet Boom of the Late 1990s caused many long-time technology industry practitioners and observers to gasp in awe at the billions of dollars in investment capital that was, basically, thrown at unproven startup companies. Every day you would read stories about some brand new "e-consulting" company receiving $50 million in venture capital, or some wireless communications startup turning away investors because it had already landed the $500 million it was looking for.

However, the crash of so many Internet-related companies during 2000 brought a bit of reality back to the world of startup companies, and turned people's attention back to a fundamental principle of starting a business: conserving cash! Now that dozens of dot-com Super Bowl ads and other such nonsense are behind us, we find struggling companies doing everything in their power to conserve their dwindling supplies of cash in order to become profitable.

So what does all this have to do with stock options? During a company's early days, management would, ideally, rather use limited cash resources for operations, marketing, and similar key business needs, rather than for salaries and other forms of cash compensation (such as bonuses). By creating compensation packages that shave a little bit — or a lot — off of the cash portion of the package in exchange for generous grants of stock options, the company can divert cash toward operational uses. In theory, better-funded operations should lead to a greater chance of business success and a shorter time to profitability, which in turn would lead to higher and higher company stock prices. And, as the company's stock price rises, those employees who accepted less cash in their compensation packages would be rewarded through gains in their stock option holdings.

(Note the close relationship between wanting to divert cash and rewarding employees and building a stable workforce. As you can probably tell, these reasons are all fairly intertwined.)

Some business leaders are very critical of the cash diversion approach to stock options, however. For example, Warren Buffett, one of the most respected investors for many years (and also one of the wealthiest people in the world), was cited in a 1999 *US News & World Report* article as being critical of stock option-issuing companies for being able to "hide" compensation expenses from their financial statements and "inflate" their earnings, leaving a ticking time bomb for investors when large numbers of stock options are exercised. The exact phrase used in reporter James Lardner's article: "fiscal chicanery — a claim against future corporate earnings that isn't reflected on the books." Now that's a strong statement!

So be warned that even when the fundamental premise of stock options works in favor of a company's employees as the company's stock price rises, macro-financial forces need to be considered in gauging the company's *true* financial picture.

Comparing the Two Main Types of Stock Options

So far, everything we discuss in this chapter has been relatively straightforward, as you might expect (and hope for) from an introductory chapter. However, one introductory-level aspect of stock options is fairly complex: the two different types of stock options.

I introduce the two types in this chapter so that you can become familiar with the terminology and the distinction between these two. Later in the book, particular Chapters 13 and 14 when we discuss taxation issues, we go into more detail about these two types. The two stock option types are:

- ✔ Incentive stock options (ISOs)
- ✔ Nonqualified stock options (NQSOs)

Incentive stock options are governed by a very tight set of Internal Revenue Code (IRC) restrictions that specify:

- Who is permitted to receive ISOs (answer: only employees)
- A statutory expiration date for ISOs (no more than ten years after the date of the option grant)
- What rules must be stated in the company's ISO documents
- How ISOs are taxed (answer: very complicated; we tackle that one in Chapter 14!)

Nonqualified stock options, in contrast, are defined as "stock option plans that for some reason don't satisfy the legal requirements to qualify as an ISO." NQSO rules and guidelines specify:

- Who can receive NQSOs (answer: not only employees, but also other people such as members of the Board of Directors)
- The tax implications of NQSOs (answer: different from ISOs, but just as complicated! Again, stay tuned for Chapters 12 and 13 rather than worry about all of those details now.)

The most important point to remember about ISOs and NQSOs is that the right-off-the-bat basics of both types of stock options are the same. Both types of stock options grant you the right to purchase shares of stock at some date in the future at a contractually guaranteed price, regardless of how much higher the market price of the stock is than the strike price. The calculations in this chapter's examples and in many of the examples throughout subsequent chapters are unaffected by whether the options are incentive, nonqualified, or a mixture of both types. It's only when we get to the "mechanics" — the nuts and bolts of exercising stock options, how long you hold the shares of stock you acquire, and how all of these various scenarios are taxed — that distinctions between ISOs and NQSOs become significant.

Beware! Some companies will give you little, if any, information about what type(s) of stock options you're being granted! Your prospective employer may provide only the most basic information about your stock options in conversation: the number of shares, the strike price, and the vesting schedule. Nothing more, though, until the stack of papers (specifically, the employment agreement and stock option agreement) are handed to you with a "sign these" command. The antidote: going into job offer discussions fully informed and knowing what questions to ask.

Even though your employment offer letter will mention whether you're being granted ISOs or NQSOs and the stock option agreement will use about 15 pages to describe all of the restrictions that are being placed on your stock option grant, just *try* and get information from your employer about how your options will be taxed or other important information that is dictated by the type of option grant you receive. In most cases, you need to figure out all of this information on your own; so you're doing the right thing by starting now.

Chapter 2

Taking Your Chances: Getting Rich or Going Broke

In This Chapter

▶ Making lots of money: the upside to stock options

▶ Understanding "underwater" stock options and why they might turn out to be worthless

▶ Finding out what happens when a privately held company never goes public or is sold

▶ Discovering the "golden handcuff" problem

▶ Knowing what to do when you're holding underwater stock options

Singer Judy Collins should have added a verse to her song "Both Sides Now" about stock options. Just like clouds, love, and life, stock options seem to have two sides: one wonderful, the other much less so.

When your options are worth a lot, just about *everything* in the world seems absolutely wonderful to you. The rain pouring down on your head? Just a lovely spring shower, that's all. The blizzard dumping two feet of snow in your yard and on your street? Perfect for building a snowman and making snow angels!

Sometimes, though, the opposite is just as true. When your stock option package is essentially worthless, the world seems to be all overcast skies and storm clouds.

Then what's the real story with stock options? Can they really make you rich? Absolutely! But could you really wind up with absolutely nothing despite years of hard work and personal sacrifice? The same answer: Absolutely! Becoming wealthy simply because you have a bucketful of stock options as part of your employment package is *not* your birthright!

This chapter takes a both-sides-now look at stock options: the up and down, the win and lose.

Making Lots of Money: The Upside to Stock Options

Your stock options package is your new best friend . . . and maybe even the ticket to early (even *very* early!) retirement if you are fortunate enough to work for a company that does the following:

- ✔ Is successful in business
- ✔ Is rewarded for that success when the investing public bids your company's stock price higher and higher
- ✔ Grants you a generous portion of stock options during the tenure of your employment

Meet Ray, a computer science major who, right after graduation, goes to work for a 1-year-old privately owned, e-commerce software company on June 1, 2001. Ray receives a package with an option to purchase 5,000 shares, priced at $1 each. Ray's package has "standard" four-year vesting, meaning that each year on the anniversary of this initial stock option grant (which, in Ray's case, coincides with the anniversary of when he started employment) 1,250 shares become vested and may be exercised if the company has gone public.

But wait, Ray's stock option grants are just beginning. At the company's holiday party, the Chief Executive Officer (CEO) gets onstage and tells the gathered crowd that because of everyone's hard work and long hours, the company's new software product is ahead of schedule and has already attracted the attention of five potential customers, two of which will be installing an early release of the product. And, to reward the employees, on January 1, 2002, every employee will receive an additional stock option grant, the exact amount of shares determined by each employee's level. In Ray's case, he gets an option to purchase an additional 2,000 shares, priced at $1.50 per share. As with Ray's initial shares, this batch is also on a four-year vesting schedule.

Six months later, Ray is scheduled for his annual review, which occurs on the anniversary of his hiring date. Ray has done a great job, and not only gets a $5,000 raise but is also awarded an option for another 4,000 shares (again on a four-year vesting schedule). The price per share on this batch is now $2. Keeping track, Ray now has options on a total of 11,000 shares, at prices ranging from $1 per share to $2 per share.

And Ray's stock options keep on coming. At the 2002 holiday party, the CEO announces that to celebrate the 12 Fortune 500 clients the company now has, another round of bonus stock options will be awarded on January 1, 2003. This time, Ray gets one for 3,000 shares, priced at $2.50 per share. And, as you can probably guess, Ray's performance review six months later is stellar: a promotion this time to accompany the $7,500 raise, plus — are you ready — an option to purchase 7,000 more shares, still priced at $2.50 per share. Ray's total on June 1, 2003: options on 21,000 shares, priced from $1 to $2.50 per share.

Next, the big event happens: Ray's company goes public on September 2, 2003, and the company's stock is now listed on the NASDAQ stock exchange. For now, don't worry about the ups and downs of the company's stock price during the first few months the stock is traded. Fast-forward to April 30, 2004, and assume that the company's closing stock price that day is $35 per share.

Table 2-1 shows a consolidated summary of Ray's stock options to this point, and — most importantly (to Ray, at least) — his profit (on paper, that is).

Table 2-1		Ray's Stock Options as of April 30, 2004		
Date of Grant	*# Shares*	*Cost/Share*	*Profit/Share (–$35)*	*Total Potential Profit*
June 1, 2001	5,000	$1	$34	$170,000
January 1, 2002	2,000	$1.50	$33.50	$67,000
June 1, 2002	4,000	$2	$33	$132,000
January 1, 2003	3,000	$2.50	$32.50	$97,500
June 1, 2003	7,000	$2.50	$32.50	$227,500

So all together, on April 30, 2004, Ray is sitting on a profit of $694,000 from his stock options. Note that no single grant has been "of Bill Gates magnitude," that is, for hundreds of thousands or even millions of shares. But a few thousand shares here, a few thousand shares there, and less than three years after Ray started working for the software company (and only three years out of college), Ray has almost $700,000 in *potential* stock profits from his stock options.

Take heed of that all-important word: potential. Can Ray exercise all of his options, immediately turn around and sell his 21,000 shares, and pocket his profit of $694,000 (before he pays taxes, of course)? Not quite. Remember that Ray has four-year vesting on each of his option grants. Assume for a moment that on April 30, 2004, Ray wants to "cash out" as much as he can from his options. Table 2-2 shows how much Ray can actually cash out of each of his option grants, based on the amount of shares that have vested to that point.

Table 2-2	Ray's Stock Options: How Much Is Vested on April 30, 2004?			
Date of Grant	*Total # Shares*	*# Shares Vested*	*Profit/Share*	*"Cash Out" Potential*
June 1, 2001	5,000	2,500	$34	$85,000
January 1, 2002	2,000	1,000	$33.50	$33,500
June 1, 2002	4,000	1,000	$33	$33,000
January 1, 2003	3,000	750	$32.50	$24,375
June 1, 2003	7,000	0	$32.50	$0

Ray's grand total of what he can tap into on April 30, 2004, is 5,250 shares, giving him a pre-tax profit of $175,875. Still not shabby, but substantially less than the $694,000 in paper profits for his total option packages.

Note that this example assumes that Ray wants to exercise whatever shares he can on April 30, 2004, and immediately sell those shares for the market price of his company's stock. Alternatively, Ray might choose to do one of the following:

- Do nothing at that point, and instead, choose to exercise his options at a later time
- Exercise options on the 5,250 shares that are vested at that point, but instead of selling those shares immediately, holding on to them as part of his personal portfolio

So what about the rest — over $500,000? Refer to our discussion later in this chapter on *golden handcuffs*.

In Chapter 6, we talk about deciding whether to exercise vested options, as well whether you should sell those shares immediately or hold onto the stock.

When Good Options Go Bad

So far, this whole stock option business sounds pretty good, right? You get to buy stock at a steep discount to the market price and, if you choose to do so, turn right around and sell those shares of stock for an instant profit — maybe even a very large instant profit. What can possibly go wrong?

The sad story of underwater stock options

Earlier in this chapter, I told you about Ray and how his stock options brought him a tidy profit. Well, meet Ray's coworker Bill, another programmer who joins the company on June 1, 2004, three years to the day after Ray does. Like Ray and everyone else in the company, Bill receives a stock option grant when he begins work. In Bill's case, the number of shares is the same as Ray had received: 5,000. However, the strike price on Bill's options is significantly more than the $1 price that had been in effect three years earlier when Ray started with the company. Because the company has since gone public, the strike price of any employee's grant, typically, is equal to the market price of the stock on the day the grant is offered. On June 1, 2004, the closing price of the company's stock is $38, so that's the price Bill gets.

On January 1, 2005, Bill receives another grant as an end-of-year bonus, this one for 4,000 shares at the market price of $40. On June 1, 2005, Bill receives another grant, this time for 7,000 shares at $40. (The company's stock price hasn't changed much over the past six months, up a little bit and down a little bit and, by coincidence, settles at that same $40 price on June 1, 2005.)

Fast-forward to April 30, 2007. Bill has received several other stock option grants along the way, at prices ranging from $45 to $55. If the company's stock price continues to edge up a little bit each year to, say, $80, then Bill is sitting on a decent potential profit on his options, just as Ray had several years earlier.

But suppose that the company's stock price goes down instead of up — way down. Why? Maybe the company has stumbled in the marketplace. Perhaps the U.S. economy has gone into recession, and most companies' stock prices have dropped significantly. The reason doesn't matter for purposes of our example; assume that on April 30, 2007, the company's stock price is $20.

Table 2-3 shows the status of each of Bill's stock option grants and the paper profit (or, more accurately, the lack thereof) for each:

Table 2-3	Bill's Stock Options as of April 30, 2007			
Date of Grant	*# Shares*	*Cost/Share*	*Profit/Share (–$20)*	*Total Potential Profit*
June 1, 2004	5,000	$38	$0	nothing
January 1, 2005	4,000	$40	$0	zip
June 1, 2005	7,000	$40	$0	sorry

(continued)

Table 2-3 *(continued)*				
Date of Grant	*# Shares*	*Cost/Share*	*Profit/Share (−$20)*	*Total Potential Profit*
January 1, 2006	3,000	$45	$0	too bad
June 1, 2006	6,000	$55	$0	still nothing
January 1, 2007	4,000	$45	$0	forget about it

Bill holds options on 29,000 shares for a total potential profit of nothing! In stock options terminology, all of Bill's options are *underwater*, meaning that for the moment at least the market price is below the strike or exercise price, and they are worthless!

Just because options are underwater doesn't mean that you can't exercise those options if you wanted. No legal restrictions prohibit you from doing so. However, Bill — or you'd be rather foolish to exercise underwater options. Stock options are the right to purchase shares of stock not at the current market price, but at some other predetermined price. When the market price is higher than the strike price of an options grant, then you are, in effect, buying shares of stock in your company at a discount. So would you want to pay *more* than the market price for shares of your company's stock? Of course not.

If Bill wanted to buy, say, 10,000 shares to hold rather than sell immediately, he would buy those shares for $20 — the current market price — rather than exercising his options and paying much more. Worse, if he wanted to buy shares and sell them immediately, then by exercising his options to do so, he would suffer a big loss by buying shares at anywhere between $38 and $45 (the strike prices of his options grants where at least some of the shares are vested on April 30, 2007) and then turning right around and selling at $20. Not a very smart move, that's for sure.

Is getting in early the secret?

At first glance, the difference between Ray's good fortune and Bill's bad luck seems to be a matter of timing. Ray got in early, acquiring what so many American workers sought during the mid- and late 1990s: very inexpensively priced options in a privately held company. Even after the company's stock dips down to $20 per share in mid-2007, all of the options Ray had received through June 1, 2003, can still be exercised and sold at a profit of at least $17.50 per share, given that the highest strike price on any single grant is $2.50 per share. (Note, though, that Ray's grants from mid-2004 and on were at the same prices as Bill's grants — assuming both received their annual review-related grants on June 1 of each year — so some of Ray's stock options are just as underwater as Bill's.)

So that's the answer, right? Get in early, before the company goes public, and you're guaranteed to make at least some money from your stock options, even if your employer's stock drops significantly at some point in the future.

Not so fast. Acquiring and accumulating inexpensive options almost always pays off *if* your employer goes public. When some semblance of sanity took hold in early 2000, and the stock prices of many Internet-related companies dropped — some a little bit, others by 90 percent or more — employees of many companies that had yet to go public learned a painful lesson. Their companies wouldn't be going public at all and in fact, might even go out of business!

Let's take a trip to an alternate dimension, where that universe's Ray goes to work for the same company on the same date and receives the same number of stock options that our Ray did. However, in the other dimension Ray's employer does not go public on September 2, 2003. Maybe the economy is in a prolonged recession; perhaps Ray's company has stumbled badly, and its product is horrible; or maybe both have occurred. Whatever the reason, the company doesn't go public. The company doesn't go out of business; it keeps plodding along, management and employees alike trying their best to produce a solid software product that will be embraced in the marketplace. However, the company's future is quite cloudy.

For Ray, April 30, 2004, is just another day. His stock options do have some value, at least in a technical sense, but Ray doesn't have a potential profit of $694,000, nor does he have immediate "cashing out" potential of $175,875 from his vested shares. Because the company has not gone public, the company does not have a market price for its stock of $35 per share. The result: no profits for Ray.

In Chapter 10, we look at several ways, including a complex formula known as the Black-Scholes Model, by which you can calculate the value of stock options in a company that has yet to go public.

However, Bill might be pleased that the company has not gone public yet. When he begins work on June 1, 2004, and receives his stock option grant of 5,000 shares, the strike price on his grant won't be $38. It will probably be some number less than $5, as determined by the company. So *if* the company ever goes public, Bill will have almost as much upside to his stock options as Ray does, despite starting work three years after Ray.

If you work for a company that never goes public (or is never acquired by a public company, as discussed in Chapter 15), you might have 10,000 or 50,000 or even 100,000 inexpensively priced stock options that you may never be able to profit from.

Stock Options as Golden Handcuffs

In Chapter 1, I mention that a primary reason companies issue stock options to employees is to build a stable workforce with as little employee attrition as possible. By giving employees a piece of the pie through stock options, those employees are (in theory) less likely to jump ship for another job.

Stock option grants vest on a multi-year schedule (typically four years) because even when a company's stock price is way up and employees are sitting on large potential profits from their stock options, they don't have immediate access to all of their profits. Stock options holders in this situation are shackled by *golden handcuffs* — potential wealth that they can't fully get to at that moment, and wealth they would lose if they left the company.

As I discuss briefly in Chapter 1, a stock option grant specifies what happens to unvested options if your employment is terminated. In Chapter 5, we further discuss the legal language in stock option agreements that dictates what happens to your options — vested as well as unvested — if you leave your company.

In most situations, if you resign your employment or are fired, any unvested options are lost, no matter how much potential profit you're sitting on.

What are golden handcuffs?

Let's go back to Ray (the Ray from this universe, not alternate dimension Ray) and take another look at the state of his stock options on April 30, 2004. As shown in Table 2-2, Ray can take profits from vested options on April 30, 2004, in the amount of $175,875, out of a total of $694,000 in total potential profits from all shares of his option grants. The difference of over $500,000 represents Ray's golden handcuffs. If Ray's stock option grants contain typical legal language that takes away all of his unvested options upon his termination, then if he were to resign his employment on April 30, 2004, he will be leaving behind the potential for more than $500,000 in profits. But remember, if the stock price tanks, his options could become worthless.

If, however, Ray continues to work at the company, nothing happens to his unvested options, even as he is exercising all of his vested options and immediately selling his shares to take his profits. The remaining options continue to vest according to the schedule described in each of Ray's stock option grants, and Ray can exercise those vested options some time in the future when he is ready.

So what are the "handcuff" implications? If Ray enjoys his job, gets along well with his coworkers, and generally isn't looking to change employers, then there aren't any handcuff implications. If, however, Ray hates his job — the long hours, the weekend work, his boss, his coworkers, the coffee in the office — then he has a very difficult choice to make.

He has two choices: He can quit and find a new job that is much more to his liking, but by doing so, he is surrendering the potential for over $500,000 in wealth that he has accumulated in his almost-three years with the company, courtesy of his stock options. Alternatively, he may decide that giving up the potential for so much money is definitely not a viable option, and therefore, he will stick it out for another year or two, no matter how much he hates his job. (And he'll start bringing in his own coffee to the office, too.)

If Ray chooses the second alternative — staying in a job he hates because he doesn't want to give up his stock option profits — then he has elected to shackle himself in golden handcuffs. Like anyone wearing real handcuffs, his movements are restrained. But in Ray's case, he's restrained from moving from a job he hates to another employer. And, as you can probably guess, "golden" is used because the restraining factor is monetary.

Conspiracy theory

Remember the Mel Gibson movie *Conspiracy Theory*, in which Gibson's character has all kinds of wacky beliefs about conspiracies? The Stock Options as Golden Handcuffs realm has its own conspiracy theory, which is a slight variation on the "classical" golden handcuffs situation I describe earlier.

The conspiracy theory goes something like this: Some companies deliberately suppress their stock price for some period of time — typically 6 to 18 months — to keep long-term employees and senior-level executives from exercising large batches of stock options, taking their profits, and resigning or retiring.

Say that BigSoftwareCompany, one of the largest software companies in the world, has had a stellar run during the 1990s. The company's stock price has gone up over 2,000 percent as sales have climbed to almost $10 billion annually. Employees have come and gone during that time, of course, as some people have elected to cash in their stock options along the way and either go to new companies or even to retire early.

In the early days of the new millennium, BigSoftwareCompany finds itself facing a changing marketplace, and the company's executive management maps out a new strategy to guide the company's next generation of products. Key to successfully executing this new strategy, however, is a high degree of continuity among key senior managers and long-time technology employees such as chief product architects — basically, the people who really know how things work at BigSoftwareCompany.

During the past two years, every time BigSoftwareCompany's stock price surges because of better-than-expected earnings or a well-received product announcement, an increasing number of senior-level managers and long-time technologists have exercised large numbers of stock options, taken the money, and resigned. No golden handcuffs for these folks; many had left more than a million dollars in unvested stock option potential profits behind, but because they were still able to cash in several million dollars' worth, they were taking the money and not looking back as they left.

Here's where the conspiracy theory comes in.

If BigSoftwareCompany's stock price were to suddenly drop and stay depressed for, say, a year or two, then perhaps other managers and lead technologists who were waiting their turn to jump ship wouldn't be quite as eager to do so, given that they wouldn't be able to cash in their options for anywhere near as much as they could have when the stock price was higher. The stock price shouldn't tank to the point where employees become so dismayed that they think the company is falling apart, and then panic and leave anyway. But if the stock price were to drop, say, 35 percent and stay around that level for a while, then the conspiracy theory scenario could be enacted. Key employees would see an improved stock price, but only *after* the company successfully executed on its strategy and launched its new generation of products. Another year or two of hard work, and then the stock price would come roaring back. Then after mentoring and training a new generation of the company's leaders, its old guard would then be "permitted" to ride off into the sunset, taking their gains with them.

This conspiracy theory scenario isn't quite the same as the typical golden handcuffs situation we describe earlier. The handcuffs in this case aren't the "gold" of right-in-front-of-your-eyes stock profits in unvested options, but rather the future stock profits in both vested and unvested options.

How common is this conspiracy theory scenario in real life? Does the scenario even exist in real life? Perhaps conspiracy theorists have gone a little bit overboard in their belief that a company's executive management would deliberately enact such a Machiavellian strategy. However, this scenario exists, and in fact is quite common in non-technology companies (for example, consumer products companies).

A leading company in a particular industry may stumble a bit, and its stock price may sink and stay depressed for a year or two. All the while, the company retrenches and in many cases, eventually recovers and goes on to new heights, and the stock price soars. Long-time employees who had planned on cashing out and leaving find themselves "handcuffed" by hopes that if and when the company's stock price recovers, then they can take out the full stock value that they had once held.

Why stock options go underwater

Anyone who has dabbled in the stock market — particularly since the late 1990s — knows how volatile stock prices can be. Stock prices go up and down for many reasons, some of them rational and others irrational. Rational reasons for a stock price increasing include a company coming out with better than expected quarterly earnings, announcing a new alliance or new product offering, or announcing that it's about to be sold to another company. Similarly, stock prices logically drop when a company comes out with lower than expected earnings or announces that sales are slowing down and the rest of the year's revenues and earnings might not be so great.

Here are few of the many reasons *your* stock options may go underwater:

- **Company-related financial reasons.** As mentioned previously, shortfalls in quarterly revenue and earnings often drive the company's stock price down. If, say, you recently received a stock option grant, and the company's stock price hasn't gone up much since that date, then when this bad news is reported, your options will most likely go underwater.

- **Other company-related reasons.** Few things will drive a company's stock price down as quickly as a large number of "insiders" (usually key executives and board members) selling large numbers of shares of your company's stock. In some cases, these people may have a valid reason — diversifying their personal assets, for example — but very often, the public perception (right or wrong) is that the people who are "in the know" have little reason to think that the company's stock price will go any higher in the near future, and instead is likely to drop. Before you can say the phrase "heavy insider selling" the stock's price is likely to head downward.

- **Marketplace reasons.** Anyone who followed or was invested in the stock market during 2000 — particularly technology stocks and Internet-related stocks — saw several periods in which most stocks dropped dramatically in price in concert with one another. Even companies with promising outlooks dropped dramatically if, say, their particular market sector fell out of favor. Consider what happened in March and April of 2000, when the NASDAQ dropped almost 40 percent, and many Internet stocks lost 50 percent or more (some, *much* more!) of the value of their stock prices. If, say, you had just received a stock option grant in January or February of 2000 — or even sometime in late 1999 — then the chances were very good that your stock options were very underwater, no matter how well your company was doing.

- **Bad timing.** As mentioned earlier, stock prices are inherently volatile. Even stocks on a long-term upward trend, like Microsoft, Oracle, and Intel, have periods in which their stock goes out of favor and drops 25 percent to 30 percent before resuming its upward climb. Now suppose you happen to start working at one of those companies just before one of those out-of-favor periods. Or perhaps you already work there but receive a new stock option grant (as a result of being promoted), again just before the stock drops. Guess what? Those stock options you received are going to be underwater. In the long run, the stock price may climb back to the strike price of your options grant or even higher, or maybe not.

Reading the Oxygen Meter on Your Underwater Stock Options

Are you totally out of luck if you are holding underwater stock options? Will they ever be worth anything? As with any attempt to predict the future, you can never tell with 100 percent certainty what will happen to your underwater stock options.

If you had worked at Microsoft or Oracle or Intel during the late 1980s or during the 1990s, then you probably had periods when one or more of your stock option grants were underwater. But you know what? You're probably still a millionaire (and you're probably not reading this book because you've retired by now, and stock options are the furthest thing from your mind). So maybe one or more of those stock option grants came at a bad time, just before a dip in the company's stock price. And when you eventually exercised your options and sold your shares, you made a few hundred thousand dollars or maybe a few million dollars less than you would have otherwise. I don't mean this in a sarcastic way, either; I can't imagine anyone who wouldn't have preferred to have received their stock option grant a month or two months or six months later at the lower price and, therefore, gained that much more in eventual profits.

But in a successful company, the dips are part of the overall long-term picture, and in the long run, you're likely to do just fine stock options-wise. Perhaps you'll even catch a few of those short-term price dips as well in future option grants, balancing out the overall picture.

Suppose, though, that sometime in 1998 or 1999, you went to work for a red-hot business-to-consumer (B2C) Internet company. The equation was crystal clear, wasn't it? Be smart enough to go to work for an Internet company and without question, untold riches were just around the corner. After all, this was the New Economy, wasn't it?

Yeah, right! Sure, many people were able to "catch the Internet wave" early enough when any company that began with "e-" or "i-" or ended with "dot-com" was a nearly foolproof road to stock option riches (or at the very least, doing pretty darn well from those stock options). But how about in the spring of 2000, when the bottom fell out of the B2C sector? How about all those B2C companies going bankrupt? How about all those B2C companies' stock prices doing what had never, *ever* been thought possible: dropping below even the ridiculously low strike prices on early employees' stock option grants? Sure, some folks may have received options to buy 50,000 or 100,000 shares of the company's stock at, say, $1.25 per share. But when the stock drops to 75 cents per share — or maybe even becomes totally worthless! — well, underwater is still underwater.

(Then there are those unlucky employees whose employers never were able to go public.)

Real companies versus fad companies

If you have underwater stock options in a real company, then the chances are pretty good that at some point in the future, your underwater options will once again be "in the money" as a result of your company's stock price being higher than the strike price of your stock options.

What do we mean by a real company?

- A company that has real customers (that is, people or other businesses that are actually buying goods or services from your company), has revenue coming in, has made a profit in the past, and has a long-term outlook and a viable strategy to achieve its objectives
- A company with a sound, tested management team
- A company with a relatively stable workforce in terms of low employee turnover
- A company that has successfully adapted to changes in its industry and has typically been considered among the top two to three companies in that particular industry

In contrast, holders of underwater stock options in "fad companies" more often will never achieve the stock option riches they dreamed of when they began working at their respective companies.

A fad company is

- Any company that is created solely to "catch a wave" in some red-hot area of the moment, such as B2C e-commerce, but doesn't have a sound business plan, profits, or much of anything other than tons of investment capital
- A "catch a wave" company that enters a particular market space very late — the 35th online drug store or the 46th e-commerce consulting company, for example — and has little to offer in terms of competing with those companies that arrived earlier in the market space

> ✔ A company that flouts the fact that it is losing tons of money, but not to worry, the company is gaining name recognition — in fact, its entire business plan is predicated around spending most of that investment capital on marketing and advertising, and losing money is an important part of its business model (and the investing public thought this was a good thing!)

Realizing failure isn't just a fad

The rules for real company versus fad company aren't very clear-cut, for example, especially when it comes to stock price. I had a personal — and painful — experience with a former employer, Digital Equipment Corporation, once the number two manufacturer of computers in the United States (behind IBM). A couple of months before the October 1987 "Black Monday" stock market crash, Digital's stock price hit an all-time high of $199 per share. The price weakened a bit over the next two months or so and then, on Black Monday, dropped to around $120 per share. Anyone who was an investor back in the late 1980s recalls that the stock market recovered about a year and a half later — and after a brief downturn in 1990, exploded even higher during the 1990s.

Alas, not so for Digital Equipment, which was a real company. The company mismanaged itself into the ground; the stock dropped as low as the 20s in the early 1990s before the company was bought by Compaq in early 1998 and now no longer exists. Digital didn't have an employee stock option plan for the masses, though there was a plan for high-level company executives. However, the company did have an employee stock purchase plan (ESPP — discussed in Chapter 11), in which most employees participated.

I know of many long-term Digital employees who had purchased and were holding shares of Digital stock, hoping for the company to right itself and to at least get the stock price back above $100 per share (forget about regaining its $199 all-time high). But it never happened, even though Digital was a real company. No doubt the executive stock option holders were left with worthless, forever underwater stock options as well.

In contrast, there's always the chance that a seemingly fad company — say the 10th or 11th one to enter a particular industry — could actually find the secret formula that enables it to blow away its competition, capture lots of market share in a real marketplace, with real customers, and actually turn into a viable, long-term real company itself. Perhaps it takes two or three or four years for that to happen, and all the while its stock price goes nowhere, then finally shoots upward along with the company's good fortunes. In this case, employees holding underwater stock options will eventually and justifiably be rewarded for their heroic efforts and long hours.

The secret is this: *Know* your company, and know it well! In Chapter 17, we talk about the many ways you can get the inside story on the company where you work and possibly predict the future, at least with regard to the potential value — or lack thereof — of your stock options.

Beware of looming expiration dates on older stock option grants you're still holding! If your company's stock price recovers and soars to new heights, but does so two years *after* one or more of your stock option grants expires (the expiration date is typically ten years after the date of the grant), you're probably out of luck!

Chapter 3

Knowing What Kind of Stock Option Situation Is Best for You

In This Chapter

▶ Determine which stock option situation is best for you

▶ Taking into account your personal situation

▶ Considering external factors such as a frenzied stock market (or the opposite)

*I*f you are already in a job where you have stock options, and (at least for now) you have no desire to do any job-hunting, then the key aspects of your stock options and overall compensation package have already been established. However, if you are considering several new employment opportunities, some or all of which come with a stock option grant, then *you* are in the driver's seat in determining how right — or wrong — any particular situation is for you.

This chapter looks at various job-related factors to match *your* attitude and philosophy with the right employment and stock option situation.

Assessing Your Attitude: Entrepreneur, Investor, or Working Stiff?

As you might guess, the right-or-wrong-for-you decision is far more complex than simply calculating the total value of your compensation package (including the stock option component, of course) and then accepting the highest-value offer. Instead, you need to carefully consider factors such as:

✔ Your tolerance for risk

✔ Whether your family obligations and other factors of your personal situation are conducive for you to accept a significantly lower salary in exchange for a chance on a big stock option payoff

✔ Whether you're willing to deal with failure, should your stock options wind up worthless, and you wind up unemployed

Like every other person, you bring a unique, personalized attitude to your job. Ideally, your attitude should closely align with the key characteristics of your job: the number of hours you work each week, how much leadership and management responsibility you have, what you do on a daily basis in your job — and how your compensation package (including your stock options) is structured. Therefore, you need to figure out if you have the temperament and attitude of any of the following:

- An entrepreneur
- A medium-duration to long-term investor
- A plain old working stiff

The entrepreneurial approach to stock options

Think about many of the stock-options-made-them-rich stories you've heard, the ones that go something like, "John Doe quit his job at Megamonolith Industries to join a dot-com startup at half of his old salary. However, within two years, John was worth over $2 million from the gains in his stock options."

These stories typically describe a person taking a big risk in hopes of a big payoff . . . in other words, these are stories of *entrepreneurship*. While many real entrepreneurs — the people who start businesses on their own — might sneer dismissively at these stories as, well, sort of wimpy as compared to their own risking-it-all tales, the important point for you to note is the entrepreneurial *attitude*. Specifically, company-starting entrepreneurs and those who seek their fortunes through large stock option packages with a startup company share an attitude and belief system that is steeped in risk-taking.

Willing to accept a lower salary

The hallmark of a stock option entrepreneur is the willingness to accept a significantly lower salary than could otherwise be earned elsewhere in a position of similar responsibility and organizational level. Basically, stock option entrepreneurs trade off a significant amount of salary for options on many shares of stock with (if everything goes right for the company) significant upside potential.

You find, of course, that the figures vary somewhat from one situation to another. But a general rule is that, if you're a stock option entrepreneur, your salary is roughly half of what you could make elsewhere if stock options weren't such a big part of your compensation. If you're a first-time stock option entrepreneur, this 50 percent rule means that if you had a salary of, say, $125,000 while working in a large corporation with no stock options (or options on only a small number of shares), then you will probably receive a salary of between $60,000 and $70,000 in your new position.

If you're a key high-level executive at a startup company with a big stock option package and you're coming from a large (for example, Fortune 50-sized) corporation, then you could find yourself with a salary that is as much as 80 percent below your former salary!

You have to deal with the obvious financial impacts of a significantly reduced cash flow (more on that later in the chapter when we talk about how to assess your personal situation).

Willing to take on a new attitude

But more important than just the impact of the raw numbers is your attitude in the face of that salary reduction and every other aspect of your new job. Specifically, you must be willing to do the following:

✔ Work in a role where you often find yourself doing many tasks that aren't part of your official job description. ("I'm going to Kinko's for copies . . . does anyone want anything from Starbucks?")

✔ Accept failure; for example, if the company winds up going out of business or needs to lay off a significant number of workers (perhaps including you!), you won't wind up in a deep personal depression.

✔ Start over after a failure in a totally new employment situation, whether that new job is another stock option entrepreneurship or perhaps a more conservative, less risky opportunity.

Almost all stock option entrepreneurs go to work at privately held companies that have neither gone public yet nor been acquired by a larger company. The strike price on most or all of the pre-IPO (Initial Public Offering of shares of a company on the market) stock options they receive is very low — perhaps even only a few cents per share, if they get in early enough.

Taking a job early in a company's lifecycle

Another key indicator of a stock option entrepreneur is someone taking a job very early in a company's lifecycle. Unlike the real entrepreneurs, they don't invest their own money in the company, and don't find themselves using their credit cards to meet payroll. But make no mistake about it, a stock option entrepreneur seeks out opportunities to get into a company very early when the "person on the street's" reaction to the company's name is "Huh? Never heard of them."

Having short-term focus

Additionally, in many stock option entrepreneurship situations you need to have a short-term focus. That is, you help build a company, you profit from the fruits of your labor along the way for several years, and then you cash out big-time, heading off for either retirement or your next entrepreneurial situation.

As a case in point, I saw a picture in *Time* magazine not long ago of the original Microsoft team from the 1970s. Aside from their almost universal horrible taste in clothes and hairstyles (but we'll give them a break, it was the '70s after all), what stood out the most was the fact that Bill Gates was the only person still working at Microsoft! The brief story that accompanied the picture detailed each person's current net worth if known, presumably accumulated largely from the value of their Microsoft stock and stock options. The only other mega-wealthy person aside from Bill Gates was co-founder Paul Allen — like Mr. Gates, a real entrepreneur. The others were all millionaires, but typically each person's net worth was somewhere in the $2 to $4 million range because they had typically moved on to other opportunities relatively early in the company's lifecycle.

Taking an early in/early out approach

And there's the pattern you often find among stock option entrepreneurs: early in, early out, taking their gains with them. Sometimes, they wind up leaving lots of money behind if the company's stock grows and grows and grows. Some high-profile company examples of the 1980s and 1990s: Microsoft, Oracle, Dell, and Cisco. (Note the "high technology" theme, another common element of many stock option entrepreneurs in terms of where they see the potential for the greatest rewards from their stock options.)

However, many other stock option entrepreneurs who pursue the "early out" strategy actually find that they get out before the company's stock price comes back to earth from the stratosphere — sometimes very quickly and very forcefully, much to the displeasure of those who still hold stock and stock options in the company. So, odd as it may seem, sometimes the behavioral patterns and attitudes of stock option entrepreneurs allow them to profit handsomely from their stock options.

Gains you can expect

You might be asking yourself if there are any tangible, quantitative guidelines for stock option entrepreneurs, other than the "expect half the salary you could get elsewhere" rule we mentioned earlier. The answer: yes.

If you're a stock option entrepreneur, you should expect gains from your stock options of at least $750,000 over a four-to-six year period. That is, by the time you call it quits and head off to some new venture or an early retirement, your pre-tax profits from your stock options should be at least three-quarters of a million dollars. If you take a close look at the number of shares for which you receive options, the strike price(s) on your option grant(s); and a realistic expectation on where your company's stock price might go, gains of $750,000 should appear to be a reasonable target.

The flip side, of course, is that if things don't go well, it's entirely possible that your stock options could be worthless. Hard work and long hours just might not result in a big payoff — the same risk-reward equation that a real entrepreneur faces.

Stock options as an investment vehicle

If you're a stock option investor, you think of stock options as an investment vehicle through which you can build a portfolio that contains substantial holdings in the stock of your employer. You may also make open market purchases in your company's stock (that is, you buy shares through your stock broker just like you would any other publicly traded stock), and perhaps you also participate in your company's Employee Stock Purchase Plan (ESPP — see Chapter 11).

The company for which you work will be either privately held or publicly traded. If you're working at a privately held company, chances are the company is past the early stages at which stock option entrepreneurs (discussed in the preceding section) felt the thrill of a company's very early days. If the company is profitable or at least has decent incoming cash flow on its way to profitability, then the chances of going public (discussed in Chapter 7) are very good. After all, building a portfolio of stock that is highly illiquid — that is, you can't easily sell or trade the shares — isn't exactly a smart, risk-managed approach to investing.

You're also likely to want to hold shares of your employer's stock, which you purchase by exercising your stock options, for a long time. The approaches you take to managing your stock portfolio are, for the most part, the same as you would take even if stock options weren't part of your portfolio-building strategy. Any "cashing out" strategy is years away, and the expectation is that, along the way, the shares of stock that you purchase at a discount through your stock options will continue to grow.

You'll also find yourself facing a salary-versus-stock option trade-off, though not as severe as the half-or-more reduction that stock option entrepreneurs wrestle with. Typically, you have to consider a reduction of 20 percent to 30 percent from what you could earn elsewhere. So the $125,000 few-or-no-options executive we discuss earlier would probably receive a salary of between $85,000 and $100,000 (higher than the hypothetical $60,000-$70,000 salary of a stock option entrepreneur, but also with options on significantly fewer shares of stock and with far less upside potential than with an entre-preneurial situation).

If you're an investment-focused stock option holder, your expected value of profits from your stock options is likely to be somewhere between $250,000 and $750,000 over a four-to-six year period. This is less than the upside that a stock option entrepreneur expects, but with a significantly lower chance of those options winding up worthless.

Finally, the employment opportunities conducive to your investment-oriented philosophy about stock options aren't necessarily concentrated in technology companies. Given the tight labor markets of the late 1990s and early days of the new millennium, companies in many different industries offer their employees stock option packages that are significant enough for their holders to build sizable portions of their respective portfolios.

Job security and a steady paycheck — but with a "kicker"

An interesting phenomenon of the economic boom during most of the 1980s and 1990s is that the ever-tightening labor markets caused companies to offer rewards to employees holding jobs as secretaries, receptionists, assembly line workers, and delivery drivers — basically, the "working stiffs" that hold the jobs that have long been the backbone of the American economy.

Few of the people holding these kinds of jobs are likely to have the philosophy of a stock option entrepreneur or even an investment-oriented stock option holder. Rather, these folks are usually unwilling — or often unable — to accept a reduction in salary of 20 percent or more in exchange for the down-the-road potential of stock options. Additionally, the uncertainty that is inherent with stock options — that they may actually never pay off at all — is likely to cause the working stiff to sneer at anyone who proposes any form of an options-instead-of-salary employment opportunity.

Nevertheless, these working stiffs increasingly find themselves holding stock option packages (though those packages are much more modest than those held by stock option entrepreneurs or investment-oriented stock option holders). Why? In a very tight labor market, many companies have no choice but to sweeten the offers to entice candidates to accept jobs of any type and to keep current employees satisfied. Companies strive to keep cash compensation gains in check, so rather than dramatically increase salaries across the board for their workforces, they often use stock options as a "kicker" to traditional salary and benefits packages.

The options-holding working stiff might eventually see a big, big payoff from those stock options. Every so often, you hear about a secretary or receptionist from the early days of some fantastically successful technology company who retires after a decade with options gains of over a million dollars. The more likely scenario, however, is that a modest upside of, say, $50,000 to $100,000 should be expected from those stock options over a period of at least ten years.

Note that the duration of the targeted gain (ten years) is a bit longer for the working stiff than the four-to-six year period for the respective targets of those with an entrepreneurial or investment-focused philosophy about their stock options. Those who are part of the working stiff category tend to have much more job stability than those in the other two categories and are likely to accumulate multiple stock option grants over that longer duration.

The stock option-holding working stiff is likely to exercise options and sell the shares immediately after or shortly after portions of the grant vest, not worrying too much about tax planning or portfolio building. To the working stiff, stock options are basically another form of cash compensation rather than a medium-term or long-term investment vehicle. And, as with salary, taxes are just something that have to be paid to get the money that's left over. Likewise, building a stock portfolio is likely to be of secondary importance to using the money left over after taxes for dental bills, tuition payments, or other basic needs.

Finally, employees with this philosophy of "don't take away anything from my salary, but I'll take a few stock options also" might find themselves working at either a privately held firm or a company that has already gone public. The potential for stock option gains at a privately held firm is usually higher than at an already-public company. The same risk-reward factors discussed in the next section faced by those with other philosophies need to be considered.

Considering Your Personal Situation

So say that deep down, you decide that you're really a stock option entrepreneur. You're certain that you can thrive in the excitement of a technology startup, and you're willing to take that big chance in order to chase after the big payoff from your stock options. But should you?

Philosophy is one thing; your personal situation is another.

Are you unmarried with a few dollars in the bank? Do you have modest living expenses and other obligations — a modest apartment payment, perhaps, and all of your student loans paid off? Do you drive a 3-year old car that's not only in good condition but is also paid off?

Or are you a married father of two, with one more on the way? Did you just buy a new home (in an expensive subdivision) last year? Do you still have $30,000 in student loans that won't be paid off for another seven years? Are you supporting your spouse's elderly parents? Did you just get laid off from a failed startup company where, for three years, you made that options-instead-of-salary bet . . . and lost?

You can probably guess where I'm headed. Entrepreneurial and risk-taking philosophy aside, sometimes you just can't make that big options-instead-of-salary trade-off to get in early at a startup software company. Actually, I'll rephrase the statement. You can make the options-instead-of-salary trade-off, but you shouldn't.

You need to take a long, hard look at all aspects of your personal situation — including current and upcoming family obligations — and be honest with yourself about whether your situation is conductive to risk-taking.

The Two Different Types of Employment Situations

In a very general sense, employment situations fall into one of two categories:

- ✔ High-risk, high-reward situations
- ✔ Risk-managed situations

High-risk, high-reward situations

Much of what we discuss with regard to the philosophy of stock option entrepreneurs (earlier in this chapter) applies directly to various employment situations. Many employment opportunities in which you will receive stock options are extremely risky, meaning the following:

- ✔ The company is almost always privately held and fairly early in its lifecycle.

- ✔ The company tends to be (but doesn't have to be) technology-focused, and its products or services are usually oriented toward emerging technologies that aren't yet widely used.

- ✔ Other competitors with substantially similar products or services are going head-to-head with your company in the marketplace, and only a handful of these companies fighting for market share will thrive (or even survive).

- ✔ The company and its industry are often part of a frenzy.

- ✔ Despite the company and industry being part of the frenzy, that company could fail and go out of business within the next one to two years.

- ✔ You get options on many shares of stock.

If you don't receive options on a substantial number of shares with a high upside potential, then you aren't in a high-risk, high-reward situation at all, but rather a high-risk, medium-reward (or even low-reward) situation, and the risk-reward balance is tilted against you! Translation: You're probably being taken advantage of!

Risk-managed situations

A risk-managed employment situation has lower risk factors than a high-risk, high-reward opportunity. Ideally, the risk and reward sides of the equation should be in balance. That is, a company that you believe is medium risky should still provide a generous stock option package with medium upside potential (related to our discussion about an investment-oriented stock options philosophy, you would be looking for between $250,000 and $750,000 in potential gains).

Likewise, a low-risk, low-reward situation means that you're working for a very stable company in a very stable industry. Even though you may have a stock option package, the upside potential is modest.

In a risk-managed employment situation, the company's infrastructure (that is, its shipping and distribution systems, its sales force, its computer systems, and so on) are usually in place by the time you arrive on the scene. The company might already be a leader in its industry, such as Microsoft in the mid-1990s or Cisco or Oracle in the late 1990s.

Also, options on the lion's share of the company's stock have already been allocated and granted to the founders, the investors, and other key executives who joined early; basically, stock option crumbs are left for you and most of your colleagues.

Putting It All Together

How do your stock option philosophy, personal situation, and employment situation all fit together? Table 3-1 matches the three different stock option philosophies to the two different personal situation possibilities, showing what kind of stock option situation is best for each combination.

Table 3-1	Matching Stock Option Philosophies to Personal Situations and Employment Situations	
Stock Option Philosophy	*Personal Situation Conducive to Risk Taking*	*Personal Situation not Conducive to Risk-Taking*
Entrepreneurial	Should go to a high-risk, high-reward situation; likely to be restless and dissatisfied in a risk-managed situation	Should probably go to a risk-managed situation to regroup or until personal situation improves, and then possibly switch to a high-risk, high-reward situation

(continued)

Table 3-1 *(continued)*

Stock Option Philosophy	Personal Situation Conducive to Risk Taking	Personal Situation not Conducive to Risk-Taking
Investment	A toss-up; either a risk-managed or high-risk, high-reward situation could be appropriate. If high-risk, high-reward, you need to be nimble and quickly find another opportunity if it looks like the company won't be a long-term success	Risk-managed
Working Stiff	Would probably lean toward a risk-managed situation	Risk-managed

Determining the Best Situation for You

Determining the best employment situation and stock option package for you is not simply a matter of looking for the appropriate entry in Table 3-1 based on your philosophy and personal situation. You also need to take a number of factors into consideration, including:

- Making certain that the risk and reward sides of a given employment opportunity are in balance with each other — figuring out if the stock option package you're offered is a fair one

- Understanding the external environment and how that factors into your overall analysis and decision-making process

The risk-reward balance and your share of the ownership pie

Don't confuse the risk-reward equation with the level of your position within a company. You could be a senior-level executive and still find yourself in a risk-managed situation — specifically, a low-risk, low-reward opportunity. Conversely, you might be an entry-level software developer at an Internet startup that is really a high-risk, high-reward situation for you because you were granted options on enough shares to give you potential gains of close to a million dollars, if the company survives!

Even if you're a stock option entrepreneur at heart and you find the perfect high-risk, high-reward situation with options on 100,000 shares — or even more — in most cases, you're getting a teensy-tiny piece of the ownership pie at that company. Even if you get in early, the founders and the investors have already staked their claim to their own pieces of that pie. You need to determine, then, if their offer to you is a fair one, or if instead you're getting only a couple of crumbs and none of the pie filling.

A final point to note is that my own stock option philosophy these days tends to be much closer to investment-oriented than either entrepreneurial or working stiff. Therefore, the minuscule one-tenth of 1 percent ownership percentage was quite significant for me.

Investors typically want some type of say in the companies in which they invest their money. For publicly traded stock we buy in the marketplace, a real voice in company business is all but impossible because of the fractional piece of ownership represented by those 500 shares of General Motors or the 1,000 shares of Cisco. With a privately held company, however, especially one in which my efforts would be a major contributor to the company's success — or lack thereof — I certainly wanted much more of a voice in company matters, as represented by the stock that I would acquire and hold through exercising my stock options.

Considering the external environment and your personal qualifications

Everything we've mentioned in this chapter is either enhanced or hindered by two additional factors you need to consider: the external environment (particularly the economic climate) and your personal qualifications.

They're printing money out there!

I wasn't alive during the California Gold Rush in the mid-1800s or the Roaring Twenties that preceded the 1929 Stock Market Crash and the Great Depression, but I've read that, in those days, if you tripped and fell, you did so because you were too busy counting your newfound wealth.

I was certainly alive during the Great Internet Boom of the late 1990s, however (as well as the Great Internet Bust of 2000, but we'll get to that later), and I can tell you that those days sure seemed a lot like those prior periods of frenzied wealth creation.

A period of extraordinary economic growth and wealth creation can affect stock option opportunities. Specifically, you should note two key points:

✔ **Your salary-versus-stock options trade-off might not be quite as severe, even in a high-risk, high-reward entrepreneurial situation.** The last few years of the 1990s were hallmarked not only by the Internet and electronic commerce taking hold and affecting many aspects of day-to-day life and business, but also by a serious shortage of qualified people to fill the hundreds of thousands of new technology-related jobs being created. Additionally, the economic boom times led to an explosion in investment capital being poured into one Internet startup after another, all chasing the fabled wealth from a company going public and seeing its stock price skyrocket. Therefore, many companies desperately seeking technically qualified executives were offering compensation packages with salaries only 25 percent to 30 percent below those of comparable, non-options-based jobs, and still giving out generous pre-IPO stock option packages.

The lesson: The economic laws of supply and demand apply to your skills and the available pool of opportunities. In very good times such as the late 1990s, you could hold out for more a more generous salary offer than you might have received for a comparable opportunity only a few years earlier. When a prospective employer replies to your salary demands with "well, we're giving you options on lots of shares of stock," you can counter with, "Yeah, so what? I *still* want a higher salary offer!" (But phrase your remarks a little more diplomatically than that, okay?)

✔ **Demand options on more shares of stock.** You can hold out for options on a higher number of shares than you might have otherwise received.

✔ *Beware:* Don't only look at the raw number of shares — 10,000 or 20,000 or 50,000, or whatever the number is — but the proportion of the company's ownership represented by those shares once they are exercised. Many technology companies are notorious for splitting their stock just so they can grant options packages with a larger number of shares. For example, a 2-for-1 stock split doubles the number of shares authorized but halves the price of those shares, so there really isn't any wealth creation from a stock split. That warning aside, in booming economic times, you'll still receive the stock option equivalent of crumbs, but at least you'll get an entire handful of crumbs instead of just a few.

The sky is falling!

So what happened to the Great Internet Boom of the late 1990s? It gave way to the Great Internet Bust of 2000. To be fair, the Internet is still very much in its infancy in an electronic commerce sense (though the Internet itself has been around for years), and it's way too early to declare that the entire Internet electronic commerce era was nothing more than a mirage. In reality, the world of Internet technologies and the companies building and marketing and offering those technologies is just retrenching in concert with economic reality, the result being a "survival of the fittest" contest in all segments of the Internet marketplace.

But what about stock options in such a climate? The answer to that question can be found in a *USA Today* headline from November 1, 2000, on the first page of the business section:

"Dot-com workers opting out of options in favor of salary"

The body of the story (by reporter Matt Krantz) notes that "increasingly it's cash, not options, that talks in the Internet business . . . Many are saying, 'Forget the stock options, just give me a good salary.'"

To read the first part of the story, you'd get the impression that employees of the late 1990s regarded stock options as a means of getting rich quick, but those feelings have since changed and options are to employees like garlic is to a vampire. However, later in the story it was noted that even with increased salaries to compensate for the probable lower upside of someone's stock option package, options were still being used as "a key tool" to attract and retain employees. "Most employees joining dot-coms still expect stock," the story notes.

So just as you should adapt your compensation expectations in we-will-all-get-rich times, you should also adapt your expectations when it seems like the sky is falling. Should you still expect to receive stock options? Certainly. But you should also *demand* a salary with less of a hit (that is, percentage decrease) than you might grudgingly accept in better times when you have a higher degree of confidence that your stock options will pay off big.

What do you offer that's unique?

Take a look at the "A small piece of a big pie" sidebar earlier in this chapter. I had such lofty expectations for a compensation package with a higher stock option component (in terms of ownership percentage) because, in the particular technology segment in which I work, I am in somewhat of a unique niche in terms of combining both consulting management experience and my name as a published author. (Shameless plug: I wrote *Data Warehousing For Dummies* prior to this book, and it's still in print!)

I bring this point up, though, to illustrate that if you have a unique background — a strong relationship with a key customer of the company where you're interviewing, a reputation as an authority in a particular subject area, or perhaps an outstanding management record — then you can demand a higher salary offer and options on a larger number of shares.

Of course, demanding a high salary and a large stock option package is one thing; whether a company is willing to give them to you is entirely another matter.

Consider the Internet boom times of the late 1990s. Almost anyone with any technical ability at all could catch on with an Internet startup — not to mention people with no technical abilities at all who were needed for roles at those companies in recruiting, human resources, and other job functions. In the big picture, however, the dot-com masses were little more than commodities, mostly interchangeable with one another. If you could write computer code in Java you could certainly find a relatively well-paying job with a decent stock option package with little effort, but to be perfectly honest, you and the tens of thousands of other Java programmers were basically interchangeable in the eyes of hiring managers.

The impacts of this interchangeability in many types of jobs are twofold:

- ✔ You will have a bit more difficulty negotiating a stock options package (and the rest of your compensation package) that is significantly above the norm as compared with your peers with similar skills and experience.

- ✔ When boom times fade away, as in 2000 when rational thought returned to the Internet and other parts of the information technology business, you don't really have much of an edge in terms of job security if industry-wide layoffs start.

Conversely, having something unique to offer may not only give you that little bit of "umph!" in negotiating for an extra-generous stock options package, but if layoffs rear their ugly head, you might have a slightly better chance of surviving the purge. Conceivably, if a company can recover from the gloom and doom to go on to new heights, you can still be around to reap the benefits of the company's recovery.

Chapter 4

The Big Guys and The Big Picture

In This Chapter

▶ Getting to know the big guys

▶ Knowing how much of your company the big guys own

▶ Looking at other big guy investment vehicles

Most likely, in your company, you're one of "the little guys." Nobody calls you to see if you'd like to be interviewed on CNBC about your company's outlook, and you don't find yourself hobnobbing with venture capitalists, rock stars, or politicians. Perhaps your position is that of a software developer or a mid-level business analyst or a quality control specialist or any one of thousands of other types of jobs. You might be making good money — maybe even six figures — but in the grand scheme of things at your company, you're not one of the privileged few who people consider to be "the big guys."

But what about those big guys? (Note: I'm using "big guys" in a gender-neutral manner, so the "guys" includes both men and women.) You know that they make more money — lots more money — than you do, and they have a significantly larger ownership stake in the company than you.

And don't forget about big guys who aren't even employees of the company — the people who sit on the company's Board of Directors, venture capitalists and other investors, and outside advisors who are tighter with your company's executives than you can ever hope to be.

At your company, what does the big picture look like, both in a general sense and in terms of stock options and other types of investment vehicles?

Recognizing the Big Guys?

An *affiliate* is a director or officer of the company. Because of the nature of such a position, any affiliate's activities in buying and selling shares of the company's stock are tightly regulated. For example, every time an affiliate wishes to sell shares, he needs to file *Form 144* with the Securities and Exchange Commission (SEC) on or before the proposed date of sale, publicly stating his intention to sell company stock. The number of the form coincides with *SEC Rule 144*, which places restrictions on company stock trading as well as certain holding periods.

Section 16 Reporting Persons are affiliates (directors or officers, as previously described) plus anyone who owns at least 10 percent of a public company (known as a *10 percent Beneficial Owner*). The term comes from Section 16(a) of the Securities and Exchange Act of 1934, which specifies that anyone who is classified as a Section 16 Reporting Person must file various types of stock ownership and "insider trading" forms, such as:

- ✔ *Form 3:* Within ten days of assuming office, a Section 16 Reporting Person must file a Form 3 with the SEC showing how much company stock he holds, and types of stock (common, preferred, different classes of common stock, and so on). Also, if a person's holdings exceed 10 percent of any securities class, he needs to file a new Form 3 indicating so.

- ✔ *Form 4:* Form 4 must be filed every time a Section 16 Reporting Person sells stock or otherwise disposes of shares (such as giving stock to charity, transferring it to a trust, and so on). So basically, Form 144 is filed when an affiliate intends to sell shares; Form 4 is filed when an affiliate actually sells shares.

- ✔ *Form 5:* On or before 45 days before the company's fiscal year closes, every Section 16 Reporting Person must file a Form 5 with the SEC indicating any transactions that somehow weren't reported on a Form 4 — either because some types of transactions don't require a Form 4 to be filed right away, or the Section 16 Reporting Person goofed and didn't file the Form 4 when he was supposed to.

Confused? Don't be. If you are, by definition, a company officer (see the sidebar "Officer, help!"), director, or are otherwise categorized as a Section 16 Reporting Person, then go immediately to have a chat with your company's compliance officer. The *complicance officer* is (or at least is supposed to be) the person who knows all the SEC rules, what forms to file and when, and all the restrictions that you absolutely don't want to violate. For example, if you think that "short swings profit liability" is some type of Big Band-era dance and don't realize that purchases and sales of your company's stock within a six-month period are no-no's and you will owe money to the company if you violate the rule, then you need to have a long, long talk with your compliance officer.

Some, but not all, of the early investors in the company where you work are categorized as Section 16 Report Persons because they may be Board members, have a very sizable (greater than 10 percent) ownership stake, or perhaps both.

However, other investors may be more of the behind-the-scenes types who don't fall under all of the SEC restrictions described in the previous section, but they may still have some degree of influence in the company's direction or a decent-sized share of ownership.

Some of these people may hold stock options in your company but more likely, they have direct ownership through common or preferred stock or some other type of investment vehicle discussed later in this chapter.

Board members

Your company's Board of Directors may be a very proactive Board — regularly involved in company affairs and with most or all members having a sizable ownership stake in the company. Ideally, a company's Board of Directors should be comprised of a mix of people from different backgrounds with different areas of expertise, but all of their respective backgrounds and expertise should be closely aligned with the company's primary business operations and its direction. Further, the board should be "independent" enough to provide an adequate level of *corporate governance*, or oversight of the company operations, policies, and behavior.

Alternatively, your company's Board could be a collection of various venture capital or other investment-related organizations that have funded the company along the way. Sure, these folks put up some money, but they have little or no experience in your company's business and actually add little to the company's business model other than playing matchmaker between your company and other companies in which they've invested.

Finally, some companies have fairly disinterested and detached Boards of Directors that have little or no ownership stake in the company's success. Often these board members are paid to attend Board meetings and have little at stake beyond that.

Hopefully, your company's Board of Directors reflects the first model described: qualified, proactive, independent, and invested. The absence of any one of those four attributes absolutely compromises a Board's abilities to perform its duties on behalf of the company's other shareholders.

"Officer, help!"

Who is considered to be a company officer in the context of all these stock ownership and trading restrictions?

According to www.mystockoptions.com, an officer "includes the company's president; principal financial officer; principal accounting officer; any vice president in charge of a principal business unit, division, or function (such as sales, administration or finance); any other officer who performs a significant policy-making function; and any other person who performs similar policy-making functions regardless of job title."

Identifying the big guys and watching their moves

You absolutely need to know who's who at your company with regard to the big guys, and unfortunately your company may not be forthcoming with that kind of information. Sure, you probably have access to an organizational chart and can look up the CEO and Executive Vice President of Operations and the Chief Financial Officer, but how about all those not-so-apparent big guys who aren't even employees of the company?

And besides knowing who the big guys are, you also need to find out who's buying stock in your company (usually a show of faith in the company's prospects, and a good sign), who's selling (not necessarily terribly bad, but worth watching), and how much the various big guys own.

Your best friend, in this case, is the Internet. You should check out:

- ✔ www.edgar-online.com and www.freeedgar.com: At these SEC sites, you can find all kinds of documents your company has filed if it's publicly traded — annual reports, quarterly reports, proxy statements, and much more. You can also find copies of the SEC Forms 144 and 4 (as well as Forms 3 and 5) filed by your company's Rule 16 Reporting Persons.

- ✔ www.insiderscores.com: Track what insiders are selling and which insiders are buying — not only at your own company but also at other companies, for your own investing purposes.

- ✔ biz.yahoo.com: Yahoo! Finance can also provide you with insider trading data for your company's directors and officers.

Understanding Other Big Guy Investment Vehicles

Many people are surprised to learn that many big guys' ownership stakes aren't comprised of, or have come about as a result of, stock options. Even big guys who do hold large numbers of stock options often have those options as "icing" on top of other investment vehicles through which they've built their sizable ownership stakes. These other investment vehicles include:

- ✔ Restricted stock
- ✔ Warrants
- ✔ Convertible debt

Restricted stock

Restricted stock is sort of a hybrid between regular ordinary common stock (the type that you would purchase on the New York Stock Exchange or the NASDAQ) and stock options.

Like the ordinary common stock, restricted stock comes with voting rights (see Chapter 1) and all of the other attributes of shares of stock. However, a company grants you shares of restricted stock subject to a vesting schedule that is basically like what you would find with stock options.

For example, suppose you join a small software company as Vice President of Product Development, and in addition to whatever stock option grant you receive as part of your compensation package, you also receive a grant of 10,000 shares of restricted stock, subject to four-year vesting. So 2,500 shares of your restricted stock would vest on the one-year anniversary of the grant, another 2,500 on the second anniversary, and so on.

In most cases, the company just grants you the restricted shares outright, and you won't have to pay anything for them. In other cases, you would pay some miniscule amount for those shares, typically a few cents per share if you receive your grant early enough in the company's life.

The "catch" with restricted stock as compared with stock options is that you have tax implications because the value of the shares (less the price you paid for them, if any) is considered ordinary income to you. With most stock option grants, if you never exercise your options because they go underwater and stay underwater, or if your company never goes public, then you won't owe taxes no matter how much those stock options might have been worth on paper. With restricted stock, however, you owe taxes on each batch of shares at the time the restrictions expire. So in this example, at the one-year anniversary, you would owe taxes on 2,500 shares; at the two-year anniversary you would owe taxes on another 2,500 shares, and so on.

You pay taxes on your *gain*, the difference between the value at the time the restrictions expire and the price, if any, that you paid for those shares.

You can, however, file a *Section 83(b) election* to pay taxes within 30 days of the grant for all of your shares, based upon their value on the grant date, which totally changes the tax picture (and introduces a risk of having paid taxes on stock that you will never be able to sell!). I discuss Section 83(b) elections in Chapter 14.

Some companies use restricted stock for many or all employees, not just for the "big guys." So you may find yourself with a mix of stock options and restricted stock as part of your compensation package.

Warrants

A warrant is very much like a stock option in terms of granting the owner the right to purchase some given number of shares of a company's stock for a predetermined price, at some future date.

Some companies use warrants primarily for nonemployees such as contractors, outside advisors, and investors. Conceivably, they could also use nonqualified stock options (NQSOs), which don't carry the must-be-an-employee condition that incentive stock options (ISOs) do.

Warrants may be *marketable securities*, meaning that someone issued a warrant rather than an ISO or NQSO could sell that warrant at some fair market value price to someone else. A company can, however, impose contractual restrictions on the transfer or sale of warrants.

Convertible debt

Sometimes, big guy investors want stock in the companies in which they invest, but investors may not want to *directly* receive stock and stock options in exchange for the funds they invest in a company, particularly a startup whose chances for success aren't all that certain. So they receive *convertible debt*, which is basically a legal IOU on the part of the company receiving the investment funds — sort of like taking out a bank loan, or issuing a corporate note or bond with some interest percentage tacked onto the principal. Technically, the investor isn't investing money, but rather lending money, at least until a conversion takes place.

And that's the key word for investors: *convertible*. If the company is successful, the investor who received and now holds the convertible debt has the right to convert that note into some specified number of shares of the company stock. The investor no longer has the right to be repaid the money that he lent, because the loan was canceled in exchange for receiving stock. However, the stock is likely to be worth far more than the amount loaned plus any accrued interest, which is the reason the investor would do the conversion in the first place.

If the company to which the money was lent/invested is not successful, the investor will not convert the debt and may receive proceeds from the sale of the company's assets.

Knowing How Much of Your Company the Big Guys Own

Every company's ownership picture is somewhat unique. However, you do have certain guidelines to go by at various stages of a company's life, as shown in this section.

The earliest stages of startup

Table 4-1 shows what the ownership typically looks like in the earliest days of a company's life.

Table 4-1	Typical Startup Stage Ownership
Group	*Ownership %*
Company founder(s)	60% to 80%
Early employees	10% to 30%
"Seed capital" investor(s)	5% to 10%

At the earliest stages, the company's founders are still firmly in control, holding an overwhelming majority of the company's ownership. Early employees — those employees who join the startup within the first few months to a year after its formation — typically hold an aggregate stake between 10 percent and 30 percent, with each early contributor's personal share directly related to his or her role and level within the company. An early Vice President may not be in charge of a large organization, but that person may have a personal stake of 5 percent of the company. In contrast, an early working stiff such as a software developer (in a technology startup) will likely have less than a 1 percent share of the company's ownership, and that's before the real money starts coming in, and ownership gets diluted further.

The "seed capital" investor(s) — the person or people who make the initial investments to get the company going — often hold between 5 percent and 10 percent of the company.

At this stage, the company founders' stake is largely in actual stock rather than stock options. The early employees may have shares of actual stock, but chances are they'll hold restricted stock (see the discussion earlier in this chapter), plus stock option grants. A "seed capital" investor such as an *angel investor* — often a friend or colleague who puts in up to a million dollars to a few million dollars to get things past the concept stage — may hold convertible debt, warrants, stock, or perhaps all three.

After the first few rounds of investment

Very often, a startup company receives multiple rounds of investment between its initial funding and the eventual IPO. For example, six months after the company began using several million dollars from an angel investor, the "professionals" (usually one or more venture capital firms) may make an investment in the company. Subsequently, more venture capital money — maybe from the same firms, or perhaps from other VCs who want to get in on the company — will make an additional investment. Table 4-2 shows what the ownership model might look as the company grows, courtesy of a round or two of investment.

Table 4-2	Typical Pre-IPO Ownership After Investment
Group	*Ownership %*
Company founder(s)	25% to 51%
Officers and key executives	5% to 10%
Working stiffs	3% to 5%
Outside investors	25% to 51%

Notice that the founders' ownership stake has greatly diminished, with a range (in this example, at least) the same as that of the outside investors. Also notice the top percentage number in the range for each: 51 percent. By the time two or three rounds of outside financing go by, there's usually a struggle between the founders and the outside investors for that magical 51 percent of the company's voting stock, signifying control of the company.

If the company's fortunes are very tightly tied to the founders in terms of some type of "value proposition" (to use consultant-speak), then the founders will likely be able to retain control of the company, but barely. However, if the company is more or less a "commodity" — just another online retailer, for example — and the founders' contributions are primarily excellent management skills rather than any type of unique value proposition, then chances are, the investors will grab control by that stage of the company's life. How? Each time additional funding is brought into the company, the founders' percentage of ownership diminishes. Once the founders' stake drops below

50 percent, the founders could conceivably be outvoted by a coalition of all of the other investors. The lower the founders' stake, the greater the chance of losing control.

By this time, the stake of the key executives and officers has dwindled a bit, down to an aggregate 10 percent at most. The earliest key contributors probably still have 3 percent to 4 percent each, but those who arrived later probably have at most a 2-percent share, most likely 1 percent or even less.

And for the rest of the folks working the 90-hour weeks (the working stiffs), if any one of them has more than ½ of 1 percent of the company's ownership, they should be very thankful. Chances are that each working stiff has options on at least 10,000 shares, but there are probably 20 million shares outstanding by this point, with the overwhelming majority being held between the founders and investors.

At this point in the company's life, stock options start to become a large part of the compensation packages for new employees at all levels, rather than stock or restricted stock grants.

After going public

Table 4-3 shows the allocation of ownership in a typical post-IPO company.

Table 4-3	Typical Post-IPO Ownership
Group	*Ownership %*
Company founder(s)	10% to 25%
Officers and key executives	2% to 5%
Working stiffs	<3%
Outside investors	15% to 25%
Investing public	20% to 30%

Not surprisingly, every group's aggregate ownership percentage has dropped to "make room" for the investing public that buys shares at the IPO and afterwards. An interesting — and often worrisome — phenomenon, however, is how small of a percentage of a company's ownership is held in aggregate by the investing public.

A company with an ownership allocation such as that shown in Table 4-3 is often referred to as being "dominated by insiders." In good economic times with a strong stock market, an insider-dominated ownership model isn't too much of a problem and can often work to a company's advantage (or at least to the advantage of their stock price). Because a relatively small number of shares are available for the general investing public, the great demand for those shares drives the stock price higher and higher in a classical supply-and-demand imbalance.

However, when the mood of the stock market turns sour as it did during much of 2000, especially with regard to the stocks of smaller, insider-dominated companies, then the ownership model can work against a company's fortunes and those of its stock price. The problems are magnified if the company starts going through a downturn in its sales and earnings.

Specifically, a company may (rightly or wrongly) be perceived as "not being real" and simply trying to dump loads of shares still held by insiders — typically the early outside investors, such as the venture capital firms, and the founders as well as early key executives — on an unsuspecting public before the company's stock price collapses.

And what about the working stiffs? Not only has their ownership percentage shrunk even more, but their potential ownership percentage is largely through stock options, most of which are filled with unvested shares. Consequently, even if the 15-hour days are becoming unbearable, they don't have quite the luxury of cashing out, at least anywhere near the extent that the big guys (executives as well as investors) do.

The Fortune 500 stage

For kicks, Table 4-4 shows what a typical Fortune 500 company's ownership model might look like. The type of company depicted here is one in which the founder is long gone — a U.S. Steel rather than a Microsoft or Oracle, where Bill Gates and Larry Ellison are still with the companies they founded and still holding sizable equity stakes.

Table 4-4	Typical Fortune 500 Ownership Model
Group	*Ownership %*
CEO	3% to 10%
Officers and key executives	5% to 10%
Working stiffs	<2%

Group	Ownership %
Institutional investors	40% to 60%
General investing public	20% to 40%

The institutional investors (pension funds, mutual funds, insurance companies, and so on) have become the new "big guys" in terms of aggregate ownership stake and influencing who sits on the company's Board of Directors, whether a CEO is fired, and who the new CEO will be — decisions that the company's founders used to make.

The "Friends and Family" Stock Program

Sometimes, it pays to be a friend or family member — or a business partner — of a big guy.

Many companies who have filed for an IPO institute a "friends and family" stock program to allow "outsiders" who don't hold stock or stock options to get in on the company's IPO. Sometimes, the friends are really friends, and "family" really means relatives. Key employees may have the option of designating a few friends or relatives that they want to be able to buy stock at the IPO price.

In many cases, however, "friends and family" stock is set aside for current and potential business partners. The argument goes that a company "is only trying to reward those who made this IPO day possible by supporting the company along the way." (Sounds like an Oscar acceptance speech, huh?) The darker side, however, is that "friends and family" stock is often intended to influence future behavior and business decisions rather than reward past alliances and support.

A typical "friends and family" program works like this (assume the company about to go public is a software firm):

1. The company and its underwriters designate some number of IPO shares that will be set aside for "friends and family" as designated by the company's management team.

2. Among the friends and family are real relatives and friends, plus consulting company executives, particularly those who are in charge of practice areas specializing in whatever discipline the software company's products fall into. These consulting companies typically have had alliances with the software company in the past, but (for you techies, I'll phrase

this in data modeling terms) there has been a "many-to-many relationship" between the consulting companies and software firms (including this one) in this particular space. That is, consulting company A has alliances with software vendors 1, 2, and 3, even though those three software vendors are competitors of each other. Likewise, consulting company B has alliances with the same 3 software vendors. So that means that software vendor 1 has alliances with at least two different consulting companies (A and B so far), who compete against each other. Got it?

3. A recipient of the "friends and family" offer will receive an official package from a stockbroker detailing the offer, including the maximum number of shares that person could purchase if he or she wishes to participate. If the IPO is over-subscribed (meaning that demand for shares is greater than supply), then assuming the company doesn't change the IPO to issue more shares, chances are that each "friends and family" subscriber will actually be offered fewer shares than he or she signed up for.

4. If the recipient wishes to participate, he fills out the form, signs it, and sends it back to the stockbroker.

5. After the IPO, the recipient is contacted by the broker indicating how many shares were actually allocated to him or her. The shares are received in exchange for sending a check, just like buying most kinds of stock through a stockbroker.

Again, you could make the argument that in the case of business relationships (as contrasted with real friends and relatives), the whole concept of a "friends and family" stock program is ethically challenged. Companies often issue "friends and family" offers to industry analysts and writers. Would they be hoping to favorably influence the for-the-public analysis of their products or services? (The shock!) Would a software company extending a friends and family offer to a consulting company's Vice President of Sales and CEO be trying to influence a tighter alliance between the two companies, even though the vendor's product is way, way behind its chief competitor's functionality and ease of use?

Loans for the big guys

The big guys get not only stock and stock options — and don't forget about lots of money — but also loans to pay for their stock and option treats.

The little guys and working stiffs who are fortunate enough to be sitting on large stock option gains may wish to exercise their options and hold those shares to gain preferential tax treatment. But if the total exercise price of all those shares is in, say, the hundreds of thousands of dollars, chances are the little guy would be forced into doing a cashless exercise — with the accompanying higher taxes — because he or she doesn't happen to have several hundreds of thousands of dollars just laying around.

But the big guys often negotiate loans for such purposes as part of their employment agreements. Not just stock options, either; loans are often available for the purchase of restricted stock. These loans are offered by the company, often with very low interest rates and prolonged repayment periods, and may even be forgiven under certain circumstances.

Not bad, huh? It's nice to be a big guy in the stock and stock option world.

Part II

Details, Details: What You *Must* Know about Your Stock Options

The 5th Wave — By Rich Tennant

©RICHTENNANT

"I read about investing in a company called UniHandle Ohio, but I'm uneasy about a stock that's listed on the NASDAQ as UhOh."

In this part . . .

This part goes beyond the fundamentals and digs deep — *very* deep — into all kinds of little details about stock options that you need to thoroughly understand. You'll explore the legalese (as well as potential problems and traps) in the stock option grant paperwork that you'll need to sign. You'll also see how you can exercise your stock options to purchase shares of stock. This part also discusses the difference between stock options in a privately held company versus a publicly traded company, as well as explaining why you aren't allowed to trade shares of your company's stock at certain times. You'll also get a guided tour of Internet resources you can use to stay up to date with the latest stock option developments.

Chapter 5

Deciphering the Legal Language of Stock Option Agreements

In This Chapter

▶ Understanding your stock option agreement as a legal document

▶ Deciphering Stock option agreements for ISOs and NQSOs

▶ Understanding the contents of your stock option agreement

*W*hile the fundamentals of stock options are fairly basic — you lock into a purchase price for shares of your employer's stock for some time in the future — the stock option agreements that you have to sign aren't quite as straightforward. If you fail to thoroughly read and understand every single clause of your stock option agreement, then you may be in for some rude, nasty, unpleasant, and distasteful surprises. (Hopefully four adjectives get the point across.)

In this chapter, we go through what you can expect to find in a stock option agreement, beginning to end. And we discuss how information that doesn't appear in your agreement can affect you and your stock options.

Knowing What an Employee Stock Option Agreement Is

In Chapter 1, we briefly mention that a stock option agreement is a legal agreement between you and your employer. The agreement document that you sign is legally binding and is the official set of rules that govern the terms and conditions of your stock options. As with most written legal agreements, the contents of the written stock option agreement supersede any verbal promises or terms that your hiring manager or a Human Resources (HR) representative made to you. (You may even find a clause near the end of the stock option agreement specifically stating that the contents of this written agreement supersede previously communicated verbal terms.)

The stock option agreement is a combination of *company-specific rules* and legal rules that primarily address U.S. tax and securities laws as they apply to stock options.

"Law is law," meaning that your employer has almost no recourse to offer terms different than those permitted by laws and regulations governing stock options. Company-specified rules stated in the stock option agreement, however, are generally administrative in nature and are not likely to be changed according to an employee's individual circumstances. Providing for terms and conditions that are applicable to all plan participants ensures fair and equitable treatment and clear parameters within which the company's stock plan administrator can work.

In many companies, you find that stock option agreement paperwork can be very, very slow. You might be told by your manager in March that you're being granted options on an additional 3,000 shares, but the paperwork may not be routed to you until October of that year. In *most* cases, a written stock option agreement will find its way to you for signature prior to the first point at which you can exercise part of that option (usually the one-year point at which your first group of shares vests), but do not assume that to be the case.

At about the three-month point after being informed of a stock option grant, start pestering your manager if you haven't received any paperwork.

Figuring Out What Kind of Stock Option (s) You Have: ISO or NQSO

Somewhere near the very top of the stock option agreement paperwork that you receive should be an indication of whether that particular stock option grant is an ISO or NQSO. You need to make sure that:

- ✔ If you were expecting to receive an ISO, make sure the paperwork indicates an ISO, and vice versa for an NQSO.

- ✔ If you hadn't been told what kind of stock option grant you'd be receiving, make sure you have in front of you the first official indication that you are being granted an ISO or NQSO.

- ✔ If your stock option grant is to be a combination of ISO shares and NQSO shares (which means you actually have two stock option grants), make sure that you receive two sets of paperwork, each appropriately labeled.

- ✔ Your employment agreement should also indicate that, at the time of hire, you are receiving an ISO grant, an NQSO grant, or a combination of both, as well as the appropriate number of shares; make certain that the details in the employment agreement that apply to the grant match the stock option agreement paperwork.

The indication on a legal agreement that the grant is an ISO or NQSO automatically includes all of the tax and securities law regulations governing that type of stock option grant, even if those regulations aren't explicitly spelled out in detail in your agreement. Therefore, make sure you fully understand the implications of the type(s) of grant(s) you receive.

Trudging Through the Details of Your Stock Option Agreements

Details, details, details. If you're like most people (including me), your eyes glaze over when you're handed a 10 or 15 page legal document with all kinds of "thereby" and "now therefore" and "whereas" clauses. Just like with mortgage agreements and car loans and insurance policies, most of us instinctively just want to zoom through the details, understand the bottom line, and just sign the documents in front of us.

Signing a stock option agreement without thoroughly understanding what's contained in that legally binding document would be a gigantic mistake.

In a stock option agreement, you will typically find clauses that deal with:

- Important dates
- The number of shares of stock covered by that particular grant
- The kind of stock the grant covers
- The strike price
- The vesting schedule
- Rules that tell you if your option is even exercisable at all if your company is still privately held
- How you can exercise your stock option (assuming, of course, that you're permitted to do so)
- Rules that govern when you must surrender your stock option and under what conditions
- When the option expires
- "Change of control" clauses that describe what happens if your company's ownership changes
- The rights you have — and don't have — as an option holder
- References to your employment agreement, if applicable (not all employees have employment agreements)
- And in case you haven't read enough legalese, even more supporting legal clauses, just for good measure

The date of the agreement

Many people don't really pay attention to the date of a legal agreement, figuring that as soon as they sign it, it's official, so what's the big deal.

In the case of a stock option grant, the date of the agreement is a very big deal. Several of the most important clauses you'll find in the agreement, such as the expiration date and the vesting schedule, are date-dependent and are tied to the date of the agreement.

As an extreme example, suppose that the year portion of the agreement date read "2002" when it was supposed to be "2001." Suppose also that the vesting schedule didn't give specific dates for when each portion of your option vested, but instead used relative dates such as stating "2,000 shares will vest one year after the date of this agreement, an additional 2,000 shares will vest two years after the date of this agreement," and so on. If you don't catch the error in the date, you could conceivably cheat yourself by delaying the various vesting dates by one year for each batch of shares covered by that grant. Whereas a good employer would likely help you resolve the matter and treat you fairly, another employer with, shall we say, a culture of being ethically challenged may take the approach of "too bad, you signed it; tough luck."

So pay attention to the date of the agreement and avoid those types of messy situations!

Note that the date of the agreement should also match any dates or events specified in your employment agreement with regard to your stock options. For example, I once received a stock option grant at the time I began a new job, and the timing of the stock option grant was to be (as stated in my employment agreement and the offer letter) on the date of the company's next quarterly board meeting, which was scheduled for six weeks after I began work. Therefore, when I received my stock option agreement for that particular grant about six months later, I made certain to verify that the date on the document was indeed the date of the company's board meeting, and that the strike price on that grant matched the company's stock price that day (it was a publicly traded company).

Even if you're beginning a job at a privately held company, you can — and need to — still ensure that the strike price on the grant is correct for the date of the agreement.

- ✔ Before you accept the job, ask what the date of the stock option grant will be (that is, your first day of work, some future event like a board meeting, or some other date or event).

- ✔ At the same time you ask about the date of the grant, ask what the price will be. Privately held companies know at least a few weeks, if not longer, before they will adjust the strike price on options grants to their existing employees and new employees joining the company.

> ✔ Make sure that when you finally get paperwork, the date and the price are what you were told. If there are any discrepancies, don't sign anything until you get matters straightened out!

Even if there is no time delay specified in your employment agreement, you should always double-check the strike price written on your stock option agreement against the date of the agreement, whether the company is publicly traded or privately held. Again, paperwork may be months in coming to you; don't overlook a simple point that could prove very costly to you if an error has been made.

The number of shares

Your stock option agreement explicitly lists the number of shares covered by that grant. You need to make sure that the number is correct based on your discussions with your hiring manager or HR representative. Specifically, you need to double-check the following:

> ✔ The spelled-out number (for example, "Thirty Thousand") matches the numeric number (for example, "30,000") if the document uses both forms.

> ✔ Throughout the document, make sure that all other references to the number of shares are the same. For example, if a specific number of shares are listed for each vesting date, make sure that the numbers of shares for all of the dates correctly add up to the total number of shares covered by the grant.

> ✔ Make sure that any percentage references to the number of shares covered by some event are correct. For example, suppose you have a stock option grant for 30,000 shares, and the agreement discusses what happens if you're laid off: "If your employment is terminated by Company, and if on the date of termination less than 50 percent of the total number of shares of this Grant have vested, then 50 percent of the total number of shares of this Grant, or 15,000 shares, will automatically vest." You need to double-check that the "50 percent number" specified is correctly stated. (In this example, 50 percent of your grant is 15,000 shares, so the number is correctly stated.)

You need to cross-reference the number of shares in the stock option agreement with any numbers specified in your offer letter and employment agreement as well.

Time is on your side. Or is it?

At a previous job, I received my stock option grant at board meeting several weeks after I started with the company. The company's stock price on my first day of employment was in the low 20s. By the time the board met six weeks later, the company's stock price had gone up 50 percent, to the mid-30s! There wasn't anything I could do about it, and I can't really blame the company for the 50 percent increase in my strike price given that the price was established by those who bought and sold the company's shares in the publicly traded stock market. However, I lost a lot of potential appreciation in the value of the shares covered by that particular stock option grant because of that delay. The opposite could have happened, of course — the stock could have dropped significantly in value, and I could have received a "bargain" in the strike price.

Beware, though, in a hot stock market, such as what we saw in the late 1990s, rapid upward movement in stock prices may be a good thing if you already hold partially or fully vested stock options that you want to cash out. However, if you're waiting on an option grant, a prolonged delay between the event that triggers that grant (such as starting your new job) and the actual date of the grant can be very costly! Not only can you lose out on a lot of value appreciation, but future significant dates, such as vesting dates, are likewise delayed, perhaps hindering your ability to profit from exercising your options if you lose that six or eight weeks of flexibility.

The primary reason for paying such careful attention to the number of shares is not because you need to make sure your employer doesn't cheat you. Instead, you're primarily looking for "cut and paste" errors that are likely to occur in situations such as:

- ✔ If you've negotiated for a greater number of shares on your option grant than was on the original draft paperwork you received as part of your employment offer package
- ✔ If an HR representative is using the word-processing document from one of your existing stock option grants as the "template" for a new grant and only changes some of the numbers in the document while creating the stock option agreement for you.

What kind of stock

In almost all situations, your stock option grant gives you the right to purchase shares of the grantee's *common stock*, as contrasted with preferred stock, restricted stock, or some other equity class. Your stock option agreement should explicitly state "common stock" in the clause that describes the option being granted to you. If your agreement with your employer is for some other kind of stock, then the document should accordingly explicitly state which type.

The strike price

You may find a term other than "strike price" used in your stock option agreement. Other commonly used terms are *option or exercise price*. Regardless of the terminology, you need to make sure that you carefully study the context of the sentence and paragraphs in which the price of your options is specified. Make sure that the sentences are grammatically and syntactically correct. (Seriously! You don't want an option agreement to turn out to mean something entirely different than you expect because of careless wording on the part of whoever wrote the agreement.)

As with the date of the grant and the number of shares, you need to make sure that the strike price is correctly stated. If wording is used in addition to numbers — for example, "an option price of Three Dollars ($3) — make sure that the words and numbers match.

Legal Unease

Several years ago, I hired a regional consulting services manager to work for me, and his offer letter and employment agreement stated that he was to receive an option on 4,000 shares. The date of his stock option grant wasn't the date he began work, but rather the date of the company's next board meeting.

About five months later, I received a voicemail message from him complaining that he had just received his stock option agreement paperwork, and the number of shares indicated was 3,000, not the 4,000 that was expected. Assuming that the paperwork was in error, I promised that I'd quickly have the mistake corrected and would have the Human Resources department get corrected paperwork to him. However, when I checked into the matter I was told by an HR representative that the paperwork wasn't in error, and in fact if I looked at the standard company employment agreement, the language read something like:

"You will be recommended to receive a non-qualified stock option grant for 4,000 shares on the date of the next Company Board meeting at the approval of the Board."

The key word in that paragraph: recommended. I was told that the person I had hired had been recommended for an option for 4,000 shares, but because there were so many new hires that quarter, the Board of Directors decided to reduce the regular number of shares for each position level in the company to accommodate the increased number of people that needed to receive stock option grants.

He (the person I had hired) was furious when I relayed this information to him; I was furious because I believed (and still do, to this day) that he was being cheated, no matter how the carefully constructed wording of his employment agreement read. The HR representative tried to smooth over the situation by promising that sometime later that year, he'd receive a new grant for the additional 1,000 shares he had been expecting plus an additional 1,000 shares on top of that, but the strike price would be different, the effective date of the grant would be different, and all in all, he was still being cheated.

Not surprisingly, he left the company a few months later.

You also need to watch out for any currency conversion issues. If you're a U.S. citizen working for a U.S. company at an office in Canada, you want to make sure that the "dollar" figures stated in your stock option agreement refer to U.S. dollars, if that's what your agreement is supposed to be. Therefore, a symbol such as "USD" (for U.S. dollars) should be included next to the price in a manner that is recognized legally.

You must make sure that the strike price is the correct price, neither higher nor lower than it is supposed to be. The downside of a higher-than-it-should-be strike price is fairly obvious. If you're expecting a stock option grant at a price of $6 per share, and the document reads $7, you would likely cheat yourself out of $1 per share profit on your stock option.

Though you might think that a strike price accidentally stated as a lower price is a bargain (for example, $5 instead of $6, giving you an extra $1 per share profit), don't let a mistake that appears to be in your favor go uncorrected. Why? Because there are usually taxation implications if you are granted an option with a strike price lower than the fair market value of the stock. In Chapter 12, we talk about how stock options are taxed. For purposes of our discussion here, though, just take note that you don't want to be unexpectedly hit with a taxation situation because you thought you'd let an error in your favor slide by. Make sure the price is correctly stated.

The vesting schedule

As we discuss in Chapter 1, stock options usually vest according to some time-based schedule, to keep employees locked into a company. If employees were to leave, they would be forfeiting large gains on their unvested shares that they can't touch. (Hey, I know that sounds cynical, but as we discuss in Chapter 2, a company isn't granting you stock options just because it feels like sharing ownership for the heck of it.)

Make sure that the vesting schedule written in your stock option agreement matches the vesting schedule you discussed with the hiring manager or HR representative.

Typically, stock options have vesting schedules from between three to five years, with four-year vesting being the most common. The way in which the vesting schedule is stated in your stock option agreement, however, could vary greatly from one document to another. For example:

✔ The vesting schedule may be specified in a paragraph that says, "twenty-five percent (25 percent) of the total number of options covered by this grant will vest one year after the date of this grant; an additional twenty-five percent (25 percent) of the total number of options covered by this grant will vest two years after the date of this grant;" and so on.

> ✔ You may see a small table with columns labeled "Vesting Date" and "Number of Shares Vested" with each row containing an anniversary date and the actual number of shares (for example, 7,500 shares) that vest on that date.
>
> ✔ You could see a small table with columns labeled "Vesting Date" and "Percentage of Shares Vested" with each row containing a date and the percentage (25 percent, 33 percent, or whatever) assigned to that date.

Your stock option grant may feature some type of staggered vesting schedule. For example, I once held a series of stock option grants that vested at 25 percent of the shares one year after the date of the grant, and the remaining 75 percent on a monthly basis from the one-year point to the four-year point. As I recall, the wording in the stock option grant went something like ". . . and the remaining (X) number of shares vesting in equal increments of (Y) shares on the 5th day of each month between (the one-year anniversary of the grant) and (the four-year anniversary of the grant)." (In the wording in the above example, "X" represented the remaining 75 percent of the total shares of each grant, while "Y" was the incremental monthly vested amount after the first year had been reached. Since I had multiple grants with different numbers of shares, the actual numbers varied from one agreement to another.)

No matter how the vesting schedule is worded — paragraph form, table, or a combination of both — and whether numbers, percentages, or a combination of both are used, make sure everything adds up correctly and is assigned to the correct dates!

You could conceivably find an exception to the typical three- to five-year vesting schedules if you're receiving a stock option grant as part of some type of special circumstances. For example, I (and all of my coworkers) once received two different stock option grants as part of an annual bonus in lieu of the cash bonus that we should have received. (Don't ask; it's still a painful subject!) The company, knowing that it had an angry mob with pitchforks and torches clamoring at the castle gates yelling, "Send out the monster!" (oh, wait, that was in *Young Frankenstein*; nevertheless, we were an angry mob, and it's a good thing we didn't have any pitchforks in the office!), established a vesting period of under six months for both grants so if the company's stock price held up, we'd receive the same amounts we had expected from our cash bonuses, but through stock option profits instead.

(As an aside, it didn't work out; the stock price collapsed just as the bonus options were vesting. Some people who were still with the company nine months later were able to take advantage of a brief jump in the company's stock and pick up a little bit of a gain, but the stock price soon headed way down.)

Split adjustment clause

Be certain that your stock option agreement also includes a clause that specifically states that the number of shares and the strike price covered by your grant will be adjusted accordingly if the company splits the stock. Otherwise, you're probably in for a nasty surprise!

Several years ago, when I was interviewing for a job, the stock option grant for that position was for 30,000 shares of the company's stock, which was still privately held. In negotiations with the company's founder, he casually mentioned that a 2-for-1 stock split would be occurring before the actual grant date, the purpose being to make more shares available for stock option grants to new employees as the company was growing. Basically, the company was close to using up all of the shares it had previously set aside for stock option grants, and needed to create additional shares.

My reply was that if a split was occurring, my stock option grant should be for 60,000 shares, not 30,000. The company founder seemed surprised at my request, and our discussions eventually ended with me declining the job offer.

What was my reasoning? In Chapter 3, we discuss making sure that the risk and reward sides of any given employment are in balance, and I explain how I almost ended up in a high-risk situation with an options grant for one-tenth of 1 percent of the company's ownership. Well, the situation here is the same one. To go into a bit more detail, without the 2-for-1 stock split, the 30,000 shares would have given me options on shares that represented one-fifth of 1 percent of the company's ownership (still nothing to write home about, that's for sure). However, with the stock split and with the company refusing to adjust the number of shares on the stock option grant, that one-fifth of 1 percent was cut in half to one-tenth of 1 percent. (Just to make sure you follow the math: The total number of shares of the company's stock would double after the split, but I would still have options on the same number of shares as if I had joined the company and received the stock option grant prior to the split, resulting in half of the percentage of ownership I would have had prior to the split.)

Consequently, I would have been compared with someone at the same level who joined the company prior to the split and had also received an equivalent stock option grant for 30,000 shares, I would have had only half of the ownership rights of my peer should we have both exercised and held our respective shares of stock.

Stock splits can also have a horrible impact on shares for which you've already received an options grant but have yet to exercise your option and purchase those shares. Consider the following example. You take a job with a publicly traded company and receive a stock option grant for 50,000 shares with a strike price of $40 per share. The company has 5 million shares authorized at that time, meaning that you have an option to purchase shares representing one percent (50,000 divided by 5 million) of the company's ownership.

So the example doesn't become overly complicated, assume that you have four-year vesting on those shares but you don't exercise the option on any of them before the entire grant vests four years later. Suppose that five years after the date of the grant (again, all your shares are now vested) the company's stock price has gone up 50 percent, to $60 per share. Not the 200 percent or 300 percent gain you had hoped for, but not too bad, and you're sitting on profits of $1 million (50,000 shares times $20 per share profit).

Before you can exercise your options, however, the company announces a 2-for-1 split, meaning that after the split the stock price will be $30, and stockholders will then each have double the number of shares as compared with their respective holdings before the split.

But how about you? Let's assume that your stock option agreement contains nothing at all about adjusting the number of shares and the share price after a split. Your agreement simply reads that you have the option to "purchase Fifty Thousand (50,000) shares of common stock of the Company at an option price of $40 per Share."

We'll get to the financial impact in a minute; first, let's look at the ownership impact. Your 50,000 shares are no longer representative of 1 percent of the company's ownership, since the company now has 10 million shares instead of 5 million after the 2-for-1 split. So you suddenly have the option to purchase ownership worth only one-half of 1 percent.

The financial impact is much worse. Think about the precise wording: "purchase 50,000 shares at an option price of $40 per Share." The current market price of the company's stock after the split is $30 per share, so you've gone from sitting on a $1 million profit to having 50,000 underwater options! Would you exercise options at $40 per share if the market price is $30 per share? No! (Chapter 2 discusses underwater stock options.)

It is possible that the company's stock option plan document(s) — not your stock option agreement, but rather the documents that govern the company's plan for everyone — make provisions for stock split adjustments. That's why, as we mention later in this chapter, you need to read the company's stock option plan documents as well as your own stock agreement to make sure! Regardless, you should insist on a split adjustment clause being part of the stock option agreement before you sign it. I've seen draft agreements that made no mention at all about adjusting for stock splits. It's possible that the company's overall stock option plan did cover splits, but not having been offered a copy of the plan to read, I couldn't make that assumption with any certainty (and I didn't go far enough along in the interviewing process to really care). Also, as we'll discuss later, don't expect to have too much in the plan that's in your favor should a dispute arise between you and your employer.

Knowing When Your Option Is Exercisable

Your stock option agreement will likely have a clause that explicitly states when your option becomes exercisable. Note that "becoming exercisable" is not the same as vesting. Whereas vesting applies to some portion of the total number of shares covered by the option grant, "becoming exercisable" refers to the option grant itself.

If you go to work at a privately held company and receive a stock option grant, your stock option agreement might specify something like the following:

"The Option shall become exercisable to the extent then vested on the first to occur of 1) a Change of Control, or 2) six months after a Public Offering of the Company's stock. Both 'Change of Control' and 'Public Offering of the Company's stock' are defined in the Company's Stock Option Plan."

Translation of the above: Unless a change of control (which we discuss later in this chapter and in more detail in Chapter 14) or the company goes public, you can't do a darn thing at all with your stock option grant.

Note that in the case of Incentive Stock Options (ISOs), one of the strategies you might employ to minimize the Alternate Minimum Tax (AMT — see Chapter 15) is to exercise your vested options even while the company is still privately held. If your stock option agreement contains an "exercisability" clause that restricts you from exercising part of your option to purchase stock shares — even those that have vested — then you won't be able to employ that particular tax management strategy.

Exercising your stock options

So, assuming your stock option grant has become exercisable, and the company has gone public, how exactly do you go about exercising part or all of your stock option?

The answer: It's usually spelled out in your stock option agreement. In Chapter 6, we discuss how to exercise options in detail. Before you even think about exercising options, though, make sure that you read your stock option agreement and that you clearly understand what is written in the document.

One of the items to which you need to particularly pay attention is whether or not your company permits you to perform a _cashless exercise_. As we discuss in Chapter 6, some companies provide you with "one stop shopping" to exercise part or all of a stock option — purchase the applicable number of shares and then immediately sell those shares in the open stock market. (With a cashless exercise, you don't have to come up with the cash — possibly large amounts of cash — to exercise a stock option if you intend to immediately sell those shares and take your profit.) Look for any specific language referring to cashless exercises being permitted.

If you don't find any specific language about cashless exercising of your stock options in the written agreement, don't despair. Perhaps your company instituted cashless exercising after the date of your stock option grant, or perhaps there are other supplemental documents, such as the company's Stock Option Plan, that explain that that capability exists. Check around.

Conditions of employment

Nearly all stock option agreements contain language that basically states the following: If you are no longer employed at this company, you have only a short period of time, if any, to exercise an option on any shares you have vested; after that period of time, tough luck, pal!

Of course, the wording in your stock option agreement is a little more diplomatic, but the meaning is the same.

If you have an ISO grant, then you legally must surrender your options after 90-days from your last day because ISOs can only be held by employees of the company.

And, even though a non-qualified stock option (NQSO) can be held by nonemployees, most employers give you the same three months.

Here's what typically happens, as specified in your stock option agreement (again, make sure you read your stock option agreement to find out exactly what rules apply to you):

1. All vesting of shares in each stock option grant you hold stops on the last date of your employment with the company, so you'll typically forfeit any unvested options upon your termination. (Hint: Sometimes you can time your last day to coincide with a new batch of options shares vesting. However, companies are wise to this trick so you may not want to give notice of your resignation — assuming you're resigning and not being laid off — until your shares vest rather than two weeks prior, to make sure they don't immediately dismiss you and deny you those just-about-to-vest shares.

2. For the next three months, you can exercise options on all shares that had vested as of the last day of your employment. So the clock is running as far as your time to exercise, but the clock is no longer running on additional shares vesting. (Like they would say in tennis, "Advantage, The Company!")

3. During those three months in which you can still exercise options, you might still be subject to any blackout periods, which we discuss briefly later in this chapter and in more detail in Chapter 8. (Just a quick preview of that portion of Chapter 8: Some high-level option holders in a publicly traded company have restrictions on when they can buy or sell shares of stock, such as before and immediately after the announcement of quarterly earnings or during merger talks.) If you were a company executive subject to blackout restrictions, you could conceivably argue that, after resigning, you are no longer an executive and therefore shouldn't be subject to blackout restrictions.

However, suppose you resign just after the beginning of a quarterly earnings blackout period and you know things won't be good on the upcoming earnings announcement. Because you are "in the know," you would conceivably be partaking in illegal insider trading if you were to quickly exercise options on all of your vested shares and sell them before the expected freefall in your company's stock price. The point: During those 90 days that you can still exercise options, you might still be subject to any blackout periods. Ask your attorney or financial advisor for guidance so you don't wind up in big trouble!

4. After the three-month period passes, any unvested and vested but unexercised options are cancelled. This means (think of the description of what a stock option really is . . . the right to purchase shares) that you no longer have the right to purchase shares that have vested. You can keep any shares you have purchased and held through exercising a portion of that option; basically, the company can't take those shares away from you. But from that moment forward, you can no longer do anything else with the terms and conditions of that stock option grant, nor with any other stock option grants you hold with the same employment-termination condition.

Termination provisions

In the preceding section, we discuss the most common reason for the termination of a stock option grant: leaving your job. You need to carefully study what other expiration conditions apply to your grant, as specified in the written agreement.

All stock option grants have an expiration date, typically ten years after the date of the grant.

Make sure that expiration dates are correct in your option agreement. If your option was granted on February 15, 2001, and the language of the expiration clause states that "The Option shall have a term of ten (10) years from the Date of Grant and shall terminate at the expiration of that period on February 15, <u>2010</u>" when the date should actually read "February 15, 2011," you could be in for trouble. Pay attention!

Under what other conditions would your grant expire? You will likely find language saying that your grant will expire because of the following reasons:

- ✔ **No longer being employed because of disability.** Typically, you will have a longer period than the 90 days we discuss in the previous section. You may have as much as two or three years, in which you can still exercise your options on vested shares; one year is the most prevalent period.

- ✔ **No longer being employed because of death.** As with disability, your estate will typically have anywhere between one and several years to exercise options on shares that were vested at the time you passed away.

- ✔ **After a Change of Control in the company's ownership** (which we discuss this topic later in this chapter)

- ✔ **If you leave the company "for cause."** (Translation: You were fired because of poor performance or something you did, such as sexual harassment.) In "for cause" situations, you may find that your stock option is cancelled immediately, and you lose any opportunity to exercise the option even for shares that have vested.

You need to cross-reference the cancellation or termination language in your stock option agreement with the "terminated for cause" language in your employee agreement. You will likely find all kinds of language defining "cause," including some rather arbitrary language along the lines of "actions that are contrary to the best interest of the Company." Be prepared for a fight for your stock option rights if you find yourself with an enemy among the company's executive ranks who seems to be flagrantly looking for a reason to fire you, even if the only problem is a personality clash or difference of opinions on company matters.

Change of control clauses

Your stock option agreement should contain a *change of control* clause that describes what happens to your stock options if the company is purchased or some other change in ownership occurs. (We discuss change of control situations in Chapter 16.)

In some stock option agreements, you'll find a lengthy, detailed discussion of all kinds of change of control scenarios and what happens to your stock options. For example, in many cases, upon the completion of a change of control event (for example, the actual date of acquisition of your company by another), all of your unvested stock options might immediately vest. Or you might find language detailing that if the change of control is being accomplished through an all-stock transaction, you will be required to immediately exercise all options — the ones that have already vested but have not been exercised, as well as those that will at that moment immediately vest — and exchange those shares for the appropriate number of shares of the acquiring company's stock.

But I've also seen stock option agreements with, shall we say, rather sparse change of control clauses, only making reference to the company's Stock Option Plan and the change of control procedures described there. You need to ask for a copy of the company's Stock Option Plan and read it as if it were an appendix to your personal stock option agreement.

Blackout periods

You may find language in a stock option agreement specifying a blackout period during which you cannot exercise any of your options, even if you have shares that have vested. If you find such a clause, make sure you understand it completely.

Create various scenarios for yourself at various points during the blackout period. For example, what happens to shares on that option grant if you resign halfway through the blackout period? What happens to your share on other option grants you may hold? What happens if the company's stock price doubles? What happens if the company's stock price drops by 75 percent? Be prepared for any situation, and completely understand how your stock options (as well as your overall financial picture) might be affected!

Replacement clause

If a stock option grant is part of a repricing event (we discuss repricing in Chapter 19), you may find language in the stock option agreement that specifically cancels your original stock option agreement(s) and replaces those agreements with the document that is now in front of you. Make sure that you thoroughly understand the terms of the repricing and exactly what the replacement clause specifies.

Also, you should compare all of the other clauses — termination, change of control, exercising procedures, and so on — in the new agreement with those in agreement(s) being replaced. Make sure your employer isn't trying to slip something by you!

Getting the short end of a long schedule

Occasionally, you will find a "special" expiration clause. A couple of years ago, I was with a company that had repriced all the employees' stock options because the market price had dropped so far that just about everyone's options were underwater (I discuss repricing in Chapter 19). On the one hand, receiving a new, very low strike price for a whole lot of shares was welcome news, considering that the stock price more than doubled within the next few months after the repricing. However, the new option grants came with a catch: a special blackout clause tied to a special expiration clause.

What the company did was keep everyone's vesting schedules as they were with the new repriced grants, but attached a blackout clause that varied according to employees' respective levels within the company. For most employees, their vesting would continue from the point at which the repricing occurred, but for the next six months they were prohibited from exercising any of their options for which they had accepted the new price. After that point, they were free to exercise to their heart's content.

For those at the vice-president level, however, the blackout restriction was one year instead of six months. After one year, we could exercise whatever shares had been vested at the point of repricing, plus whatever shares vested during the one year between the repricing and the end of the blackout period.

Sounds good, right? Well, one teensy little catch wound up costing me — and many of my coworkers — big-time. Because a special blackout period was attached to the repricing, if an employee resigned during the applicable blackout period (as I did, during the one year after my options had been repriced), all repriced options held by that employee would automatically expire on the last day of employment, even if thousands of shares had vested. Basically, the combination of the special, lengthy blackout period and the special expiration superseded one of the basic aspects of a stock option agreement: vesting.

So beware of expiration terms and conditions in stock option grants you receive in special situations. The odds are definitely tilted against you.

Restrictions on rights

Most of the clauses I discuss in this chapter describe the details of the stock option itself, what may be done with the option, and what may not be done. However, you will also find language in your agreement that describes various rights (or, more accurately, the lack thereof) ascribable to your stock option grant. For example:

✔ **Employment rights.** You don't have any! Just because the company hires you and grants you a stock option, it can still fire you or lay you off if it feels like it! You'll probably find a clause titled something like "No Employment Rights" that specifically states "Guess what? We can terminate your employment at any time, so don't forget it!" Okay, maybe the language will be a little bit more diplomatic, but make no mistake, the language will still be just as explicit. One "Employment Rights" clause in front of me right now is only two sentences long, and it uses the phrase "terminate at any time" twice!

- ✔ **Shareholder rights.** You don't have any! As we mention in Chapter 1, shares obtainable through exercising a stock option are not the same as shares of a company's stock. But just to be absolutely certain you understand those restrictions, your employer will usually be kind enough to spell those restrictions out for you in your agreement, noting that until you actually exercise part or all of your stock option and take delivery of the company's stock, you have no shareholder rights.

- ✔ **Transfer rights.** Unlike publicly traded stock options — puts and calls, which we briefly mentioned in Chapter 1 — ISOs and NQSOs are not marketable securities, meaning that you can't sell your stock options to anyone (even to another employee of the company) or trade your stock options for something else (or a 1951 Mickey Mantle baseball card). The only exception is if you die while you're still an employee and have one or more active stock option grant. Your estate can, during the "after you die" period specified in the expiration clause (which we discuss earlier in this chapter), take ownership of your stock option grant(s) and exercise them during the specified length of time until expiration. You might, however, have limited transferability to family members *if* your company permits.

References to your employment agreement

At several points, we refer to the importance of cross-referencing your stock option agreement with your employment agreement (if you have one — not everybody does!). We want to briefly revisit that relationship because it related to ways in which you could possibly wind up losing your stock option rights.

Your employment agreement contains many clauses that prohibit you from doing things like stealing company secrets or going to a new job and trying to recruit your former coworkers to join you. In your employment agreement and possibly in your stock option agreement, you will probably find language noting that, if you violate the terms of your employment agreement, you not only can be fired for just cause but you will automatically and immediately be required to surrender all of your stock option grants, even if you have vested shares that are "in the money" (that is, the strike price on those shares is below the current market price and you have a profit just waiting for you).

If you violate the terms of your employment agreement, it's fair that you should not only be subject to having your employment terminated but be subject to losing your stock option rights as well. However, you need to consider the following question: How fair is your employment agreement?

In general, you should probably shy away from taking a job with an employment agreement that is excessively restrictive. For example, I've seen clauses in consulting companies' employment agreements that say something like, "if you voluntarily resign from The Company you are prohibited for a period of two years from working for any competitive consulting organization that has an office in a state in which The Company does at least 3 percent of its annual revenue." (Actually, the language is typically much more legalese, but you get the idea.)

Many people read some of these highly ridiculous clauses and figure that the restriction is unenforceable anyway and just go ahead and sign the agreement when taking the job. And perhaps they're right; many highly restrictive employment agreement clauses are likely to be legally unenforceable in many states, so you probably don't have to worry about taking a job with a competitor, as long as you don't violate other portions of your employment agreement like recruiting people away from your now-former employer or going after clients where you worked.

But what about your stock options? I've heard — but have not seen personally — that some technology companies (not only consultancies, but also hardware and software companies) are putting clauses in their employment and stock option agreements that require an automatic cancellation of the 90-day period after you resign during which you can still exercise options on vested shares, _if_ you go to work for a "competitor" (and "competitor" is somewhat loosely defined).

The point to remember is that you should not take anything for granted (no pun intended) with regard to restrictions written into your employment agreement and how they might affect your stock options. So read everything, and make sure you understand it all.

The rest of the legal language

No legal agreement of any type would be complete without all the rest of the legal language mumbo-jumbo, near the end of the document. Since your head is usually spinning by the time you come across this stuff your brain usually interprets it as "blah, blah, blah, yada, yada, yada, ba, ba, ba, ba barbara ann" or something along those lines.

However, in the interest of completeness, this section briefly lists the remaining clauses that you can expect to find in your stock option agreement:

- **References to the company's stock option plan.** Be sure to ask for a copy! Why should you sign a legally binding document that keeps referring to language in "The Plan" when you haven't read "The Plan?"

- **An applicable law clause that specifically mention the legal jurisdiction that covers the interpretation and enforcement of the stock option agreement.** Pay attention: Just because you live in California and you're going to work for a company based in Arizona, if the stock option agreement says that Arizona law governs that agreement, then Arizona law applies to you, even if you never set foot in the Grand Canyon State. (You really should, though, but not in most parts of the state during the summer, unless you want to find out for yourself how much of a fallacy that dry heat business is.)

- **Notice clause.** This "pen pal" clause says "if you want to write us, here's our address, and if we want to write you, we'll use the address we have on record for you."

- **"Supersedes verbal" clause.** You may find a clause along the lines of "this written document contains the entire agreement between Company and Grantee" with some more mumbo-jumbo that basically says, "Even though we may have promised you all kinds of things, if you don't see it written down, then forget about it, it's not gonna happen."

Signature blocks

Actually there is one more very important, often overlooked part of your stock option agreement: the place where signatures go. Make sure you get a signed copy with your signature and the signature of a company official (and that person's job title). Even if the stock option paperwork is on the slow side, don't fall for "we'll keep a copy in your employee file for you." Get a signed copy!

Chapter 6

Exercising Your Stock Options

· ·

In This Chapter

▶ Understanding the four reasons for exercising your stock options

▶ Preparing all of the exercising logistics

▶ Understanding how to exercise your stock options

▶ Exercising pre-IPO options

▶ Exercising the cashless way: advantages and disadvantages

· ·

*E*xercising stock options is a formal, rigidly defined process through which you purchase a given number of shares of your company's stock at a predetermined price. (The purchase price was established at the time your option or options were granted — see Chapter 1 for the details of how stock options are priced.)

This chapter focuses on the important aspects of exercising stock options, particularly the mechanics of exercising your stock options. Additionally, this chapter also provides you with guidance on when and why you may choose to exercise stock options.

The Four Reasons to Exercise Stock Options

You can exercise stock options for any one of the following four reasons:

✔ **"Show me the money":** You want to immediately convert some of your on-paper stock option profits to cash.

✔ **"Save the money":** You have very bad feelings about the fate of your company and its stock price, and you want to salvage whatever you can.

- **Diversification:** You take a long, hard look at your portfolio and decide that it's too heavily weighted in your company's stock, and you want to reallocate your assets.
- **Tax management:** You exercise options and continue to own the shares you purchase (rather than sell them immediately), with the hope of having even further gains in your company's stock price receive favored tax treatment.

"Show me the money"

Your company's stock is now publicly traded, and the value of your options keeps going higher and higher. Along the way, you've been working very long hours, maybe even scrimping from paycheck to paycheck because you accepted a lower salary than you could have received elsewhere to join your company and receive its stock option package.

Many stock options "experts" advise that the most critical decision you need to make with regard to your stock options is how to pay the absolutely lowest amount of taxes on your gains. If you view your stock options from an investment-focused perspective, then most (but not all!) of the factors that go into deciding when to exercise stock options will be based on tax management strategies, as discussed later in this chapter and in Chapter 3.

However, if you're like me and have just a plain old working stiff philosophy about your stock options, then your top priority in deciding to exercise options is to finally get your hands on some of that wealth that has been building up. Sure, you'll forego future gains in the value of those shares, but you'll have converted some of that paper wealth into real cash.

Reason number one for exercising options: To convert some of your paper wealth to cash as quickly as possible.

"Save the money!"

If you wake up each morning thinking of the latest round of problems at your employer and you're more certain than ever that your company's stock price will soon be heading lower (maybe much lower!), then it's time to exercise options on as many vested shares as you can and then immediately sell those shares. As with the "show me the money" reason for exercising your options, tax considerations should be secondary as you try to salvage as much as possible from your stock option profits (which are probably dwindling away by the time you find yourself thinking "save the money!").

Reason number two for exercising stock options: Salvage as much as you can from your stock option profits that most likely are steadily shrinking away.

Diversification

If you're fortunate enough to find yourself holding stock options that have skyrocketed in value, you need to carefully consider pulling some of that money away from being invested in your company, and diversifying your portfolio. If your company makes a major blunder in the marketplace, and its stock price goes into a freefall, you don't want to find yourself with the majority of your net worth potentially wiped out (or at least badly damaged) in a very short period of time.

Reason number three for exercising options: diversifying your portfolio.

Tax reasons

One of the primary reasons you would want to exercise options and continue to hold the shares you purchase (rather than selling those shares immediately) is to start the "long-term capital gain" clock running on *future* gains in the value of those shares. ("Future" meaning gains that occur after the date you purchase those shares.) Chapters 13 and 14 discuss the various tax implications of nonqualified stock options (NQSOs) and incentive stock options (ISOs), respectively, including some of the strategies available to you to minimize your overall tax impact by exercising and holding shares. You could conceivably hold off exercising your stock options as long as possible and then, when you finally exercise, sell those shares immediately. Doing so will keep the cash to buy those shares in your pocket as long as possible rather than having to be used to buy the shares of stock. However, the "wait as long as possible" strategy means that all of your gains in the value of your options to the time you exercise those shares will be taxed at higher rates than if some portion of the overall gain occurs after you exercise your options and continue to hold the shares of stock.

The key point to remember, though, is that by not "taking the money and running" — that is, holding your shares of stock rather than selling them immediately and pocketing the proceeds — you are, essentially, making a bet (hopefully, an informed bet) that the stock price will go higher over time and not drop precipitously between the dates you purchase those shares and eventually sell them.

Reason number four for exercising stock options (take a deep breath): gambling (yes, I said gambling) that you can minimize the overall taxes you'll eventually have to pay even while you hold shares of stock and hope their value doesn't collapse on you.

Procrastinators, Beware! Getting All of Your Paperwork in Order

Long before you even think about exercising stock options, you need to make sure that all of the necessary paperwork has been completed, double-checked, and triple-checked.

What kind of paperwork? Situations vary from one company to another. On the simple side, some pre-IPO companies may have one form for you to fill out. Or you might not have to fill out any paperwork at all: You might just have to write a letter to the company (possibly its board of directors or stock option plan administrator) stating your intention to exercise options along with all of the details (which shares from which grant, for what price, and so on).

However, paperwork becomes a bit more complex if your company's stock is publicly traded and if your company supports cashless exercise programs (discussed later in this chapter). In these situations, you will likely need to complete paperwork to open an account at the company's selected stockbroker (if you don't already have an account there), and then possibly complete even more paperwork for another investment company that acts as the company's stock option plan administrator.

In some cases, the broker and administrator are the same firm. In other cases, your company may administer its own plan using in-house resources. In still other situations, your company might use a third-party administrator that isn't a broker. Make sure you understand the "who's who" lineup for your company's stock options!

Make absolutely, positively certain that you complete all of the paperwork that you need to — correctly — and that you thoroughly understand all of the documents. If you have questions, or are unclear about what needs to be entered in a certain field on a given form, do not guess or leave the field blank. Instead, ask your company's Human Resources (HR) department to either directly provide guidance to you or to point you to someone in the company who is designated to assist stock option holders.

You can also try to find out guidance on your paperwork from pages on your company's internal Web site or from co-workers who have previously completed paperwork and have already exercised options; you know that they either got it right the first time or, if they made mistakes, they corrected their errors.

Increasingly, companies are shifting more and more of their paperwork to online registration and completion as part of their "B2E" (business-to-employee) e-commerce movements. So in addition to enrolling in your preferred health insurance plan online, you may be able to complete the necessary paperwork for your stock option plan online as well. Some of that paperwork may not be administered by your company, but rather by outside parties acting as the stock plan administrator or the company's broker. You need to make sure that you have paper copies of all forms that you fill out online. Not only should you print out copies from your own computer and keep them in your file, but also request official copies of the paperwork to be sent to you by the stock brokerage and administration companies. This way, if any disputes arise regarding lost or missing paperwork when you try to exercise options, you have paper copies that prove you completed your paperwork in a timely manner.

Watch for changes in exercising procedures and paperwork along the way! If you join a company before it goes public, the exercising procedures (if allowed by your stock option agreement) may be as simple as requiring you to write a letter. However, five years later after the company has gone public and grown dramatically, the procedures may involve formal paperwork. Pay attention to those changes and make sure that, as the procedures are modified, you do whatever is necessary in a timely manner.

The Mechanics of Exercising Stock Options

The exact procedures for exercising stock options vary from one company to another, depending on the complexity of paperwork and the number of parties involved. These sections describe a typical exercising procedure for a publicly traded company. But again, remember that your company's exact procedures may differ slightly (or a lot!) so use the material here as a guideline so you know what to expect at your company.

Be sure to write (or call)

Typically, you kick off the exercising stock options sequence of activities when you either call or write the designated stock plan administrator and communicate the precise details of

- The number of shares you will be purchasing
- Which option grant(s) you will be using to trigger your purchase
- Whether this option exercise will be a cashless exercise or if you will be holding those shares and, therefore, paying the total purchase amount of those shares to your company for the shares

If your company uses a brokerage, you may have a designated specific stock-broker who will be the point of contact for you and your fellow employees when it's time to exercise options. Keep in mind, though, that if only one person has been designated, then you could conceivably find yourself waiting in a long line (on the phone, at least), if you work for a fairly large company whose employees try to exercise options all at the same time. If you're trying to exercise *and* sell in a time-sensitive situation, such as when your company's stock's price is heading down (so you're exercising to "save the money," as discussed at the beginning of the chapter), then getting caught in a traffic jam can be a bad thing. By the time you finally get through and get to the point where you have the shares to sell, you could be looking at some fairly serious deterioration in the gains you thought you had locked in.

Note that the definition of "exercise date" varies among companies. Some companies use the actual sale price for cashless exercises but the closing price on the date of exercise for cash exercises. Make sure you understand your company's rules for your stock options so you correctly determine the fair market value of the shares you purchase when tax time comes.

The actual "I want to exercise" phone call often lasts only two or three minutes, assuming all of your paperwork is in order *and* the brokerage has accurate, up-to-date records of your stock option grants, the number of shares vested, and so on. However, don't just assume that after that short phone call, everything is automatically in order. You will likely receive several different types of confirmations in the mail (or perhaps electronically as well).

Check all of the details and make sure they're correct! In addition to the obvious items to check — the number of options, the price you're paying for those shares, and so on — you absolutely, positively need to make sure that the brokerage has correctly recorded the option grant(s) you specified that you are using. For example, shares from incentive stock option (ISO) grants and nonqualified stock option (NQSO) grants are taxed differently. (Part IV discusses tax considerations.) So catch any errors and make sure they are corrected.

What do you get when you exercise?

When you buy any kind of stock, you are eligible to receive an attractive certificate, suitable for framing. In many cases, however, you would leave your certificate under the control of your stockbroker. (Perhaps because the walls in your home are already cluttered enough, and there's no room to hang your framed stock certificates?) Instead of the old-fashioned manner of taking physical delivery of a stock certificate, you receive electronic and mail confirmations that indicate your ownership of some number of shares of a company's stock. In fact, your stock may be held in your name or in the "street name" (that is, in a broker's overall account).

Shares of stock purchased by exercising your stock options work the same way. You may want to take physical possession of a stock certificate if you want to transfer those shares to the control of another stockbroker, as discussed later in this chapter. Otherwise, you may choose to leave the certificates under the control of the brokerage through which you exercised your options and purchased the shares.

If, however, you are doing a cashless exercise, there are no certificates to either take possession of or to leave at your broker, because you immediately sold those shares right after purchasing them, and you don't own any of those shares after receiving cash for them.

Reading the tax forms when they arrive

In January or February of the year after you exercise stock options, you will receive tax forms that specify the details of your options exercise(s). These forms arrive around the same time as your W-2 statement(s) from your employer(s) or the various types of 1099 forms (interest, dividends, mortgage interest, and so on).

If ISO cash exercises, nothing shows on your W-2. For NQSO exercises — cash or cashless — your NQSO income will be shown in various boxes. If you did a cashless exercise, you will also receive a 1099 form that will show your gross sale proceeds.

If you don't receive tax forms from the brokerage that handled your options exercise by the end of January, call the brokerage company immediately. The company may be running a week or two late (that happens occasionally), or your transactions may have been overlooked, or the forms may have been lost in the mail. Make that phone call if you don't have all the paperwork you're expecting. And read each form carefully and make sure the details are correct.

Exercising Pre-IPO Stock Options

Part IV discusses the tax implications of exercising pre-IPO stock options in detail. For now, the main point for you to note is that you need to double-check your stock option agreement and see if you're even permitted to exercise pre-IPO options.

You exercise pre-IPO options for tax reasons — to start the long-term capital gains clock running in pursuit of overall preferential tax treatment for your stock — not because you want to sell vested shares. There is no market for those privately held shares as there is for publicly traded stock.

How Much Money Do You Need to Come Up With?

Not surprisingly, many options holders are surprised, shocked, and horrified when they realize that exercising stock options can be a very expensive proposition. Stock options guarantee you the right to purchase shares of stock for a predetermined price. But how do you pay for those shares?

The cashless exercise

The cashless exercise is the simplest way in which you can exercise stock options. Suppose that you want to exercise an option on all vested shares from the first NQSO grant you received at your employer. The total number of shares on that grant was 10,000, and today 5,000 of those shares are vested. The strike price is $5 per share, and yesterday's closing stock price was $9.75 per share.

1. In a cashless exercise, you call the company's stockbroker and/or plan administrator and indicate that you want to do a cashless exercise for 5,000 shares and that all of those shares will come from your first NQSO grant with the strike price of $5 per share.

2. The broker confirms your instructions and tells you that you will either get a call back shortly with a confirmation of the transaction or that you should call back in an hour (or two).

3. And then you wait.

   When you next talk to the broker (or someone else at the brokerage), you will receive the confirmation, indicating that you bought 5,000 shares for a total of $25,000 and then sold those 5,000 shares for $10 per share for a total of $50,000. The difference is $25,000 ($50,000 proceeds minus $25,000 purchase amount), which is the money you made. You will receive a check in the mail in the next few days with taxes taken out of the proceeds.

The key points to note about a cashless transaction:

✔ You *don't* have to come up with the purchase amount ($25,000 in this case) because you will be immediately selling those shares (or, more accurately, your broker will be immediately selling those shares). The brokerage basically does a very short-term loan for you for the purchase amount and then pays the loan back out of your total proceeds.

✔ You need to pay attention to how your company's stock price is moving before you do a cashless exercise. In the preceding example, yesterday's closing price was $9.75 per share. But that was yesterday; this is today. The price you receive when you sell your shares is not yesterday's closing price, nor today's closing price. Rather, you receive the market price at the moment the brokerage places the sell order for you, just like any other stock you're selling. In this example, the stock price actually went up 25 cents per share, meaning that your proceeds will be a bit more than you had anticipated. The opposite could happen, of course. The price you receive could be lower than yesterday's closing, or even lower than the price at the moment you called the broker to issue your cashless exercise instructions.

✔ The brokerage withholds taxes from your proceeds, so even though your gross proceeds are $25,000, the actual amount of cash you receive will be less.

In a worst-case scenario, if your company's stock is moving rapidly to the downside while you're trying to do a cashless exercise, you could wind up with much less than you had anticipated. In the absolute worst case, you could conceivably wind up with a loss on the entire buy-and-sell transaction if the stock price moves below your strike price (underwater stock options are discussed in Chapter 2), meaning that you might actually have to come up with additional cash when you had been expecting to actually receive money.

Paying for stock with real money

Suppose that you don't want to do a cashless exercise but rather purchase and hold shares in the pursuit of preferred tax treatment on future gains.

Aside from the market risk you'll be subjecting yourself to (that is, the price of your company's stock could drop significantly while you're holding those shares waiting to eventually sell them), another potentially serious consideration is paying for those shares. Unlike a cashless exercise, there are no immediate proceeds from the sale of stock from which the purchase price can be extracted.

Sometimes, coming up with the stock purchase funds is relatively easy. If you're exercising an option to purchase 10,000 shares with a strike price of $.10 per share, then you would only have to come up with $1,000. In most cases, that may not be too big of a deal.

Suppose, though, that you want to exercise an option for 50,000 shares at $3 per share, for a total of $150,000. If you have an extra $150,000 just sitting around, then no problem. But for many people, the large sums of money needed to exercise stock options and hold the stock are beyond their means.

What then? If you need to come up with a large amount of cash that you just don't have, you have several choices available to you. You can borrow the money from a family member or friend; borrow the money from a stock brokerage (a margin loan); borrow money against your house through a home equity loan; or borrow money through your company's loan program (if your company has one) to help employees, like yourself, exercise stock options. (This program is sometimes available to senior executives — see Chapter 4.) You can also sell other assets you have, such as stock in other companies or personal goods, and use those proceeds to purchase shares when you exercise your options.

I don't know about you, but from my perspective, none of these options sit very well with me. In stock market boom times such as the 1998 through 1999, Internet frenzy, borrowing to buy stock — whether as part of a stock option exercise or just in general — very often paid off. But suppose you're looking at market conditions such as those prevalent through most of 2000, when stocks broadly and sharply sold off. Here's a worst-case scenario:

1. You borrow money from one or more of the sources listed above and use that money to purchase shares of your employer's stock when you exercise a stock option.

2. During the time you're holding that stock, waiting for the clock to tick to the point at which you would pay lower taxes on your profits, your company's stock drops significantly to the point where there are no profits because the stock price is below that which you paid.

3. The result: Your stock option profits have evaporated, and you still have loans to repay.

If you don't think this sounds too bad, put some numbers in this scenario. Suppose you join a publicly traded company and receive a grant for 20,000 shares, priced at $25 per share. Five years later, all shares have vested, and the stock price is $75 per share. Your paper profit: a cool million dollars.

You are confident the stock price will continue to rise, and you want to exercise shares now and continue to hold them, meaning that future gains will be taxed at the lower long-term capital gains rate (see Part IV). Because you don't have a half million dollars (20,000 shares × $25 per share purchase price) laying around, you borrow $250,000 from a company loan program for executives and another $250,000 against the value of your home.

So far, so good, until six months later when your company issues an earnings warning, the CEO resigns, and your company's two closest competitors each come out with products that leapfrog your company's technology. Before you know it, the stock price — which had been eroding a bit ever since you exercised your options — has been hammered down to $15 per share.

Before the stock drop, you had net assets related to your stock holdings of $500,000 ($1 million in the total value of your stock, minus $500,000 in loans). Now, after the stock's freefall, you have net assets of minus $200,000 (–$200,000), calculated as follows: stock worth $300,000 (20,000 shares × $15 per share), and debt of $500,000 through your loans. (Actually, the picture is a bit worse, because you've most likely been accruing interest on that debt. Six months of interest at, say, 7 percent on $500,000 is another $17,500 you owe!)

Sorry about the doom and gloom, folks, but I want to make absolutely certain that I make the point that exercising stock options and being single-mindedly focused on minimizing the taxes on future gains in the value of those shares can be a very risky proposition.

Do you always face the same degree of risk in an exercise-and-hold scenario? No. The riskiest situations are when you join a publicly traded company and receive options on a large number of shares for any price above a few dollars per share (in the preceding example, the strike price was $25 per share). The risk is directly proportional to the amount of money you will have to pay to purchase shares that you intend to hold: The more total money you pay, the higher the risk because you are putting a lot of money at risk sitting in company stock.

If you go to work at a pre-IPO company and have options on a large number of shares, as long as the price per share is relatively low — say, under $1 per share — then your risk of losing cash is minimized. However, even with "cheap" option strike prices, the risk in a pre-IPO situation will increase proportionally to the number of shares involved. Someone holding options for 500,000 shares priced at an average of $.50 per share could still have a total of $250,000 exposed by exercising options and holding all 500,000 shares, if loans are needed to pay for the stock.

Risk is very much a person-by-person case. If you have a substantial amount of assets and don't need to borrow money to buy and hold shares, then by all means you should consider exercising and holding rather than doing a cashless exercise. Also, your stock option philosophy (see Chapter 3) factors into your decision process. If you are investment-focused, then you might be willing to take on debt to purchase and hold stock that you believe will appreciate in the long term. If, however, you are a working stiff who views stock options as another piece of your compensation that you want to tap into as quickly as possible, then you really aren't a candidate for borrowing money to buy and hold stocks by exercising options.

You may think you sold at the top, but you didn't. You bought at the top — a big, and very expensive, difference!

Chapter 7

Differentiating Pre-IPO and Post-IPO Stock Options

In This Chapter

▶ Understanding what an IPO is

▶ Receiving stock options in a privately held company

▶ Receiving stock options in a publicly traded company

"*I*'m looking for a job with pre-IPO stock options." During the latter half of the 1990s, the sentence above was probably uttered millions of times as people attempted to describe what they were seeking in a new employment opportunity. They didn't just want stock options; they wanted pre-IPO stock options. What's the big difference between pre-IPO stock options and options in a publicly traded company? This chapter explains the difference.

What Is an IPO?

Ah, those magic initials: IPO. The holy grail of entrepreneurs, venture capitalists, and tens of millions of employees of small companies. But what exactly is an IPO?

An *IPO (initial public offering)* occurs when a company sells shares of stock to the public for the first time. (Well that seemed sort of obvious, didn't it?) Up to the point of an IPO, a company is considered to be *privately held*, meaning that the company is owned by a relatively small group of individuals — various investors such as venture capitalists and angel investors, along with the key executives of the company who typically own special classes of the company's stock. Members of the general public have no way of buying into that exclusive ownership club, because unlike IBM, Coca-Cola, McDonald's, Microsoft, and thousands of other companies whose stocks are listed on a public stock exchange, a privately held company's stock isn't listed on the New York Stock Exchange, the NASDAQ, or any other stock exchange.

Aside from the lack of a stock market listing, another reason that outsiders can't usually buy into a privately held company is that the stock held by the insiders is usually governed by restrictions prohibiting a stockholder from selling part or all of an ownership stake to an outsider.

In addition to the true owners of a privately held company, there is a group of individuals called "owners in waiting." These _owners in waiting_ are the employees and others (such as contractors) who hold stock options, which at some point in the future permit them to purchase shares of stock.

If you own stock options, you do not have the same ownership rights as someone who actually owns a company's stock — see Chapter 1.

IPO basics

The IPO is the event at which time a predetermined number of the company's shares of common stock are made available for general purchase. A typical sequence of events leading up to an IPO include:

1. The company's management selects one or more investment firms that will become the chief participants in the firm's IPO.

2. The company's management files paperwork with the Securities Exchange Commission (SEC) indicating its intent to "go public" and offer shares of its stock. Typically, these filings occur three to six months before the anticipated IPO date. The company employees are usually "primed" with a general time frame for when an IPO is expected (the purpose being to keep them motivated and working very hard — in anticipation of the big day).

3. At some point, the investment firms and the company's management select an IPO day, and even more paperwork is filed. An anticipated price range for the offering is established (for example, between $8 and $12 per share), and the company calculates how much money it will receive from selling those shares and makes a formal statement about what that money will be used for (for example, paying down debt, funding international expansion, and so on).

4. A selected number of IPO shares are made available to "friends and family" of the company (discussed in Chapter 4). For example, a software company that is planning an IPO will often offer a small number of shares to executives of consulting companies that have recommended or sold its products. If one of those consulting companies is privately held, then it will likely return the favor and offer IPO shares to key executives of that software company for its own IPO.

5. In the weeks leading up to the IPO, brokers do their best to find investors who want to get in on the IPO. For several years in the late 1990s, many IPOs were _over-subscribed_, meaning that many more potential buyers

existed than shares of stock. In many cases, the company and its investment bankers raise the IPO price because of the huge demand, thus bringing in even more money to the company from the offering.

6. Finally, IPO day arrives. The shares are sold to the subscribers, and the stock becomes listed on a public stock exchange (often the NASDAQ, especially for technology stocks). At that point, the stock becomes traded just like McDonald's, Coca-Cola, Oracle, or any other publicly traded stock. Many people who got in on the IPO will flip their shares, meaning that they immediately sell part or all of the stock they bought for a quick gain.

7. In a hot IPO market, a company's stock price almost always gets a *first day pop,* meaning that even if the offering price turned out to be $15 per share, the stock's price may rise significantly higher, ending the day with a significant gain. During the frenzied days of mid-1999, a few companies going public saw first-day pops of over 600 percent! And hundreds of companies saw first-day pops of at least 100 percent, meaning that those shareholders who bought in at the IPO price saw their money at least double in one day.

Many academic studies have shown that companies' stock prices tend to decline within a few months after IPO events. These post-IPO declines occur even during normal market times (if there is such a thing as "normal" market times), not to mention when massive waves of selling drive stock prices down — like what happened to Internet stocks during 2000. Therefore, many financial advisors caution investors against chasing hot IPOs and buying shares on the open market during or after a huge first-day runup. In many cases, those investors will be sitting on losses in the not-too-distant future unless they can time a quick-in, quick-out purchase and sale of those shares that have just become available.

How about your stock options?

So this IPO business sounds pretty good, right? Lots of money flying around; stock prices usually going higher, and often much higher. So how much money do you, as a stock option holder, get when your company goes public? The answer: in most cases, nothing!

Whoa! How could that possibly be? Isn't the IPO the "we've finally made it!" milestone that everyone who joins a privately held company impatiently waits for?

Read your stock option agreement again. (Refer to Chapter 5 for guidance in interpreting the language and clauses.) In most cases, IPO day is simply a switch of sorts that moves your stock options from one classification to another. The first classification, before the IPO: "I sure hope that someday these options will be worth something, because I sure can't make any money off of them now." The second classification, after the IPO: "If the stock price doesn't collapse within the next few months, then I can probably cash in some of these vested shares and get a few bucks out of this whole deal."

Okay, maybe the previous paragraph has a bit of a pessimistic, cynical tone to it. But the key point to remember is that for several reasons, IPO day does *not* equate to "stock option payday."

- ✔ **Reason 1:** You almost always are subject to a *lockup period* after an IPO, meaning that you can't exercise any options or sell any shares during that time, often for six months after the IPO. (I discuss lockup periods in Chapter 8.)

- ✔ **Reason 2:** Depending on how long before the IPO you joined the company and the vesting schedule on your stock option grant(s), you may have very few — if any — vested shares that you could cash in even if you weren't subject to a lockup period.

So that's a real bummer, huh? All that work and along comes the event that you and your co-workers have been waiting for, the day your company finally goes public, and you don't get anything out of it at all!

Well, not right away, but the IPO does signify an important milestone along your path to (hopefully) stock option-fueled profits. Because after the IPO has occurred, two very important things happen.

First, the clock is now counting down to a definitive point in the not-too-distant future when you can do something with option shares that will be vested by that point, if you choose to exercise your options and either hold those shares or cash them in. Before the IPO, the countdown clock was sort of frozen in "some day in the future" mode with regard to your options becoming exercisable.

Second, the price of your company's stock is no longer set by internal valuation mechanisms (see Chapter 10), but rather by the investing public as your shares are bought and sold every day on a stock exchange. When the stock market in general is moving higher, valuation by the investing public usually works to your advantage, because many people want to own stock, and stock prices become more richly valued by traditional measures such as comparing the stock's price to the company's earnings.

However, the reverse is also true. In a down market, even well-run, profitable companies often see their stock prices hammered down to the point of being cheaply priced by historic norms. Previously, when your company was still privately held, the valuation of shares you held and those for which you held options was done in an impartial manner based on various metrics and calculations. Now, however, your shares are at the whim of the investing public, which as you know doesn't always act rationally. Sometimes, that irrationality works in your favor (such as when stocks are rocketing higher). Other times, irrationality works against you and can adversely affect the value of your holdings, at least for a little while.

Receiving Pre-IPO Stock Options

Even after factoring out overly enthusiastic (and erroneous) assumptions about pre-IPO stock options, you're still looking at one of the most sought-after compensation components in the U.S. job marketplace (and in many other parts of the world). So this chapter takes a brief look at some of the particular nuances of pre-IPO options.

Pre-IPO option pricing

One of the most attractive features of stock options in a privately held company is that they are almost always priced very low. Pre-IPO option prices typically range from a few cents per share for the company founders, chief investors, and others who get in very early to a few dollars per share. Over time, as the basis for valuing existing options and pricing new ones (see Chapter 10) increases, the strike prices will increase, but usually not by very much. In a company that is formed with the intention of going public in a relatively short time (such as within a two to three year time period, or perhaps even sooner), strike prices are usually under $10.00 per share at their highest. And, even at their highest, those prices are typically at least 25 percent to 30 percent below the expected IPO price.

Until a company goes public, the pricing of its options is mostly within the control of the company's management and guided primarily by fairly formal valuation guidelines. Management could, at its discretion, disregard those guidelines in some cases and price certain options grants favorably, that is, less expensively than they otherwise should be priced. In most of these circumstances, the receiver of a "specially priced" option grant will have some tax consequences to consider.

What can you do with your stock options before your company goes public?

You can't do much with your stock options before your company goes public. I already discussed the "waiting game" that you need to play with your stock options along the way to your company's IPO. In most cases, about all you can do is watch and wait, watch and wait.

Some companies, however, do permit you to exercise options while the company is still privately held. You absolutely, positively must check your stock option agreement for the specifics on when your option grant becomes exercisable.

For example, your stock option agreement may specify that your option is exercisable to the extent that it is vested when one of several events occurs: either a change of control, an IPO, or at some definitive point in time such as three years after the date of the grant. If, at the three-year point, your company has neither gone public nor been acquired by another company, you are finally allowed to exercise your option for the shares you have vested. If your option grant has a fairly typical four-year vesting schedule, then at the three-year point, you can exercise 75 percent of those shares.

But you most likely can't sell those shares after you exercise them! Remember that exercising a stock option allows you to *purchase* shares at a predetermined contractual price. *Selling* those shares is entirely another event, even if you're doing a cashless exercise (see Chapter 6) where the buying and selling events seem to be linked as one.

So why in the world would you want to exercise options to buy shares that you cannot sell and, in fact, may never be able to sell? The answer: for tax planning reasons. In Part IV, I discuss the factors you need to consider when deciding to exercise options on pre-IPO shares. However, the main point to remember here is that you might be able to exercise options and buy shares while a company is still private, but you need to carefully read the language in your stock option agreement to determine if you can and at what point that may occur.

What happens to your pre-IPO options when your company goes public?

As I note earlier in this chapter, the key event on IPO day is that the count-down clock starts running, leading up to a now-definitive point in the future when you can sell shares and take profits from your stock options if you choose to do so.

While doing additional research into stock options for this book, I came across several sources that discuss stock option grants in a pre-IPO company in which all shares automatically vest upon a company's IPO. I have personally never seen a stock option agreement that specifies automatic vesting of shares in the event of an IPO as is often done in the case of a change of control. Indeed, one of the key features of stock options, from the employer's perspective anyway, is to keep employees locked in their "golden handcuffs" of unvested option profits (see Chapter 2).

However, I suppose that it's possible to find a stock option agreement in which automatic vesting of all of your shares occurs when the company goes public. If you do and if you really hate your job at that point, then all you have to do is wait out the lockup period and then exercise options on all of your shares, sell some or all of those shares to give yourself enough money to live on, and tell your boss good-bye as you walk out the door forever.

What happens to your pre-IPO options if your company doesn't go public?

Suppose that one of the following situations occurs at your company:

- ✔ Your employer issues a broadcast e-mail message to all employees indicating that because of weak overall stock market conditions, the company's IPO has been pulled — either deferred indefinitely, or altogether canceled.

- ✔ All employees receive a voicemail message from the company's chief financial officer indicating that the anticipated IPO date a month from now has been pulled, but you receive no explanation for the reason, and the company management gets very tight-lipped when asked to explain what happened.

- ✔ When you joined the company six years ago, the recruiter and your hiring manager had mentioned that the company's business plan called for an IPO sometime in the next three to four years; the company is still privately held, and no IPO is on the horizon.

Many relative newcomers to the workforce, especially those who work in technology-related companies, are often surprised to learn that not all privately held companies go public. Indeed, even though statistics vary over time, most privately held companies never go public (let alone turn out to be one of those one-in-a-million dynamos like Cisco, Microsoft, or Dell).

The 1990s, and particularly the last few years of that decade, grossly distorted the going-public picture in many segments of the economy, but particularly in the technology arena. Simply put, the rules changed, if only for a few years. Specifically:

- ✔ Investment funds, particularly venture capital for brand new companies, was available in unprecedented quantities.

- ✔ The general U.S. economy kept expanding and expanding and expanding, year after year after year.

✔ The financial markets in general were in one of their up cycles in which IPOs were very popular. Hot IPO markets seem to occur in cycles of two to three years, with cold periods (that is, a general lack of interest in IPOs) taking hold in between each hot market.

✔ One of those revolutionizing technologies that takes place every couple of decades had taken hold — this time the Internet.

Consequently, all of these situations came together to create an environment in which almost anyone could put together a business plan and not only get bucketloads of investment funds to get a company off the ground, but an IPO in the not-too-distant future was almost a certainty. In so-called normal times, a company usually had to meet criteria such as profitability or the expectation of near-term profitability before the financial markets would embrace an IPO, but the rules in the late 1990s had changed.

Many investors look back and laugh sheepishly as they lick their wounds from their Internet company losses, but for a while, the collective mantra was "profitability is bad; spending as much money as possible to build brand identity and market presence is good."

So enough with the brief commentary on financial days in the not-too-distant past. The point to remember is that aside from unique periods such as the last few years of the 1990s — an environment that may not be repeated for decades — just because you go to work at a privately held company and receive stock options does not automatically mean that your employer must go public. There is no cause-and-effect between your receipt of stock options and those options ever being usable on publicly traded stock of your employer.

So if your employer never goes public, that's bad, right? You've wasted several years (or maybe even longer) working long, hard hours for less money than you could make elsewhere, and have nothing to show for your sacrifices, right? Not necessarily!

You must be able to make a distinction between your company's success in business (or lack thereof) and the direction your company takes with regard to its financial structure. Even though IPOs have become closely associated with cashing in on the investing public's voracious appetite for equity in young, growing companies; in reality, an IPO is little more than a change in the financial structure of a company.

Instead of a limited number of stockholders who represent the ownership population of the company, suddenly ownership is open up to the general public at large. Additionally, an IPO brings a whole new group of restrictions and constraints to a company's operational and financial management. Suddenly, the company must report earnings (or losses) in great detail on a quarterly basis, along with regular reports of the company's assets and liabilities, cash flows, and other financial measures. Regular filings with the Securities Exchange Commission (SEC) must also take place.

But aside from the paperwork (which the company's management should be doing anyway even when privately held), becoming a publicly traded company changes the game with regard to how the company is financially managed. Suddenly, a whole lot of know-it-alls at investment houses and stock brokerages make public statements about where they expect your company's earnings to be in the upcoming quarter or next year, or maybe even make bold predictions that your company's stock will underperform that of your closest competitors.

Basically, a whole new set of external factors come into play following a company's IPO. But the primary reason a company goes public is not to subject itself to those external factors, but rather to unlock value in its ownership and allow early investors and employees who hold options to partake in (hopefully) increasing stock prices.

However, your company's management may decide that going public isn't really for them at all. Maybe the stock market conditions are poor enough that IPOs are far and few between and even those companies bold enough to attempt an IPO are finding their shares priced significantly below what they would have fetched only a year ago. Or, maybe, the company's business strategy changes in such a way that the company would be better off maintaining a privately held structure.

Or, along the way, your company's management might receive an attractive enough offer from another company that they decide to sell the company in its entirety rather than pursue going public. See Chapter 16 for a complete discussion of what happens in general and to your stock options when your employer is acquired by another company. (Hint: Usually, the result is pretty good for your stock options!)

Of course, if your employer cancels an IPO or never even files to go public, the reason could be because the company has turned out to be a flop. (You knew there was a dark cloud hanging over this discussion after all, didn't you?) Even though many of the high-profile Internet companies that failed in 2000 were companies that had already gone public, thousands of failed companies never even made it to IPO day.

If you join a privately held company with an anticipated IPO, and the expected going-public window passes with no IPO, you must get concrete answers as to the company's plans and how your stock options are affected. You need to find out:

- Whether the company is in financial trouble and that's the reason there is no IPO (or a canceled IPO)

- Whether an IPO is still on the horizon

- Whether the company's management has decided, after further review, that going public is not in the best interest of the company for some reason

In the latter case, you need to figure out what the impact is on you and your stock options. Sure, the company's management may decide for whatever reason that retaining a closely held ownership of the business makes the most sense. But how about the options-holding "working stiffs" out there writing computer programs, packing boxes, laying communications cable, answering telephones, or doing whatever jobs are part of that company's business operations?

Perhaps management will be instituting a new bonus plan to disperse a portion of the company's annual profits to employees in proportion to their direct stock ownership and the number of shares on which they have options, while still allowing employees to retain their options in case the company is acquired.

Or, perhaps, the company will automatically vest all outstanding options and give employees the right to buy those shares at the various strike prices, and then profit-based bonuses will be distributed — but only to actual shareholders, not to option holders who haven't exercised options on their shares.

Whatever the new situation will be, you need to find out. Don't just "float along" hoping that company management will be fair and equitable to you and your fellow option holders. Quite possibly, you will be treated equitably and even though the post-IPO payday you had expected won't materialize, you will find yourself receiving profit distributions or other financial compensation to make up for the lack of exercising options on publicly traded shares. However, you have no guarantee that you will be treated fairly, so find out the true picture as quickly as possible!

Receiving Options When Your Company Is Already Publicly Traded

Going to work for, and receiving a stock option grant from, a company whose stock is already publicly traded has advantages and disadvantages compared to a pre-IPO employment opportunity. A chief advantage is that the uncertainty associated with a privately held company with regard to its ability to go public (and even the basic viability of the company) is negated. The company is already publicly traded, so at some point in the past, the investment community had embraced your new employer and supported an IPO.

Even if the company's form of ownership were to change down the road — if it were acquired by another company, or if the ownership model were to shift from publicly traded to privately held (that does happen on occasion) — your stock options are usually protected, as long as the Change of Control clause in your stock option agreement specifies that all of your shares vest upon the Change of Control.

Sometimes, you need to look beyond the exact wording in your stock option agreement to the details of the company's stock option plan that governs your agreement. If your agreement contains a brief, somewhat vaguely worded Change of Control clause that refers to "Details of the Company's Plan," then you absolutely, positively need to obtain a copy of the stock option plan and make sure you completely understand what happens to your options in any type of change in company ownership.

The chief downside to the degree of security you obtain through options on publicly traded shares is the *likely* decrease in upside potential on your profits from those options. If you joined Microsoft in 1988 (shortly after the company went public), or Dell, or Oracle, or Cisco, or some other grand stock market winner of the early 1990s, then chances are you did much better on your options than someone who joined a successful privately held company later in the decade.

But very often your timing in joining a publicly held company and receiving stock options can be way off, so you need to be careful.

Riding the waves: How your stock options are affected by normal peaks and valleys in your company's stock

Stock prices go up and down. Big surprise, huh? Most everyone who even knows what a stock is knows that even the most successful companies regularly see their stock prices drop 10 percent, 20 percent, or maybe even more before resuming their upward climb. Sometimes, a significant decline in a company's stock price is due to factors beyond the company's control, such as a weak overall stock market. Other times, the reasons are directly related to company operations and financial performance, such as a surprisingly weak quarterly earnings report or the announcement of a significant shift in company strategy that isn't enthusiastically embraced by the financial community.

If you have a long-term, investment-focused perspective about your stock options and your future at your employer, then for the most part you can afford to ignore the peaks and valleys in your company's stock price. You won't become overly enthusiastic when the stock price jumps 15 percent after a good quarter, but you also won't find yourself in a deep funk when the stock price drops 20 percent as part of an overall stock market pullback. You can stay focused on your job and your day-to-day activities and deliberately take a step back from the mood swings the stock market often seems to be trying to cause you to fall victim to.

You do, however, need to monitor your company's stock performance even if you aren't focused on intra-day price movements, trying to calculate how much your options gained or lost in value over the past hour. As you approach planned or possible points at which you might be exercising options on shares, pay attention to price patterns, such as *trading ranges* (that is, over the past year, your company's stock price seems to pull back whenever it hits $50 per share but never really drops below $35 per share).

The profit potential of your stock options, however, is very much affected by those peaks and valleys in your company's stock price. Suppose that over a two-year period your company's stock price repeatedly tops out at $50 per share and bottoms out at $35 per share, but then, after tremendous success in the marketplace with new product introductions, the stock price rises to $75 per share.

Very often, the timing of your stock option grants and the price you receive are out of your control when you work for a publicly traded company — meaning that the strike price(s) you receive will be determined more by the market's perception of your company's performance.

On occasion, you may have the opportunity to influence the timing of your stock option grants, such as accelerating a grant following a drop in your company's price or deferring a grant following a big stock price runup. My advice: Don't play that game, it's too dangerous!

For example, suppose that you recognize the $35 to $50 trading range and you anticipate that you will be getting a performance-based grant for another 5,000 soon. Now you see the company's stock price go from $40 per share to $50 per share in the matter of a few days, and you're tempted to tell your boss to hold off for a little while with the stock grant. You run the risk of trying to influence that delay just at the point when your company's stock price takes off on its run up to $75 per share. So in your eagerness to try and hold off for a better price on your options, you wind up costing yourself $25 per share paper profit if you finally grudgingly receive your grant with a price of $75 per share.

The danger point: Joining a company right after a post-IPO stock price runup

In mid-1999, a former colleague of mine called me to discuss some of the new employment opportunities he was considering after bailing out of a failing, publicly traded consulting company. One of the possibilities for which he had a job offer was another consulting company specializing in e-commerce that had gone public only a few weeks before, and the company's stock price had already doubled from its IPO price.

He expressed his concern to me that he might be too late in getting in there, at least from the perspective of potential stock option gains. The company, like most Internet-related consultancies at the time, wasn't even close to showing a profit, and he felt that the doubling of the company's stock price was due to the mania at that time for "all things Internet." (I agreed with his analysis.)

He was also a bit nervous because the company recruiter with whom he was dealing was still pitching the company with the same "high risk, high reward potential" story that really didn't apply now that the company had gone public. Chief among my friend's concerns: a salary that was decidedly below market compensation for someone with his background and expertise.

He decided to decline that position and pursue an opportunity as an independent consultant for a while. And about three months later, when the e-commerce consultancy's stock price tripled from the point at which he and I thought the price was way too high, we both felt sort of foolish.

Jump ahead to the waning days of 2000, though. The e-commerce consultancy is still in business, and it's still losing money. However, as I note earlier in this chapter, the investment community had since decided that companies that were losing lots and lots of money might not be quite so desirable as investments after all, and the company's stock price is now below $5 per share, or a small fraction of its IPO price.

The point of this story: Even in those rare days when investment mania ruled the day on Wall Street (like 1998–1999 for Internet stock), it's often not the best idea to take a job with an employer that has just gone public and that has seen a tremendous runup in its stock price since its IPO.

If the company has adequately and correctly shifted its employment philosophy following its IPO and has increased salaries for newcomers (because the potential for tremendous profits from stock options has greatly diminished), then you might find working at such a company to be a pleasant experience, even if stock option-driven riches won't be bestowed upon you.

If, however, you are interviewing with a company that has just gone public, and its stock has increased dramatically and they're telling you that they can't pay you anywhere near as much as you'd make elsewhere because of your stock options, then my advice is to run far, run fast, and don't look back; they're likely trying to take advantage of you. Even though you might be passing up one of those one-in-a-million companies like Microsoft, Cisco, or Dell whose stock keeps flying for years after its IPO, the chances are much better that you'll be avoiding an employment situation that you'll be looking to get away from in the not-too-distant future.

Chapter 8

No Trading Allowed! Lockups and Blackout Periods

· ·

In This Chapter

▶ Dealing with post-IPO lockups

▶ Strategizing your way through a blackout period

· ·

*O*ne of the fundamental principles of stock options is vesting (introduced in Chapter 1 and discussed throughout this book). Because your stock options vest over several years, and you don't have access to unvested shares, you can't capitalize on all of your paper gains at once.

But you may find yourself facing other situations in which you are prohibited from exercising stock options and selling shares — even vested shares!

Specifically, you might find yourself subject to a *post-IPO lockup* or a *blackout period*. This chapter will provide you with the guidance you need to handle these types of situations.

Understanding Post-IPO Lockups

Chapter 7 discusses what happens when you work for a privately held company that completes an initial public offering (IPO). From the perspective of your stock options, the most significant occurrence is that if you have in-the-money stock option shares (that is, shares with an option strike price below the current market price) you can exercise your option(s) and sell some or all of those shares if you want to.

But not immediately!

The day your company goes public, the clock starts running on the lockup period. In the simplest sense, a *lockup period* is a time in which your stock options as well as actual shares of stock in your employer are, as implied by the term, "locked up" — meaning that you are prohibited from selling those shares. A post-IPO lockup period is typically about six months long, though you may find a shorter lockup period (that is, five months) or perhaps something a bit longer, say seven to eight months.

The primary purpose of a post-IPO lockup period is to prevent company insiders from immediately cashing in on huge paper profits — that is, pursuing a "take the money and run" strategy with regard to the company. An IPO is the time that the general investing public can first get shares of your company's stock, but a large part of establishing and supporting your company's market stock price is faith on the part of those new investors that the company's operations will continue without serious disruption. And if a large contingent of the company's executives and employees cash out and walk away from the company within days or weeks of the IPO date, well, I'd certainly call that somewhat of a disruption.

Actually, the details behind lockup periods are a bit complex because you are actually being subject to a combination of two different lockup periods, each instituted by a different entity. The first lockup period comes to you and your fellow employees courtesy of the Securities and Exchange Commission (SEC). SEC regulations specify that for a 90-day period after a company goes public, employees and other insiders (such as Board of Director members) are prohibited from selling shares of company stock.

The SEC actually has several sets of rules that specify lockup periods for insiders. If you're a "big guy" in your company (see Chapter 4), then SEC Rule 144 governs the period in which your shares are locked up. For "non-big guys" (or more formally, non-affiliates), SEC Rule 701 governs the lockup period. The simplest way to find out which SEC rule governs you: Find the authority on your company's stock option plan — usually the company's compliance officer — and ask.

The no-selling restrictions don't end there, however. Beyond the SEC-imposed 90 days, the investment firms that underwrite (basically, sponsor) the public offering of the company's shares impose an additional period. That additional lockup period is typically in the two- to five-month range, giving a total post-IPO lockup of five to eight months.

Look in your stock option agreement to find out what the total post-IPO lockup period that governs your stock options is. You usually won't find wording that specifies the 90-day SEC period plus the additional underwriter-specified period, but you may find a reference to the total post-IPO period during which shares cannot be sold. You may also find lockup-related language that specifies that you can neither sell shares you own nor exercise options and hold those shares for the specified post-IPO period of time. So again, make sure you check the language in your stock option agreement and if the rules aren't crystal clear, ask your company's compliance officer for clarification.

Getting Through Blackout Periods

In many cases, as soon as the post-IPO lockup period ends, employees are free to exercise options and sell shares — the only prohibition being that unvested shares are still inaccessible.

However, some employees still won't have total freedom to exercise options and sell shares any time they wish. Typically, a company's executives, top managers, and other key insiders are governed by *blackout periods*.

What is a blackout period?

In some ways, a blackout period is just like a post-IPO lockup period: If you're one of the people subject to a blackout period, you can't sell shares of your company's stock until the blackout period ends.

However, a blackout period also prohibits those affected by it from buying shares of company stock. Furthermore, whereas a post-IPO lockup period ends and doesn't reoccur, blackout periods do reoccur . . . frequently!

A blackout period typically occurs in two situations:

- ✔ During the period leading up to a company's release of its quarterly earnings and for a short period of time afterward
- ✔ When "special situations" occur with regard to company operations and ownership

The philosophy behind blackout periods is that company insiders must be prohibited from taking advantage of likely stock price movements by having a sneak peak at the news that may drive price changes. From the quarterly earnings side, if the company will be releasing earnings with a nice "upside surprise" (that is, earnings are higher — maybe much higher — than expected) and the company revises its forecast for the next few quarters to reflect a higher earning, the company's stock price may rise. Even though company insiders would probably love to buy shares of stock because the stock price is likely to rise, that's a big no-no called "illegal insider trading."

Similarly — and this is where stock options come into the picture — if a company's earnings will be less than expected and the company will also announce a revised downward forecast, the company's stock may take a big hit. Insiders who know what's coming in the way of a disappointing earnings release and who anticipate the company's stock price dropping may be tempted to exercise stock options and unload their shares before the expected stock price drop, preserving as much of their on-paper gains as possible (minus the gains on unvested shares, which can't be sold). Again, a big "illegal insider trading" no-no.

So to prevent the temptation and to (hopefully) prevent shareholder lawsuits and problems with the SEC, companies impose blackout periods surrounding the release of earnings. Insiders subject to the blackout period are legally prohibited from buying or selling shares of company stock or exercising options during a blackout period.

Aside from the period surrounding company earnings releases, blackout periods will also be imposed when a company is about to announce "something big," which is also likely to move the stock price. The most common "something big" news is usually related to mergers and acquisitions. However, companies may impose blackout periods for other significant events at their own discretion, again under the premise of preventing shareholder lawsuits or problems with the SEC in case insiders were found to have benefited financially from advance knowledge of some price-moving event.

Who is subject to a blackout period?

How do you know if you and your stock options are subject to blackout period restrictions? Simple: You'll be told.

If you're a formally designated "big guy" (see Chapter 4), then without a doubt you will be subject to blackout periods. But even "sort of big guys" who aren't "insiders" (again, see Chapter 4) according to SEC definitions may be designated by the company as subject to blackouts.

What is your blackout period strategy?

Consider the implications of being subject to blackout periods. Suppose that the company's blackout period surrounding quarterly earnings is seven weeks long: six weeks from the end of a quarter until the earnings announcement, and continuing for one additional week after the announcement. That's 28 weeks total in any given year — at least! Additional blackout periods caused by acquisitions or other announcements may add four or five or more weeks onto your no-trading periods. So, basically, anyone subject to blackout periods must very carefully plan when to exercise options and sell shares as well as have a contingency plan in place.

In some situations, holding off exercising and selling may be the right thing to do. If you work for a well-respected company, and the drop in its stock price seems to be a one-time phenomenon, perhaps due to overall market weakness, you might be better off waiting for the stock price to recover before exercising and selling shares.

However, you have no guarantees that the stock price will ever recover. So if you had specific plans for the money you would have received from selling those shares, and your confidence in your company's prospects is starting to wane a bit, then you may want to proceed with your post-blackout exercise-and-sell plans anyway, even though you will wind up with less proceeds than you may have otherwise received. Remember, a little bit of gain is better than no gain!

The price of patience

When I worked at Cambridge Technology Partners, my first batch of shares from my first option grant were about to vest in the summer of 1998. During a blackout period related to quarterly earnings, the company's stock price went to almost $60 per share, a record high. Given that my strike price was much lower, I decided to do a cashless exercise on those vested shares as soon as the blackout period ended and cash in at least a little bit of my paper gains, while the unvested shares would still sit there hopefully going even higher in price.

Right around the time of the earnings release, the stock price began to weaken a bit; and then when the quarterly earnings were announced, the stock price weakened even more to the low $40s, even though the company did hit its revenue and earnings target for the quarter. So by the time the blackout period ended, the stock price had dropped about $16 per share from the price when I had originally decided to exercise and sell.

So, silly me, I decided to hold off on exercising the option and selling the vested shares, assuming that the price drop was only a temporary dip. After all, why settle for $16 less per share than I would have received only weeks earlier if I hadn't been subject to the blackout period?

Well, the stock price tanked to the $30s and then down to the low teens. Eventually my options were repriced, with a whole new blackout period imposed on those repriced options. (The sad story of those repriced options is told in Chapter 5 as part of my caution to carefully check the language in your stock option agreement for what happens if you leave the company.)

The lesson of my blackout period story: Very often a blackout period will work against you, especially if your company's stock is particularly volatile. However, if you find yourself in a situation like mine — planning to cash in a certain number of shares whose value drops during a blackout period — don't just automatically cancel your plans to exercise.

Chapter 9

Finding Stock Option Information Online

In This Chapter

▶ Information-packed Web sites that you must check out

▶ Other online resources

*Y*ou might be thinking, as you make your way through this book, that there's a whole lot of information to keep track of. You might wonder whether it's possible to stay up-to-date on the latest developments in taxation and stock option agreements and exercising strategies and everything else. And aside from your co-workers, you might wonder whether there's a way to confer with other option holders or even experts.

Certainly! As you probably know, the Internet is a wonderful source of information for just about anything you want to find out about. This chapter takes you through a guided tour of several Web sites that you absolutely have to check out and monitor frequently to stay on top of the latest stock option developments.

myStockOptions.com

The first stop is myStockOptions.com (www.mystockoptions.com).

The home page has a *Register now* link to register for membership. Getting an account at myStockOptions.com is free, fast, and easy, so the first thing you should do when you visit the site is register for a new account.

The myStockOptions.com home page is packed with all kinds of information, including links to articles and regularly updated, frequently asked questions (FAQs). Additionally, the site has a number of tools — Calculators, My Records, and Modeling Tools — that you can use to help manage and plan for your own stock options.

The site features an Ask Our Experts question and answer section. (***Note:*** The first time you go beyond the home page, you'll be asked for your user ID and password.) You can ask very detailed, personalized questions about your own stock option situation and receive an expert answer that cites various rules and regulations, as applicable. By all means, if you have questions that you're having trouble getting authoritatively answered by your company's stock option plan administrator or someone else at your employer, then you have this forum as another option (no pun intended) for seeking information. You'll find an *Email the Expert Now* link throughout the site.

If you want to look up stock option-related terminology, myStockOptions.com contains a glossary of terms. Sometimes you might want to exchange stories and information with other option holders in addition to (or even instead of) the experts. The myStockOptions.com site contains a Discussion section that covers a broad range of topics. Chances are that you can quickly find a discussion about almost anything you're looking for.

This Web site also contains an Articles section with several categories — Alternative Minimum Tax, Basic Overview of Stock Options, Broad Based Plans, and so on. You can e-mail the site's editor to submit or suggest an article that you think other stock option holders would be interested in.

Also at mystockoptions.com is a feature called Greed and Envy. As you can probably tell by the contents of this book, I strongly believe that many of the mistakes people make in dealing with their stock options — from choosing the wrong employment opportunity to holding overvalued shares of company stock way too long — are the result of being greedy or envious. So you should check out these articles available through this section to supplement the material I've included in this book.

The information on the calculator is *parameterized*, meaning that you can do calculations based on all of your options or only selected options, such as those that are exercisable or, conversely, those that are still unvested.

In addition to the basic calculator, myStockOptions.com includes tools oriented toward specific needs. Finally, the site features another modeling tool that you can use to help determine whether you should exercise options and move the proceeds into another investment. You enter your expectations about your company's future stock price performance and expected returns from alternative investments to receive guidance.

MyOptionValue.com

MyOptionValue.com (www.myoptionvalue.com) is a membership site, meaning you need an account to access the site's contents, and getting a free account is easy.

One of the features at the MyOptionValue.com site is the MOV (My Option Value) School, an online, step-by-step tutorial program that covers many different topics about stock options.

The MyOptionValue.com site features an Options Portal to a broad range of information external to the site. You can follow the links available on that page to access other Internet information about how stock options are valued, careers, company research, and many different articles from various publications.

You can use MyOptionValue.com as a resource to track your options. You can also run simulations using advanced valuation techniques such as the Black-Scholes Model (see Chapter 10) to see how changes in factors affecting your stock options — the company's stock price, interest rates, or even how volatile your company's stock price is — will affect the future value of your employee stock options.

StockOptionsCentral.com

To access information at StockOptionsCentral.com (`www.stockoptionscentral.com`), you first sign up for a free account at StockOptionsCentral.com. You fill in personal information about yourself, your tax filing status and state tax rate (used in the site's calculations), and your company and its stock. The site retains this information for you and uses the information in its various modeling and calculation engines.

www.stock-options.com

The home page for stock-options.com (`www.stock-options.com`) has three main links: one to the site's calculator one to stock option information, and the other for discussion forums with other users.

The Links section contains links to related sites, including that of the owner-operator of the site (Krieger, Ruderman, and Co., LLC, an investment advisory and brokerage firm). You can also link to the National Center for Employee Ownership (NCEO), whose Internet-available resources are discussed later in this chapter.

In the Calculator section, most of the entry forms for your data are similar to those at the other sites discussed earlier. However, one interesting set of entry forms available on stock-options.com allows you to enter information about your company's stock splits. This way, the effect on your stock option from those stock splits (discussed in Chapter 6) can be automatically adjusted without any manual intervention required on your part.

MyInternetOptions.com

Another site to check out is MyInternetOptions.com (`www.myinternetoptions.com`). This site offers a variety of services (for a fee) related to your stock options, most of which are associated with calculating (in their words) the *extrinsic value* of your stock options.

In Chapter 10, I mention that *extrinsic value* is a fairly complex manner of valuing your stock options using the Black-Scholes Model, and incorporates a number of variables (volatility, interest rates, and so on) in addition to the basic pricing information. Extrinsic value contrasts with *intrinsic value*, which is, basically, calculating the difference between the value of your options at grant time and today (or any other time) through simple subtraction. Check out the discussion in Chapter 10 for more information.

The pages at MyInternetOptions.com are similar to those mentioned earlier in this chapter — the site has a glossary of terms, links to information about options, and so on.

The National Center for Employee Ownership (NCEO)

The National Center for Employee Ownership (NCEO) has a Web site at `www.nceo.org`. Even though this site goes beyond stock options and covers a broad variety of issues relating to ownership of your company's stock, you can find a great deal of information about stock options as part of the overall employee ownership picture.

In addition to information about stock options, though, you can also find detailed information about employee stock purchase plans (ESPPs — see Chapter 11) and employee stock ownership plans (ESOPs, which are another investment vehicle through which to purchase your company's stock).

The NCEO also sponsors events such as workshops and conferences about equity-related subjects for employees. You can get on the NCEO's e-mail list by sending a message to `nceo-nceo.org` to find out if there are workshops or conferences near where you live or work that might be of interest to you.

EDGAR? Who's That?

You can also find information online about your company or perhaps a company where you're considering an employment offer through the many different filings with the SEC — specifically at Electronic Data Gathering and Retrieval, or EDGAR. One site — FreeEDGAR.com at www.freeedgar.com — contains no-cost information about IPO filings and other company-related matters. Or you might want to check out "the big site," EDGAR Online at www.edgar-online.com, which contains a wealth of information, including all-important data about insider trades by your company's executives (or the executives at a company where you may soon be working).

Note that www.edgaronline.com (no hyphen) also connects you to www.edgar-online.com, so you can enter either of those spellings to access the EDGAR Online site.

At the EDGAR Online site, you can register for either free or subscription services, whatever is of interest to you.

Part III
Money!

The 5th Wave   By Rich Tennant

"SELL."

In this part . . .

*I*n the end, stock options are all about money. This part gives you the information you need to know to figure out how much your stock options are worth at various times (when you first receive them as well as at various points in the future). You'll also see how your stock options fit into your overall portfolio: a very important topic to help reduce your overall risk should your company's stock price plummet suddenly.

Chapter 10

Determining What Your Stock Options Are Really Worth

In This Chapter

▶ Knowing the value of your stock options when they were granted to you

▶ Understanding the current value of your stock options

▶ Discovering what your stock options should be worth now

▶ Figuring out what your stock options might be worth in the future

▶ Getting help online

*I*f you're like most people who hold employee stock options, you probably have a spreadsheet on your laptop or desktop PC that you access frequently to track the value of your stock options and how much more — or less — they're worth than when they were granted to you.

Hopefully, your options tracking doesn't border on obsessive behavior — plugging your company's stock price into the spreadsheet several times a day and continually recalculating your profits or losses. So much for taking a long-term approach, huh?

But of course, the value of your stock options *is* important to you. In fact, you need to have a fairly good idea of the value of your stock options at several points in time: past, present, and future:

✔ When your stock options were first granted to you

✔ Right now in the present (whenever "now" might be)

✔ At some given point in the future, such as when your first batch of shares vests or when you think you might want to exercise and cash in some shares so that you can plan a major purchase

Additionally, you need to have some idea of what your options *are* worth as contrasted with what they *should* be worth to help you decide whether to exercise options and what to do with those shares after you exercise — whether to hold them or sell them immediately.

Seem complicated? Don't worry, this chapter makes it all clear.

Valuing Stock Options

On the simplest level, the value of your stock options is easy to calculate: Multiply the number of shares on which you have options by the current price per share. However, like most aspects of life, valuing your stock options at the simplest level is usually slightly askew to their *real* value. Two reasons are

- ✔ If your company is publicly traded, you have ready access to information about the price per share simply by finding your company's current stock price on the New York Stock Exchange, NASDAQ, or whatever stock exchange on which your company's shares are traded. If, however, your company has yet to go public, access to current price per share is much more difficult to ascertain and, more important, may not be subject to dispute or confusion.

- ✔ Stock options aren't the same as shares of your company's stock because of factors such as vested versus unvested shares and the lack of voting and ownership rights. Therefore, the simple equation of "current value minus original value equals profit or loss" seems to be straightforward, but it doesn't always present a precise picture of your options' value, as I discuss shortly.

When you read about or calculate the value of stock options — yours or others' — you need to pay attention to whether the value represents the *total value* of the stock options or the *gain in value* (that is, profit) of those options. For example, the following equation represents the *total value:*

```
number of shares x current price per share
```

However, the following equation is equally as simple and represents the *gain in value* (assuming that the current price is higher than the strike price):

```
number of shares x(current price per share - strike price per
          share)
```

Both total value and gain in value are important numbers for you to know, but *either* value may be referred to as "value of your options." Make sure you understand the difference!

Another way of looking at the difference between total value and the gain or loss in value of your stock options is presented by Robert Pastore in his book *Stock Options: An Authoritative Guide to Incentive and Nonqualified Stock Options* (PCM Capital Publishing). Pastore describes the *intrinsic value* of a stock option as the difference (either higher or lower) between the current price and the *fair market value.* The *fair market value* is, as I describe above, the total value of your stock options (or any given stock option grant, if you have received more than one). So on the date of your stock option grant, most likely the intrinsic value of your stock option is zero — no gain or loss — because you were granted an option at the fair market value of the moment.

Knowing your options' value: Why it's important

Aside from the sometimes irresistible urge to track how much you're ahead or behind on your stock options, there are some sound reasons for why you should be able to quickly and accurately figure out how much your stock options are worth and your gain or loss, even if that gain or loss is on paper. Richard Friedman, Vice President of the Benefits & Group at The Ayco Company, in "What Are My Stock Options Worth?" — an online article written for and available on www.myStockOptions.com (see Chapter 9 for information about myStockOptions.com and other online resources) — lists the following reasons:

- ✔ Taxes and tax planning
- ✔ Estate planning
- ✔ Divorce situations
- ✔ Evaluating new job opportunities and the implications to your current stock option packages

Getting complicated: The Black Scholes Model

So if the simple approach to valuing a stock option (or more than one) is to calculate the price difference from when the option was granted and multiply that difference by the number of shares covered by the option, what's the complicated approach? The Black-Scholes Model, developed by Fischer Black and Myron Scholes, two Nobel Prize-winning finance professors, applies mathematics — very complicated mathematics — to determine the real value of a stock option. The model is one of those typically complex, difficult to understand formulas with a whole bunch of Greek letters, embedded parentheses and brackets, and exponents.

The model factors in variables representing volatility, interest rates, time, and when an option can be exercised along with price to determine the value of an option. The model was developed for European-style stock options, meaning that a key assumption of the model is that an option can only be exercised on the expiration date, not at various vesting points during the life of the option. There are also other assumptions regarding stock market efficiency, interest rates, commissions and dividends, and other factors that you don't need to worry about. If you're really interested, though, the best explanation of the Black-Scholes Model that I've found is available on the Internet at `bradley.bradley.edu`, where you can read all about the history of the model and study the assumptions, formula, and variables.

So what good is the Black-Scholes Model and how does it apply to your stock options? To be honest, you really don't have to think much at all about the model, unless you're a chief financial officer (CFO) or someone else in charge of establishing stock option grant prices for your company. Very often, the Black-Scholes Model is used to establish grant guidelines (prices and number of shares to grant).

Additionally, companies often use the Black-Scholes Model to calculate the value of their stock options in financial statements, such as those filed with the SEC. If you are trying to do sophisticated financial analysis on your employer, then you probably want to take a look at the financial statements and any mention of stock options and how they are being valued.

Terminology alert: You may come across the term *extrinsic value* in your research. According to MyInternetOptions.com (`www.myinternetoptions.com`), extrinsic value is "the difference between the option value and the intrinsic value. This is determined via the Black-Scholes formula, and requires important inputs such as the volatility of the stock."

The Value of Your Stock Options at Grant Time

You have four primary points of interest with regard to your options. The first point of interest is when you receive a stock option grant. In almost all situations, your intrinsic value is zero — that is, no gain or loss over the fair market value, because you will have received the grant at fair market value.

Occasionally, though, one of the big guys — Directors or company officers, as discussed in Chapter 4 — may receive a stock option grant in which the intrinsic value is not zero — that is, the option is granted with a built-in profit premium. Basically, the strike price of the option grant is below the current market price per share, thus allowing immediate profit.

If you're one of the big guys and you are fortunate enough to receive an option grant with a below-market strike price, beware. Sure, it's great to start off with a built-in profit, but chances are you'll have to pay taxes on that profit even if you don't exercise the option for many years.

Consider the following description from www.nceo.org of nonqualified stock options, more formally referred to as *nonstatutory stock options*: "A nonstatutory stock option is taxed to the employee at grant, but only if it has a readily ascertainable fair market value at that time (most stocks do not have readily ascertainable fair market value unless publicly traded)." In other words, as long as your NQSO grant is at the fair market value of the stock, you won't have any tax implications at grant time.

Concerned? Confused? Don't be! Whether you're one of the big guys or not, when you receive a stock option grant, simply ask your company's stock plan administrator if there are any grant-time tax implications because of the strike price of your stock option.

In almost all cases, then, the most important thing to remember is that when you receive a stock option grant, you're starting from square one. You have no gain and no loss. If, hypothetically, your entire option was vested at grant time, and you could exercise the option and immediately sell all shares — and you did — then you'd make nothing (and lose nothing) because the price per share you'd receive would be exactly the same as your strike price.

Even though technically your option has some calculable total value at grant time, I stick with the simple calculation of the number of shares × current price per share because none of your shares on that grant have vested yet. It's dangerous to think that, say, your option is worth $300,000 because it covers 10,000 shares, and the strike price is $30. Sure, in the "purest" sense the fair market value of the option might be $300,000, but it's not like your company just handed you $300,000 in stock or cash. Remember that a stock option gives you the right to purchase shares at your strike price. But you could, if you wanted to and if your company's stock is publicly traded (and you had the money), purchase 10,000 shares on the open market for the same $300,000 without having to exercise your option.

So my recommendation is to forget about trying to calculate any kind of value of any one of your stock option grants at the time it's granted to you. Actually, until you get within three or four months of the vesting date for the first batch of shares covered by an option or if your company is about to be sold (see Chapter 16). I'd forget all about trying to figure out how much your stock options are worth, because you can't do anything with them anyway.

Determining What Your Stock Options Are Worth Now

If several years have passed since you've received a stock option grant(s), how do you figure out the value of your stock option(s) at this very moment?

If your company's stock is publicly traded, then the simple-versus-complex discussion presented at the beginning of this chapter applies. The total value (or fair market value) of your stock options is calculated as

```
number of shares × current price per share
```

That's the simple side of the picture. Or, if you really want to play around with the mathematics and take a walk on the complex side, you could apply the Black-Scholes Model or some other mathematical model to your option grant(s) and come up with a complex value.

Remember, though, that applying the Black-Scholes Model or some other complex model is really only an academic exercise. Even if you determine, for example, that, because of the particulars of your company's stock price and the various assumptions on interest rates, volatility, and so on, your stock options are worth significantly more than the value determined by the following calculation, so what?

```
number of shares × current price per share
```

You can't sell your stock options to someone else, and you can't exercise vested shares and sell those shares for a price higher than the current market price. Sure, it might be interesting to know that your options are more valuable than they might otherwise appear to be, but you're not going benefit financially from the results of those calculations.

Where Black-Scholes or another model does come into play in determining what your options are currently worth is if your company is still privately held, and there is no New York Stock Exchange or NASDAQ stock price you can use to determine the current price per share. In theory, you could use the Black-Scholes Model to calculate the value of each of your options now and you could then subtract the grant-time value from the current value to calculate your gain or loss.

However:

- If your company's stock is still privately held, determining via Black-Scholes or another model that you're sitting on substantial gains is nice, but you can't benefit from those gains until your company goes public or is sold.

✔ You don't need to worry about dabbling in a complex modeling exercise, especially if you're mathematically challenged, because your privately owned company actually does so for you. Why? Because your employer is regularly using the Black-Scholes Model or some other type of valuation to determine the strike price on new option grants, and to avoid tax consequences for grantees by avoiding a "readily ascertainable fair market value" (refer to the earlier discussion based on information from www.nceo.org).

Therefore, if you work for a pre-IPO company and you want to figure out what all of your stock options are worth, you can use the simple calculation (number of shares × current price per share) and simply plug in the price your employer is using for new stock option grants for the current price per share. And, if you want to figure out your total gain or loss, you can use this formula on each of your option grants:

```
number of shares ×(current price per share minus strike price
            per share)
```

Plug in the various strike prices into each calculation and use your company's current strike price for new options for the current price.

Even if your stock options have appreciated considerably from the times they were granted to you, I still recommend being cautious in your perception of either their total value or your gains, especially if a substantial number of shares covered by your option(s) are still unvested. Sure, it's nice to think of yourself as being very well-off — maybe even a millionaire — but remember that your wealth is mostly on paper for now. And, not only is your wealth on paper, but in the case of unvested shares, you can't even tap into that paper wealth if you want to.

So you might want to calculate the total value of your options and your gains in two different parts: One part for shares that have vested (or might be within a couple months of vesting), and a second part for shares that will vest at various points in the future. This way, you'll have a good idea of what wealth you can access now if you choose to or need to, and what wealth is still out there.

What Your Stock Options Should Be Worth

If you follow the stock market, you've probably heard the terms "overvalued" and "undervalued" in reference to a stock's current price. Basically, a fundamental premise of equity investing (that is, investing in stocks) is the *efficient stock market theory,* meaning that in general, stocks are priced as they should be, based on the current information that's available regarding a company's current performance and future outlook, along with environmental factors such as interest rates and economic outlook. However, at various points, the efficiency in a company's stock price might get out of whack, and the company's stock price is higher or lower than it *should* be.

And that's the key word: should. According to theories about stock markets being efficient, when a stock's price gets out of whack, it will eventually get back to where it's supposed to be. And along the way, investors can supposedly profit from those movements from where stock prices are to where they should be.

I say "supposedly" because like just about everything else with stock investing, making what's supposed to happen is more difficult than you would think. Sure, it's easy to look back at various points in stock market history and, with 20-20 hindsight, detect stock price anomalies that eventually corrected themselves.

Take the rise and fall of Internet stock prices during the late 1990s and 2000. With hindsight, it's easy to look at some no-earnings, low-revenue dot-com company whose stock went up eight or nine times above its IPO price and realize the following:

- ✔ If you had been a pre-IPO employee of that company, then at the peak of your company's stock price you would have entered a few numbers into your PC's spreadsheet and cackle with glee because on paper, you're rich, rich, rich!

- ✔ Your company is overvalued, and its stock price should really be lower than it is. How do you know this? You apply stock valuation measures such as those I discuss in a moment and realize that there is a big discrepancy between your company's current market valuation and what that market valuation should be.

  So you exercise your options on all of your vested shares, sell those shares immediately, and hope that more of your shares vest before reality catches up with your company's valuation and the stock price does a great imitation of a Navy dive-bomber plane.

The opposite situation — your company's stock price is undervalued — also occurs and, in retrospect, you should be able to profit from those situations as well. If you look at various periods in the recent past — the early 1990s during a brief U.S. recession, and the few years before the stock market began skyrocketing in 1982 — you might have had an inkling that your company's stock price should be higher than it was at the time. Maybe you purchase shares of your employer's stock with the expectation that sooner or later, the investing public will apply the proper valuation to your company's stock and the supposed efficiency in the stock market will elevate the stock prices.

Of course, without the benefit of hindsight, determining if a company's stock is overvalued, undervalued, or priced just about right (sounds like the three bears, huh?) is a rather difficult proposition. Take a look at technology stocks in general, and Internet-related stocks in particular. What we now recognize as dramatic overvaluation was occurring as early as the 1996–1997 time frame, yet it wasn't until early spring of 2000 that rationality finally starting hitting many companies' stock prices.

Along the way, many investment professionals tried to profit from what they believed to be overpriced stocks by shorting those stocks. (*Shorting,* or *short-selling*, is an investment technique used to bet that a stock's price will drop by borrowing shares to sell and — hopefully — buying those same shares back later at a lower price.) Because technology stock prices kept going higher and higher, many short-sellers wound up taking very large losses, even though in retrospect they were right about the overvaluation.

So what's the deal then? Does overvaluation or undervaluation in your company's stock price matter at all, or should you just not worry and stick with tracking your employer's actual stock price movement? After all, neither of the simple formulas used throughout this chapter to calculate the total value of your options, or your gain or loss, have any variables for what you think your company's stock price should be.

I'd recommend that you at least have some idea of whether you think (you'll never know for sure, though) your company's stock price is overvalued or undervalued, or if it's sitting about where it should be. Why? To help you make better decisions about what to do with your stock options, such as whether you should immediately sell shares that you purchase from exercising an option or hold them for preferred tax treatment.

If you exercise options and you believe that for whatever reason, your company's stock is highly overvalued, then you would likely want to sell those shares immediately even if you'll pay higher tax rates than if you hold those shares for several years. Conversely, if you believe that your company's stock is undervalued or fairly valued, you might choose to exercise options but hold those shares because you believe the chance of a major price slide is negligible. Or, at the very least, any major price slide would be because of overall economic or market conditions rather than the investing public suddenly coming to their senses and unloading your company's shares en mass.

Enough generalities. How can you try to figure out the overvaluation-undervaluation situation? There are many, many formulas you can use, each of which has its strengths and shortcomings. Two of these formulas are:

> ✔ **Price-earnings ratio:** One of the classics — in which your company's stock price is compared against its earnings per share, either historically (often the past 12 months) or against projected earnings (for example, projections for the next 12 months). Basically, the higher the ratio, the more expensive the stock is. However, a key shortcoming of valuation

based on price-earnings ratios is that one company growing much faster than its competitors or other similar companies might "deserve" a higher price-earnings ratio than those slower-growing companies.

✔ **Price-sales ratio:** Basically substituting a company's revenue (sales) per share for earnings, and calculating a ratio just as you would for price compared to earnings. Price-sales ratios are useful to try to determine the value of a company that doesn't yet have positive earnings (that is, it's still losing money). The same deal applies: The higher the ratio, the more expensive the stock is. However, a chief shortcoming is that price-sales ratios don't take into consideration if a company will ever have positive earnings.

You can find many other ratios and formulas that you can use. Check out *Investing For Dummies* (written by Eric Tyson and published by Hungry Minds, Inc.) to study different techniques you can use to analyze your company's valuation.

Regardless of what formula or formulas you use, you need to remember one key item: A stock's price is supposed to represent the present value of a future stream of earnings. (Remember that earnings means profits, not just gross sales.) A lack of earnings — or miniscule earnings, or earnings that come too late in a company's life cycle — means that you'll be lucky if your company's stock price isn't measured in cents rather than dollars. Or, for that matter, you'll be lucky if your company is still in business — witness all the Internet-related companies that shut down in 2000 because of lack of current earnings and no confidence that there would ever be earnings. And, just as a reminder, here's a little equation you should take to heart:

```
No earnings = No company = Worthless stock options
```

Maybe, just maybe, you'll get lucky and wind up at a company that is riding a tsunami wave of (to quote Federal Reserve Chairman Alan Greenspan) "unbridled enthusiasm," and the above equation will be negated for a little while. Look at all of the people who were able to take some stock option profits away from Internet-related and other technology companies that eventually went down the tubes, even after going public. But sooner or later, the above equation will come back into play. Therefore, you should always pay attention not only to your company's stock price and how it changes over time, but also to price movement in relation to what you believe the price should be.

Determining What Your Stock Options Might Be Worth in the Future

Once again, here's the classical stock option dream scenario, the one that caused you to create that how-much-I'm-worth tracking spreadsheet I mentioned at the beginning of this chapter. The dream scenario goes something like this:

You join a sound, solid company early in its life, before it goes public. Or, if the company has already gone public, its stock price hasn't yet gone to the stratosphere; it's still "cheap," that is, undervalued (or at least fairly valued). The company's original products or services are well-received in the marketplace, and revenues and earnings grow steadily, year after year. (Or, to keep the short-sighted folks on Wall Street happy, make that "quarter after quarter" instead of year after year.) And just at the right time, the company comes out with new products or services, or expands into new markets, and growth continues unabated.

There may be a hiccup or two along the way. Maybe earnings are a bit light one quarter, and the stock price drops 15 percent or 20 percent. But then things get back on track, business-wise, and the stock price recovers and continues its march upward.

You can find many companies that fit this profile: Microsoft, Intel, Cisco, and Dell are among the biggest successes of the recent past. But you don't have to restrict yourself to technology companies when looking for examples of "dream stock option" companies. Or, for that matter, you don't even have to restrict yourself to relatively young companies. General Electric, for example, enjoyed spectacular growth from the early 1980s under the leadership of CEO Jack Welch, and GE is hardly a new company. And for a number of years, Disney fit the steady-growth, ever-rising stock price profile.

Now you're probably wondering where I'm heading with all of this. It's simple: Trying to predict the future value of your stock options is fairly straightforward if those stock options were granted by a company (your employer) that has positioned itself for the long term. Why? In the previous section, I mention that a company's stock price is supposed to reflect the present value of a future stream of earnings. When a company is positioned for long-term, steady growth in all aspects of its business — market share, product or service lines, and most important, revenues and earnings — then you can predict that future earnings stream with some degree of confidence. And, therefore, the valuation formulas that rely on results several years down the road are likely to have a high degree of accuracy.

In contrast, consider many of the startup companies of the late 1990s that offered dreams of stock option-driven wealth to their employees and prospective employees. Looking at many of these companies now — admittedly with 20-20 hindsight — it's easy to find numerous cases of little or no long-term earnings prospects. Too many dot-com business plans were predicated on gaining dominant market share as the single most important company objective, with surprisingly vague ideas about future earnings. To be fair, more than a few business plans for companies applying to go public included wording to the effect that "we aren't making money now; we won't make money in the near future; and we have no idea if we'll ever make any money."

So when it came time to try and predict the future stock prices — and future values of employees' stock options — at these companies, models based on confidence in future earnings were supplanted by the stock market equivalent of "a wing and a prayer." Many stock option-holders at these companies fell back to overly simplistic thinking that went something like this: I'm holding pre-IPO options on 10,000 shares, all at strike prices under $1. If we go public, our IPO price should be at least $10. I'll be conservative and assume that stock price will go up 50 percent on IPO day (but I hope it doubles or triples!). One year after the IPO, the stock price could be sitting at $20 (but I hope it's actually at $40 or $50!). After another year, the stock price could go up 30 percent to $26 (but I hope the stock price is really at $75 by then!). After another year passes, it could to up another 30 percent to $33 (but I hope by this time, the stock price is over $100, and it's split at least once!). Okay let me plug these numbers into my spreadsheet and figure out how rich I'll be three years after we go public.

Anyone who has engaged in thinking along these lines has made one very serious mistake: thinking about a company's stock price as an entity in and of itself rather than as a reflection of a company's success in business and (I know I'm getting repetitive, but it's an important point) of its future earnings. It's quite possible that the preceding scenario — even the optimistic sides of each milestone, such as one year post-IPO having a stock price that has gone up 400 percent instead of 100 percent — could actually happen. But the chances of phenomenal growth and stock option riches are greatly increased in a company that actually has a business strategy and on-track operations to achieve growth and profitability, as compared to companies based solely on "interesting ideas."

So when you try to predict the future value of your stock options three or five or ten years down the road, keep this one item in mind: Don't simply plug numbers like 10 percent or 20 percent into your handy dandy spreadsheet as your assumptions for your company's stock price's future growth. Try to correlate your stock price assumptions to the reality of your company's business success (or lack thereof). You must have some idea of how your employer is doing in your market: if sales are growing, if you're profitable, when new products will be released, and so on. You can't just focus on your little corner of the world and have little or no visibility beyond your day-to-day job tasks.

So it comes down to this: If you can predict your company's future sales and earnings with some degree of confidence based on past and current business success, then your projections for the future value of your company's stock — and the value of your stock options — may well be on the mark. Conversely, if you have to rely on wild guesses about where your company's sales and earnings will be several years down the road — or if you truly, honestly don't believe that there ever will be earnings — then predicting the future value of your stock options is about the same as trying to pick winning lottery numbers.

Maybe, just maybe, you'll get lucky and "win the lottery" because the investing public will bid your company's shares higher and higher, despite the lack of business success. But eventually, reality will set in, and all of your long-term projections will be down the tubes.

Getting help on the Internet

In addition to your handy dandy stock option tracking spreadsheet that I mention in this chapter (come on, admit it, you do have one on your PC, right?), you can also find help on the Internet. For example, MyInternetOptions.com (www.myinternetoptions.com) has a fee-based service that proclaims, "Do you know what your Options are worth? We Value your Employee Stock options. Its not as simple as just Stock Price minus Strike Price."

Additionally, as I discuss in Chapter 9, you can find a few Internet sites with a broad set of services, including calculators, available for tax planning, test exercising, and other purposes such as valuation. For example, myStock Options.com (www.mystockoptions.com) has a calculator that you can use to enter your assumptions about your company's future stock price along with information about your options (number of shares, strike prices, and so on), and you can find out your after-tax net gains. So in addition to facilities you set up yourself, you should check out online resources available for your use.

Chapter 11

Stock Options and Your Overall Portfolio

. . . .

In This Chapter

▶ Figuring out the number of eggs and the number of baskets

▶ Understanding the "paper wealth" challenge

▶ Protecting gains on unvested shares

. . . .

This chapter is about eggs and chickens. Or, more accurately, folk sayings about eggs and chickens.

The first saying: "Don't put all your eggs in one basket."

The second saying: "Don't count your chickens before they hatch."

The third saying: "Why did the chicken cross the road?"

I'm joking about the last one. But with regard to stock options and your personal portfolio, the first two sayings actually do a pretty good job of summarizing the contents of this chapter.

The value of your stock options may zoom skyward or fade away into oblivion; such is the nature of the stock options game. But when the news from the stock option front is bad, you don't want your overall financial well-being to fade away along with the value of your options.

The secret recipe: Three parts cautious enthusiasm, combined with two parts balance, and then mixed with a healthy portion of careful monitoring.

Counting the Baskets

Suppose that you choose your favorite mode of time travel, such as a flux capacitor-powered Delorean (from *Back to the Future*), and you go back in time to March 1987. Suppose also that you find yourself working as a software developer at Microsoft, a company that had gone public only a year earlier. At that time, Microsoft was already a fairly successful firm from its various PC software systems and packages (such as the MS-DOS operating system and its relatively new Excel spreadsheet program), but its phenomenal industry leadership position was still several years away.

Oh, yes, you also open your desk drawer and find that you hold options on a bucketload of shares of stock.

Because you're from the future, you know that in about seven months — on October 19, 1987, to be exact — the U.S. stock market is going to crash, with the major averages dropping more than 20 percent in a single day. But you're not worried, even though Microsoft's stock will get hit that day along with nearly every other company's shares. Because you know that by holding on to your stock options and the shares you acquire from exercising those options, by the turn of the millennium you'll be very, very wealthy. In fact, you also pour every spare dollar you can scrape up into buying additional Microsoft stock as often as you can.

You make a very conscious decision to put all of your eggs in one basket, the Microsoft basket.

Now suppose that your method of time travel has a bit of a glitch, and instead of winding up at Microsoft you find yourself employed as a software developer at Digital Equipment Corporation, at the time the second largest computer company in the world. You still know the stock market crash is coming in October, but you also know that Digital's stock price will peak in August 1987, and never, ever recover. Therefore, you wait until August and sell all of your Digital Equipment stock and exercise your stock options on all of your vested shares. Then, following the crash and for the next couple of years as the company's stock price ratchets lower and lower, you regularly do a cashless exercise of all options as soon as they vest (if they're still in the money) and take whatever profit you squeak out. And you never, ever buy any shares of Digital Equipment stock on the open market.

In this case, you go out of your way to not put any more eggs in your Digital Equipment basket. In fact, you quickly remove any eggs (that is, newly vested shares from your existing stock options) from that basket and deploy the proceeds elsewhere.

Time travel, Microsoft, the late Digital Equipment Corporation, and eggs. So what's the point here?

Unlike our two time-traveling examples, you have no idea whether your stock options will soar or sink. If you reversed the two strategies I previously describe — cashed out as quickly as possible at Microsoft, or "kept the faith"

and stubbornly held onto your Digital Equipment stock and stock options —
you would have either cheated yourself out of tremendous profits from your
Microsoft stock options, or watched your personal net worth dwindle away
as your Digital Equipment stock options went underwater and turned out to
be worthless.

Like the rest of us, then, you have to deal with a high degree of uncertainty
about the fate of your stock options. I look at some basic strategies that will
help you.

Understanding the Principles of Personal Financial Planning

Volumes and volumes have been written about personal financial planning. I
won't attempt to address all the important points here; however, because you
must think about your stock options in the context of your overall financial
picture, I want to emphasize a few key points that should guide your thought
processes.

(If you are looking for detailed information about how to manage your personal financial picture, then you should check out *Personal Finance For
Dummies* and *Investing For Dummies,* both written by Eric Tyson and published by Hungry Minds, Inc.)

You need to keep the following principles in mind throughout this chapter:

- **Allocating and diversifying your assets.** You shouldn't put all of your
  financial assets (eggs) into a single basket. Sure, if you happen to guess
  right (and the correct word is *guess)* and concentrate the majority of
  your assets in an investment like your company's stock and if that investment outperforms most others, your overall returns will be stellar, but:

  - Your chances of guessing right month after month, year after year,
    are pretty much nonexistent. Sooner or later, you'll pick the wrong
    investment and wind up facing significant losses.

  - Even sophisticated investors and entrepreneurs who do hit the jack-
    pot and wind up with fantastic gains from a single investment even-
    tually take some of their profits and rellocate those funds to other
    investments — in effect rebalancing their respective portfolios.

- **Establishing a time frame for your asset allocation goals.** The optimal
  asset balance for an unmarried person under age 30 with no significant
  financial obligations will vary greatly from the preferred allocation for
  someone who just turned 50 who is putting three children through college.

As you look at stock options as assets in the context of your overall portfolio, you will need to regularly reevaluate how those stock options relate to the rest of your assets.

✔ **Looking ahead.** As you figure out how to adjust your assets — stock option-based and otherwise — you must not only consider your financial picture today (for example, kids in college) but also what's coming three to five years down the road (for example, kids who will *then* be in college).

✔ **Continuing to plan proactively.** Don't just assume that the appropriate balancing of your assets will happen by magic. You need to be extremely protactive in your personal financial planning, employing whatever outside assistance (such as from an accountant or Certified Financial Planner — CFP) you need to fully understand implications such as taxation.

Considering Your Equity (Stock) Holdings

An important component of most peoples' financial assets is *equity investments* — that is, stocks and other investments based on stocks (such as mutual funds).

One of the chief reasons to invest in stocks directly or through mutual funds is that over time, equity investments outpace inflation as well as other investments, such as bonds. However, the key words are *over time*. As you hopefully understand if you're reading this book, stocks fluctuate in value, and any given stock or mutual fund you own could drop in value below the price you originally paid. That risk, however, is mitigated through diversification (that is, owning a variety of stocks and mutual funds), varying your allocation and diversification strategy over time and in accordance with your personal situation and goals, and proactive planning.

Additionally, you can further mitigate equity risk by finding out as much as possible about the companies whose stock you buy or the mutual funds your purchase (that is, study their performance history under various market conditions, understand the investment objective of the fund, look at the fund manager's track record, and so on).

And in most cases, the equity investment that you will have the most knowledge about is your own employer.

The company loyalty trap

Don't make the same mistake that many first-time stock option holders (and more than a few repeat stock option holders) do: Don't hold on to your employer's stock or your stock options out of a misguided sense of loyalty when you should be diversifying your assets.

You might think that if you sell some of the company shares of stock you're holding, or exercise stock options and sell those shares, that company management might see you as "disloyal," and that "disloyalty" will reflect on your position at the company, costing you promotions and salary increases.

Hah! Do you think that your company's chief executive officer (CEO) and chief financial officer (CFO) worry that you and your colleagues will think that they are "disloyal" when they exercise options and sell shares, or sell shares of stock that they are holding? No way! Sure, the big guys need to be careful not to give the investment community the perception that they are dumping their shares and losing faith with the company's future, but that's entirely another story.

The big guys diversify their assets; and so should you. Nobody will think the worse of you for selling shares of your company's stock if doing so is in your best financial interests.

And besides, what you do with your assets, even company stock and stock options, is nobody's business but yours (and your family's).

Investing in Your Employer

You have at your disposal three primary ways to invest in your employer:

- ✔ Your stock options
- ✔ Shares of your company's stock that you buy on the open market
- ✔ Shares of your company's stock that you buy through a special program, such as your employer's Employee Stock Purchase Plan (ESPP)

Buying additional stock in your company

Just because you hold an option grant (or more than one grant) for shares of your employer's stock doesn't mean that you can't also buy shares of the company's stock in the open market (that is, on a stock exchange such as the New York Stock Exchange or the NASDAQ). If you have a high degree of confidence that you're working at a winning company with a bright future ahead and if you have enough spare cash available, then buying company stock may very well be a smart move.

However, don't put all your eggs in one basket. Sure, if your company's stock shoots higher, then you'll make a nice profit from your investment, but what happens if your company's stock slides lower and never recovers? Now you run the risk of holding not only underwater stock options that may never be worth anything but also an equity investment that has shrunk in value (maybe by a lot).

Suppose that Ralph, a close friend of yours from high school, went to work for a 6-month old Internet company in mid-1999. At the time, Ralph was granted an option on 30,000 shares with a strike price of $8 per share. The company went public a month later at a price of $10 per share, and the stock price took off from there, rising to $75 per share by the end of the year.

Along the way, Ralph — feeling flush from his on-paper gain of more than $2 million, figures that he wants to make even more money and buys 500 shares of the company's stock on the NASDAQ in the waning days of 1999, at prices ranging from $50 to $70. Every one of those 500 shares is showing a profit along with Ralph's stock options at least until the bottom falls out of the company's stock during the dot-com crash that begins in the spring of 2000. Ralph's employer's stock spirals downward with so many other business-to-consumer (B2C) dot-com companies, eventually winding up at a price of $3 per share, where it sits today.

Not only are Ralph's options underwater (assuming he hasn't exercised any of them and sold those shares), but he also suffered a tremendous loss on the shares he bought directly. Suppose that the average cost of those shares was $60 (250 shares purchased for $50 per share, and another 250 purchased for $70 per share). Sitting at a post-crash of $3 per share, Ralph has lost $33,500 *in real money.* Sure, his options are underwater, and that's a terrible situation by itself, but at least Ralph isn't directly out any money since he hadn't exercised any of them. But since he had gone to high-risk, high-expected-reward company and had accepted a position for a much lower salary than he could have earned at a more stable, mature company, the $33,500 loss really hurts.

Think it can't happen? By the end of 2000, the NASDAQ was littered with companies showing losses of 60 percent, 70 percent, 80 percent (like the drum-beating bunny on TV commercials, "still going . . ."), 90 percent, and — get this — even close to 100 percent that happened over the course of less than a year!

As I mention at the outset of this chapter, you have no way of knowing if your company's stock price will soar or nose-dive. So absent any kind of future-predicting device, you should think twice (or even three times) before buying additional shares of your company's stock if you are already heavily "exposed" through your stock options. Instead, you are often better off putting the money you would use to purchase those shares into some other type of investment to at least mitigate your overall risk in case your company's stock price goes down the drain.

Your company's Employee Stock Purchase Plan (ESPP)

A special case of your invest-or-not decision in your company's stock is when you can buy shares through an Employee Stock Purchase Plan (ESPP). In almost all cases, you should fully participate in an ESPP, but you should also be careful. After I explain the basics of an ESPP, I tell you what you need to watch out for.

ESPP basics

An ESPP is an investment vehicle set up by your company through which you can periodically purchase shares of your company's stock, usually at a discount and through money set aside through payroll deductions. ESPPs are almost always established in companies that have publicly traded stock rather than a privately held company.

Many of the rules of an ESPP are actually prescribed by the Internal Revenue Code (IRC), so even though your employer's ESPP may vary slightly from that of another company, many of the details in your ESPP are actually established by law.

You can set aside between 1 percent and 10 percent of your gross pay each pay period to put into the ESPP. This money is taken out of your gross pay just as taxes and other withholdings (like health insurance) are.

In a typical ESPP, a six-month "ESPP enrollment period" is established. On the first day of the ESPP enrollment period, the company's closing stock price is recorded. And then, on the final day of the ESPP enrollment period, the company's closing stock price that day is also recorded. Whichever stock price — the first day's or the last day's — is lower becomes the basis for determining the number of shares to purchase with the money set aside from your paychecks. And then, to give you an extra treat, take 85 percent of this basis to determine the number of shares you can purchase with your ESPP money now in the custody of your company.

Confused? Don't be; here's a very simple example.

Your annual salary is $50,000, and you decide to enroll in your company's ESPP program to the fullest extent permitted — 10 percent, or $5,000 per year. (To simplify the example, assume that your salary doesn't change during the year.)

Your company's plan is established in six-month enrollment periods, meaning that during the first six months you're enrolled, $2,500 (one-half of the $5,000 annual total) will be set aside in equal increments from each of your paychecks. Your company's closing stock price on the first day of the enrollment period is $20. Your company's closing stock price on the last day of the enrollment period is $25. Therefore, the lower value, $20, becomes the basis for establishing the number of shares you can purchase.

Your company's purchase discount is 85 percent of the lower of the two prices, meaning that your actual purchase price per share is $17 ($20 × 85 percent). Because you set aside $2,500 and your purchase price per share is $17, you purchase 147 shares ($2,500 divided by $17). Actually, the correct number for 2,500 divided by 17 is 147.0588, but most ESPPs don't permit you to purchase fractional shares. This means that if you purchase 147 shares at $17 per share, you actually pay $2,499 (147 × $17) for those shares, not $2,500. Don't worry; you don't lose the "leftover" dollar, it stays in your ESPP account and is available for the calculations during the next period.

Now stop and think about this for a moment. You now own 147 shares of your company's stock, worth $25 per share (the closing price at the end of the period), but you just paid only $17 per share. You have an automatic profit of $8 per share, or a total automatic profit of $1,176. And all for just being enrolled in the ESPP!

The cycle repeats for the second six-month ESPP enrollment period. Assuming that your salary is still $50,000 per year, then the same amount will be set aside from each of your paychecks as in the previous period. So if the stock price ends the first day of the second enrollment period at $25 (let's say there was no change from the previous day's close), and on the last day of the period your company's stock price closes at $30. You would have $2,501 in your account (the $1 left over from the previous period, plus the $2500 withheld from your paychecks), and your purchase price would be $21.25 per share ($25 × 85 percent). You will then purchase 117 additional shares ($2,501 divided by $21.25). Your actual total purchase price is $2,486.25 (117 × $21.25), and the leftover money remains in your account for the next period. And again, instant profit, because you purchased shares at $21.25, and the stock price is now $30 per share!

Sounds pretty good, huh? But what happens if your company's stock price falls during an ESPP period? No worries; remember that the lower of either the beginning or ending price is used as the basis before the 85 percent calculation occurs. Therefore, if the stock price begins an ESPP enrollment period at $30 and has dropped to $25 at the end of the period, your calculations would be the same as previously described for the second period with the same numbers ($25 and $30). The only difference: Your automatic profit at the time of purchase is less if the stock has dropped during the ESPP enrollment period than if it had risen.

Keep in mind that the only two dates that matter during the ESPP enrollment period are the first and last dates and the prices on those days. For example, if the stock price on the first day is $30 per share and two months later it drops to $10 per share, but by the last day, the price has recovered to $25 per share, you will have a purchase price of ($25 × 85 percent), *not* ($10 × 85 percent). The lowest stock price during any given ESPP enrollment period only matters if that price occurs on either the first or last day of the period.

The most serious ESPP gotcha!

Two ESPP programs in which I participated differed in only one minor detail. In the first company, my employer had set up an electronic transfer system tied to its ESPP program. The day after my ESPP calculations were made and the number of shares I could purchase had been determined, those shares were electronically transferred to the control of a stock broker, and if I wanted, I could immediately sell those shares and take my automatic profit. The important point to remember: I had immediate access to those shares to sell and receive my cash, if I wanted to do so.

However, the second company did not have any kind of electronic share delivery system set up, and instead, enrollees received paper stock certificates that they could then deliver to whatever stock broker they used. (The first company had this option available to me as well, if I wanted to use my own broker rather than the one theyhad their electronic system.) However — and here's the catch — employees usually waited about six weeks before the actual stock certificates would be delivered. In the meantime, nothing at all could be done with those shares that had just been purchased!

So what's the big deal? Well, when the company's stock was steadily climbing, there really wasn't any big deal. Even if an employee wanted to sell those shares, by the time the certificates had arrived the stock price would usually be a few dollars higher than it had been at the close of the ESPP enrollment period, meaning that an even greater profit would result.

But when the company's stock started heading downward, then that six-week delay turned into a trap. More than once, by the time certificates for ESPP-purchased shares had arrived, the company's stock price had dropped below even the discounted (85 percent) purchase price, meaning that that automatic, "guaranteed" profit had turned into a loss! For example (the following numbers are fictional, but they illustrate the point):

An employee makes $50,000. The company's stock price at the beginning of the period is $30 per share, and at the end of the ESPP period, the price has dropped to $25 per share, meaning that 117 shares would be purchased at $21.25 per share. ($25 × 85 percent = $21.25, and $2,500 @ds $21.25 = 117).

So far, so good, right? The stock is heading south, and you think it will continue to do so, but you have 117 shares with a $3.75 (the $25 current price minus your $21.25 discounted purchase price) per share profit. But wait — by the time you receive your stock certificates six weeks or so later, the stock price has dropped to $19 per share. Goodbye, profit! Hello, loss!

Your ESPP and your stock options

In case you're wondering why I spend so much time discussing ESPPs, here are several reasons:

- ✔ ESPPs are actually a form of stock options, with a special set of tax calculations established by the Internal Revenue Code. So even though the primary discussion of the book is stock options of the ISO and NQSO variety, in the interest of completeness, I wanted to describe how ESPPs work.

- ✔ More to the point of this chapter and this overall section on investing in your employer's stock, ESPPs are a key mechanism through which you can invest in your employer in addition to when you exercise stock options. Therefore, the example earlier in this section, with Ralph's money waving bye-bye because his dot-com employer's stock price got hammered, would also apply to shares of your company's stock that you purchase through your ESPP and hold, rather than sell immediately.

Keep in mind that you are under no obligation to immediately sell your shares that you purchase through an ESPP, just as you are not required to immediately sell shares you acquire by exercising a stock option. You may choose to hold onto those shares as part of your portfolio because you will receive preferential tax treatment by holding those shares long enough to turn them into a long-term capital gain, or you believe those shares will continue to appreciate in value even after you take possession of them.

When you decide to hold or sell ESPP shares, consider your philosophy about your stock options (see Chapter 3). If you have either an entrepreneurial or investment-oriented perspective about your company's shares, then you probably want to hold ESPP-purchased shares rather than immediately sell them — if you have some confidence that the company is stable and over time, its stock price will rise. (Again, remember that you have no crystal ball so you cannot know for sure which way your employer's stock price will go.) You will gain preferential tax treatment of those shares, plus you can manage your portfolio balancing and rebalancing (that is, sell some of those shares and put the proceeds into some other type of investment or some other stock) according to your own schedule.

If you are concerned about your company's future prospects even if you are entrepreneurially focused or investment-focused, you should consider immediately selling some or all of your ESPP-purchased shares as soon as you receive them. (See Chapter 17 to see how to look for hints and clues that might indicated either upward or downward trending in your company's stock price.)

If you are a member of our third philosophical category — the working stiffs — then you probably not only want to exercise in-the-money stock options as soon as they vest and sell those shares for your proceeds (see Chapter 3), but you will also likely want to have the same immediate sell-upon-receipt strategy for ESPP-purchased shares. Sure, you'll pay higher taxes than if you hold the shares for a longer period of time, and you may lose out on future appreciation in the value of those shares if your company's stock price rises, but your philosophy is that you want the "sure thing" from your stock options and your ESPP. You see both of those equity investment programs as, basically, extensions of your base salary, and you want your money to spend as little time exposed to risk as possible.

No matter which of those three philosophies you hold, if your company does not make your ESPP-purchased shares available to you immediately, either electronically or though actual physical delivery of stock certificates in a day or two, then you should not automatically enroll in your company's ESPP program. Instead, only do so if you have enough confidence in your company's future that you don't see an overwhelming risk in waiting four to six weeks (or longer) for those certificates.

And, for what it's worth, if you honestly think that a four- to -six-week period is an unacceptable waiting time because you're so confident that the company's stock is heading down below your discounted ESPP purchase price, then you should start updating your résumé and exercising options on whatever in-the-money shares you have vested (and immediately selling those shares) because your company — and your stock options — are most likely in big trouble!

You're Wealthy! But Is Your Wealth Real or Only on Paper?

Take another quick look at those stock options held by your fictional friend Ralph (the one who was so overconfident in his dot-com employer's future prospects that he bought an additional 500 shares of the company's stock — see "Buying additional stock in your company" earlier in this chapter). Recall that Ralph began working for the company in mid-1999, and by early 2000, his option on 30,000 shares gave him a gain of more than $2 million because the company's stock price rose to $75 per share after going public, and the strike price on his grant was $8 per share.

Two different kinds of paper wealth

For a moment, forget about the dive that Ralph's employer's stock price will soon take. At that giddy moment in early 2000 when the company's stock price is sitting at $75, is Ralph really a millionaire?

No, that's not a trick question. Remember that at that moment, all of Ralph's profits are on paper — meaning that he hasn't exercised options on any shares. If Ralph's option grant contains the normal four-year vesting with 25 percent of the shares vesting on the one-year anniversary of the grant, then he can't exercise options on any of those shares, even if he wanted to!

And thus we arrive at the Great Stock Option Paper Wealth Philosophical Question, the stock option equivalent of "if a tree falls in a forest and nobody is there, does it really make a sound?" The stock option version goes like this:

If your stock option(s) shows a paper profit of lots of money because your company's stock price is far above the strike price(s) on your option(s), but most or all of those shares are <u>not</u> vested, are you really wealthy?

You need to understand a very important difference between several scenarios that may both be categorized as "paper wealth." Say that, like your friend Ralph, you also hold an option on 30,000 shares from your employer with the exact same strike price and current market price as Ralph's company, but all of your shares have now vested. Even so, you have yet to exercise any part of that option.

Many people would categorize your situation as one of paper wealth: Your options are worth a lot of money, but you have yet to take advantage of your contractual right to acquire those shares. However, at any given point in time (except for any blackout period to which you're subject, as I discuss in Chapter 8), you could immediately exercise your option and acquire all 30,000 shares. If you hold on to all 30,000 shares, then your portfolio will contain a whole lot of stock worth a whole lot of money, at least at that moment in time. If you sell all of those shares, then your portfolio will contain a whole lot of cash that is, of course, worth a whole lot of money (considering that cash is money, right?).

However, now consider Ralph's no-shares-are-vested predicament. Even if Ralph woke up one morning in February 2000, and his instincts scream at him that the company's stock price can't possibly stay up around $75, that sooner or later the bubble will burst, he is powerless to do anything with those 30,000 shares on which he has an option. Ralph's situation might also be categorized as paper wealth, just as they would describe your situation. The difference between your situation and Ralph's is obvious, though. Your so-called paper wealth could be converted to real wealth in a snap simply by exercising your option on those 30,000 shares. Whereas in Ralph's case, his wealth is truly only on paper. (So would we say that Ralph has "unreal wealth"? Or how about "surreal wealth"?)

The two key points for you to remember are

- ✔ Sometimes stock option-driven wealth isn't real in the sense that you don't have ready access to either the underlying shares of stock or the proceeds from selling those shares because of the vesting schedule in your stock option grant. Very often, an extremely rapid rise in your company's stock price soon after you receive a stock option grant is the worst thing that can happen to you! Sure, the value of the shares covered by your option grant skyrocket, and chances are that on paper, you're sitting on a profit of tens of thousands, hundreds of thousands, or even millions of dollars. However, you are, for the most part, powerless to do anything except hope that your company's stock price doesn't come plummeting back down before you can at least salvage some of your profits when your first batch of shares vests.

✔ You shouldn't even consider profits on unvested shares to be part of your near-term usable assets unless those shares are about to vest soon and you don't have a major volatility point coming up for your stock price before that vesting occurs. A *volatility point* might be the company's next quarterly earnings report, and the general consensus in the investment community is that if your company doesn't meet expected earnings, then the stock price is going down, down, down.

Previously, I use the phrase "near term usable assets." Near the beginning of this chapter, I mention that you should make sure that your portfolio allocation is aligned in concert with your current and anticipated needs and obligations. Here's what I mean: Suppose that you are holding an in-the-money stock option with some — but not all — of the shares vested and are showing a very, very nice profit based on your company's current stock price as compared with the strike price on your option grant. Suppose also that, within the next six months, you have a major expenditure coming up — purchasing a house or a car, or paying college tuition for your child — and you anticipate using part or all of your stock option profits as payment for part — or even all — of the upcoming purchase. My suggestion: Take some of that stock option paper wealth that you can access off the table by exercising a portion of your stock option, selling those shares, paying the taxes on your gain, and stashing away your proceeds. Sure, you'll wind up paying more taxes than if you exercised and held onto those shares, or just kept holding all of your option without exercising any part of it. But if you anticipate using part of those gains in the near-term, you should not risk a precipitous drop in your company's stock price putting an end to (or at least delaying) your housing, vehicle, or child's college plans.

Don't think that can't happen, either! As I noted earlier, take a look at all of the Internet companies with stock price drops in a few short months of anywhere between 60 percent and almost 100 percent. I know there's a lot of stock option holders who wish they could jump into their own flux capacitor-powered Delorean and go back in time to a point where they could have exercised options on whatever shares they could and immediately taken profits before their respective companies' stock prices took the big plunge. No doubt, untold thousands of people's plans went down the tubes along with those stock prices.

Of course, you may be better off tax-wise if you had anticipated a future expenditure several years in advance rather than several months and exercised part of your option then, holding the stock to receive preferred tax treatment on future gains as I discuss in Part IV. Keep in mind, though, that sometimes you can't be as proactive as you'd like solely for tax-managed purposes. For example, if you anticipate needing $150,000 two years from now, but only $50,000 of your total $400,000 on-paper stock option profits are vested, then (assuming your employer's stock price doesn't crash), you will likely exercise an option on whatever shares you can as soon as they vest (the ones that yield the $50,000 profit). Then you will have to "make up" the remaining $100,000 over the next few vesting periods, even though some of those shares will have to be exercised and sold before qualifying for preferred tax treatment.

The key point for you to remember is that you need to do your tax planning for your stock options in the context of your overall financial planning for you (and, if applicable, your family), and sometimes you will have to do a give-and-take between tax-driven considerations and the timing of your anticipated needs for proceeds from your stock options.

Protecting (or trying to protect) your unvested stock profits

Don't try this at home! This section should be labeled the same as one of those automobile commercials showing a car slaloming at high speeds or bouncing all over a bounder field: "Professional driver on closed course."

In Chapter 1, I briefly discuss publicly traded (listed) options such as puts and calls, and note that they are very different than the types of stock options covered by this book (for example, ISOs and NQSOs).

Some professional investment advisors propose strategies to "insure" your stock option profits on unvested shares — as well as profits from vested shares, or even profits from shares you've exercised and are holding to obtain preferred tax treatment. Some of these strategies involve puts or calls or sometimes both. Other strategies involve stock market indices or other investment vehicles.

Some strategies are applicable to your stock options only if your company's shares are publicly traded, while others apply to pre-IPO options as well.

As with insurance policies in general, the premise of many of these strategies is to try and lock in profits by sacrificing a smaller amount of money that will be lost (or worth less) if your stock options do what you want them to do: hold their value or, better yet, increase in value. However, should your company's stock price do what you don't want it to do — sink to the point where your options go underwater and wind up worthless — the insurance investment pays off with compensating gains. Typically, the insurance investment is set up to be one that will automatically move in the opposite direction of your company's stock price, that is, increase in value if your company's stock price drops.

Other protection strategies involve investments that don't quite possess the official inverse relationship from your company's stock price, instead relying on investments that should move in the opposite direction from your company's stock price.

I won't even attempt to describe these strategies, because you absolutely need to work with a highly qualified financial planner or accountant if you are even considering using listed options or some other financial instrument in concert with your stock options.

I will note, however, that if you have either an entrepreneurial-focused or investment-focused philosophy about your stock options, then you might want to look into some of these strategies if your company's stock price is a bit more volatile than you'd like it to be, and you have some uneasiness about your company's future prospects. Keep in mind, though, that some companies prohibit these types of "hedging" strategies, so make sure you fully understand what you are and aren't allowed to do.

If, however, you have a working stiff perspective to stock options, then I don't recommend even thinking about these types of strategies for a single moment. Chances are that you're not totally comfortable with even some conservative investments, and your stock options are basically an add-on to your salary, so you want to avoid overly complex investments that could conceivably turn against you and cause you to lose money.

Sector Exposure

Sometimes, diversification isn't really diversification.

No, I'm not double-talking or talking in circles, but am simply pointing out that just because you take some stock option profits off the table and put the proceeds into other stock investments, you could still find yourself subject to an across-the-board downturn in your portfolio, affecting not only your stock options (and other holdings of your employer's stocks) but your other investments as well.

For example, suppose you work for a company in my favorite target for this chapter, a business-to-consumer (B2C) dot-com online retailer. You do the smart thing when your company's stock price skyrockets: You exercise options on some of your vested shares to reduce your exposure to the fates of your company's stock, selling those shares (and paying taxes on your gain). However, you take half of your after-tax proceeds and invest them in the stock of another B2C dot-com company, and put the remaining half in a sector mutual fund that invests exclusively in companies in one industry or several closely related industries — in this example, Internet B2C companies.

So on the one hand, you have diversified your assets a bit, but on the other hand, you are still just as susceptible to taking a big hit in your portfolio if the stocks tank.

Many investment professionals use a measure of portfolio volatility called beta as part of their asset allocation decisions. *Beta* predicts how a group of assets should perform relative to overall market performance. A portfolio with a beta of 1 means that those assets, taken as a whole, should move up or down just about the same as the overall stock market. So if the market goes up 10 percent, then those assets should also increase 10 percent; if the market drops 10 percent, so too will those assets. A higher-than-1 beta means portfolio increases and decreases should be more than the increase or decrease, respectively, in the overall market. A beta between 0 and 1 should mean a lower-than-market increase but also, in the case of a declining market, a lower-than-market decrease. Finally, a negative beta means an expected inverse gain or loss as compared to the overall market.

Unless you want to really get into portfolio management, you don't need to worry about trying to calculate the beta of your collective assets. Instead, think of managing your sector exposure this way: As you divide your investment eggs among a number of different baskets, make sure that not too many of those baskets look the same as each other.

Part IV

Pay Up! Taxes and Stock Options

The 5th Wave   By Rich Tennant

PHIL HARRISON VISITS HIS TAX ATTORNEY

©RICH TENNANT

The new tax law goes on to say that "...all taxpayers shall be exempt from these extra charges except...", and this is the part that bothers me, Phil, "...except for Phillip Harrison of 120 Colby Ave., Patterson, New Jersey."

In this part . . .

Your stock options giveth, but the tax man (or woman) naturally wants a cut of your gains, if you're fortunate to profit from your stock options. The tax rules for stock options vary depending on what kind of stock options you receive — nonqualified options, incentive options, or maybe both. You'll explore the basics of taxes and then find out about all the little details that apply to both kinds of stock options. You'll also get a look at that "great wild card" of the tax world that you need to watch out for: the alternative minimum tax (AMT).

Chapter 12

Understanding the Basics of Taxes and Stock Options

In This Chapter

▶ Developing your personal philosophy on paying taxes

▶ Heeding some warnings and surprises

▶ Understanding the basics

▶ Considering state tax and international tax issues

*J*ust like The Grateful Dead put it: "Every silver lining's got a touch of gray." The silver lining: exercising in-the-money stock options and benefiting from the long hours and personal sacrifices that you've made for your job. The touch of gray: the tax man (or woman) waiteth, hand held out.

In this chapter, I focus on the basic and fundamental principles that you need to understand before turning your attention to specific options-related tax situations, which Chapters 13 through 15 tackle.

Deciding How Much You Want to Worry about a Tax Strategy for Your Stock Options

Some people approach every decision they make with regard to their respective stock options with one single thought: how to minimize the taxes they'll owe on their gains. Decisions about when to exercise, how many shares, which shares, and how long to hold those shares before selling are all based solely (or at least primarily) on minimizing that tax bill.

Sometimes, the fates are with someone falling into this category, and that person not only minimizes the taxes owed but also continues to profit from a steadily increasing stock price, yielding even greater gains from a stock option package and the shares acquired from those options.

In other situations, though, fixating on tax considerations can cause a person to make ill-advised decisions about his or her stock options, and what was once a sizable paper profit evaporates into nothingness. Worse, sometimes the strategies someone employs to minimize taxes on options, such as borrowing money to pay taxes so shares can be held rather than sold, can result in the value derived from those stock options sinking into nothingness, perhaps leaving the person in debt — perhaps seriously in debt.

So where am I headed with this discussion? Before getting into the tactical aspects of taxation related to stock options, such as whether you'll owe taxes when you exercise various types of stock options, you need to consider what your philosophy will be related to taxes and your stock options.

In addition to the applicable tax laws and how they affect what you'll have to pay, you need to take the following factors into consideration as you make decisions about exercising options and selling shares:

- ✔ The timeframe in which you will need access to the after-tax profits from your stock options

- ✔ The current state of your company: how it's doing financially, its stability, its outlook over the next one to two years, and so on

- ✔ The overall health of the stock market and economy

- ✔ Other aspects of your financial picture (and that of your family)

Stock option gains, especially sizable gains, are hardly a "gimme" — you need to be working at the right company at the right time in the right stock market climate in the right economic environment. (Got all that?) It's a shame, though, when those who are fortunate enough to have their stock options greatly increase in value end up having their gains diminish, even vanish, solely because they are so obsessed with minimizing taxes. They make foolhardy decisions about waiting too long to exercise their options, or holding shares too long waiting for the favorable tax rates to kick in.

So as your stock option adventures go merrily along, keep in mind that you need to make key decisions with more thought than simply and mechanically following a laundry list of steps that will result in lower taxes, if the value of your stock doesn't collapse in the meantime!

Warnings and Possible Surprises Waiting for You

Tax laws related to stock options are complicated enough, but muddying the waters a bit more are two additional realities. First, tax laws frequently change. Second, you may find yourself owing taxes even though you haven't received any cash.

Tax laws change frequently

Anyone who has been in the workforce for more than a few years knows that tax laws and all the accompanying rules and regulations that govern your tax returns frequently change. Heck, I still remember oldies but goodies from the 1980s such as income averaging, gasoline tax deductions, and deductible credit card interest that have long disappeared from the annual tax return ritual. And if you've been filing tax returns for 10, maybe 15 years, then you've seen the tax rates and holding periods related to capital gains (which I discuss later in this chapter) change frequently.

Which brings me to the heart of this version of "the only constant is change." One of the key items you need to factor into the decisions I discuss in Chapters 13 through 15 is the difference between long-term capital gain rates and ordinary income rates. Under current tax law (circa 2000–2001), most people see a fairly substantial difference between these respective tax rates. However, not too long ago, there was no difference between ordinary income and any kind of capital gain rates.

So because of tax law changes, the decision you might make today about exercising options and selling shares could very likely be different than the decision you may have made in the not-too-distant past.

Not only do you need to stay on top of tax law changes as they occur, but after a significant modification of the tax code, you should also reevaluate your entire stock option portfolio and your strategy to determine the impact on your stock options and shares of your company's stock you are holding.

When the rules of the game change, ask your accountant for advice, especially if you have a valuable stock option package with sizable paper profits. Also, you should check out the various Internet stock option sites that I discuss in Chapter 9 for the latest and greatest news and opinions from the experts.

Owing taxes even if you haven't received any cash

Many of the scenarios that I discuss in Chapters 13 through 15 involve your having to pay taxes after some particular action you take, such as exercising options, even though you don't receive any cash as a result of that action. You might be wondering how you are supposed to pay taxes even though you're not getting any money out of the deal?

Unsettling as these situations may be, if you think about it, they aren't all that uncommon. Other situations not related to stock options, but with similar consequences, include:

- ✔ Receiving a capital gains distribution from a mutual fund you own and automatically reinvesting that distribution in additional shares of the fund. Even though you don't receive any cash, you do owe taxes on the amount of that distribution.

- ✔ Winning a non-cash prize in a raffle or somewhere else (like a game show); because you are receiving something of value, you need to pay taxes on those goods just as if you had received cash.

- ✔ If you are a partner (in legal terms) in a business, the partnership's net income or loss is allocated to you and the other partners to be included on your respective tax returns.

So don't assume that just because you "do something" with your stock options (typically, exercising) and you don't receive any cash that you won't find yourself facing a tax bill.

Key Tax Concepts

Tax laws are very complex. And that's just talking about U.S. federal tax laws; just wait until I discuss state taxes and international taxes later in this chapter. Filtering through this complexity, though, four key concepts stand out as arguably the most important with regard to understanding the tax implications of your stock options:

- ✔ Ordinary income
- ✔ Short-term capital gains
- ✔ Long-term capital gains
- ✔ The alternative minimum tax (AMT)

Ordinary income

For most people, the most significant portions of their annual earnings are classified as *ordinary income*: your salary or income from a self-employed business that you own, for example. Ordinary income is taxed in *brackets* that under current (early 2001) tax law range from 15 percent to 39.6 percent.

Of course, along the way, you can take IRS-authorized deductions from your ordinary income (mortgage interest, for example) before you have to calculate the tax you owe.

With regard to your stock options, the important point to note is that often times your stock option gains become classified as ordinary income with the aforementioned tax rates applying. And many of the tax-driven, hold-or-sell decisions you make after exercising options will be driven by the difference between ordinary income rates and long-term capital gains rates, which I discuss shortly.

Short-term capital gains

When you buy and sell various types of assets — stock, real estate, and even collectibles such as comic books — capital gains take center stage. A *capital gain* is, the gain you make by buying and selling assets — or, more accurately, capital assets. (A capital loss, as you might expect, is a loss you incur from selling a capital asset for less than you had purchased it for.)

Under current (early 2001) tax laws, a short-term capital gain occurs when you sell an asset you have held for one year or less. The tax rates for short-term capital gains are the same as ordinary income rates.

Long-term capital gains

One of the most beneficial aspects of tax law in general, and stock options in particular, is long-term capital gains: assets sold after being held for a year and day. Long-term capital gains can result in huge *after-tax* stock option profits . . . or in broken hearts for taking too much of a chance in search of locking in those supersized stock option gains.

Under current tax law, long-term capital gains are taxed at a rate of 20 percent, even though you may be in the 39.6 percent tax bracket (or any other tax bracket) because of your ordinary income. The only exception: If you don't have a lot of taxable ordinary income and you're only in the 15 percent tax bracket, then your long-term capital gains are taxed at only 10 percent.

So where does the heartbreak come in? As I discuss in the next few chapters, you may choose to hold the shares you acquire from exercising your options rather than sell them immediately, your objective being to hang on to them for a year and a day to have them qualify as long-term capital gains rather than short-term capital gains. However, if the stock price drops significantly while you're holding onto the stock, then the amount of your long-term capital gain could significantly diminish, perhaps to the point where you wind up with less after-tax gains than if you had simply sold at exercise time and paid the higher short-term capital gains taxes at the ordinary income rates.

In the worst case, your gains could entirely evaporate if the stock drops too much, turning your anticipated long-term capital gain into a loss.

So hang on and wait until the next few chapters when I look at your "options on your options" in more detail and help you decide what path you should take at various decision points.

Alternative minimum tax (AMT)

I discuss the AMT in all of its ugliness in Chapter 15, but in the interest of completeness I introduce it briefly here. Way back in the 1970s, the IRS was getting fed up with people abusing *tax shelters,* basically, investments whose primary purpose was to generate sizable tax losses to dramatically lower taxes that would otherwise have to be paid on high income. You used to see all kinds of books and articles that touted how to teach you to pay zero taxes even though you made hundreds of thousands, maybe even millions, of dollars. The IRS had had enough, so tax laws were changed to outlaw many kinds of tax shelters.

Aside from outlawing all kinds of tax shelters, the folks who create tax laws came up with the idea for the *alternative minimum tax*. Despite the awkward wording, the AMT is exactly as described by the term: an alternative way of calculating your taxes to make sure that you pay a fair minimum tax.

But with tax shelters on the wane, why the need for the AMT? The tax law folks figured that high-income people with "too many" deductions and credits may be able to escape paying their fair share of taxes. So you have to use an alternative set of tax rules for income and deductions to figure out if the AMT applies to you and, if so, what your tax bill will be.

Now with regard to stock options, the AMT comes into play with incentive stock options (ISOs) — when you exercise an ISO but do not sell the stock in the same calendar year. Stand by for Chapters 14 and 15 for more details, but be forewarned, it might not be a pretty story if you don't play your cards right.

State Tax Considerations and Michael Jordan?

What does Michael Jordan have to do with taxes and your stock options? Directly, nothing. However, you may work for a company that complies with what is sometimes called "The Michael Jordan Law." During the 1990s, some states enacted laws that required everyone who worked (more on that later in this chapter) in the state to pay taxes on their earnings in that state — not only residents and part-time residents, but even nonresidents.

The catalyst for these laws is sometimes attributed to high-paid athletes who travel from state to state for road games. The rationale used by the proponents of these ridiculous laws is that if someone like Michael Jordan was earning income in, say, California — even if only for a few days each year — then Michael Jordan should darn well pay taxes in California for the portion of his income earned there, even if he were a resident of Illinois or wherever he lived when he played basketball. The same was true of his Chicago Bulls teammates (even Dennis Rodman), of baseball players, and basically every professional athlete.

However, the states didn't stop with athletes when they enacted these laws. They specified that everyone who worked in their respective states should be subject to the same rules as the athletes. Several important points:

✔ The definition of *work* usually means actually performing whatever services an out-of-state, nonresident employee does for a living: a computer consultant doing consulting work for a client, for example. Typically, attending training at an out-of-state location doesn't qualify as "working" for purposes of figuring out if you would owe taxes in some state you visit during the year.

✔ Not all companies comply with these laws, even though they're supposed to. For example, a computer consulting company may only withhold taxes for each employee in his or her own home state, even though they are supposed to allocate those tax withholdings to all states in which their employees work. Technically, you are supposed to do your own cross-state, multiple-state tax calculations and estimated tax payments, but most people don't bother to do so.

✔ Most states have some type of "equivalency" provision for their residents, in which *some* of the taxes withheld by another will be credited against what a person would otherwise owe in his or her home state. However, you still could find yourself ripped off, big-time. For example, my home state of Pennsylvania has a flat state tax rate of 2.8 percent. Pennsylvania residents who can credit taxes paid to other states can only credit up to the amount they would have paid in Pennsylvania (2.8 percent of the taxable income) even though the other state's rate may be much higher, such as in California or New York. From Pennsy-lvania's point of view, I agree that's fair; otherwise Pennsylvania would find themselves short-changed just because other states have higher tax rates if they allowed you to credit everything you pay to every other state. But from your point of view if you're subject to this silliness, you're still paying more than you would have to if you were only paying taxes in your home, low-tax (or even no-tax) state.

✔ Many companies who comply with these "Michael Jordan laws" help their employees by providing a "state tax equalization program" in which they figure out what you would have paid in state taxes if you were only paying in your home state, versus what you had to pay to all of the states in any given tax year, and then they pay you the difference to make it up to you.

So where am I going with all of this? When you have some taxable event related to your stock options, you not only have federal tax implications but also state tax implications! Make no mistake about it, your home state will probably want its share of your taxable stock option events, so you need to understand exactly what the tax laws are in your state with regard to stock options: ordinary income, capital gains, and anything else.

But the state tax implications don't stop with your home state, if you travel extensively for business, and your company fully complies with all states' Michael Jordan laws. And sometimes, you can get very . . . well, I can't think of the appropriate word to conclude this sentence, I'm sure my editor won't let me write the one I want to use.

Consider California — my favorite example for how messed up all of this is. Suppose you are a computer consultant earning $200,000 per year, and you live and work in Pennsylvania. During a calendar year, you work for a couple of days at a client site in California, and your company allocates your income proportionally to your home state of Pennsylvania as well as California and other states in which you work. So say that $4,000 of your income is deemed to have been "earned" in California.

Now you might think a sensible way to calculate how much you owe in California is to simply figure out what the tax is on $4,000 of income. According to the tax table in California's booklet of instructions and forms for nonresidents and part-year residents for the 1999 tax year, the tax would be $40, or 1 percent. That sounds fair, right?

But no. California doesn't do it that way. You have to go through a long and complicated sequence of calculations that, basically, requires you to figure out the tax you owe California as if <u>all</u> of your income had been earned in that state, and <u>then</u> you figure out the percentage of your time spent in that state and pro-rate that tax calculation. The result: If you have a sizable salary, you could end up paying California's top rate (just under 10 percent) on that California-earned income even though you only spent a few days in that state — costing you a lot of money.

Now you may think I've gone off on a tangent here, doing a Dennis Miller-style rant (minus the profanity) about the idiocy of this whole nonresident taxation business. But don't worry, I haven't forgotten about stock options.

Basically, you could wind up paying far more total state tax on your stock option gains than if you were only paying taxes in your low-tax home state. Even aside from the "more taxes" problem, you also have the additional problem of just trying to understand how all this works and if you have any safety valve for your stock options.

To pick on California one more time, consider this little tidbit from the same 1999 California booklet for nonresidents and part-time residents describing adjustments you are allowed to make (page 30):

> **"Exclusion for compensation from exercising a California Qualified Stock Option (CQSO).** To be eligible for this exclusion your earned income from the corporation granting the CQSO must be $40,000 or less; the market value of the options granted to you must be $100,000 or less; and the total number of shares must be 1,000 or less. If you included in federal income an amount qualifying for this exclusion, enter that amount in column B."

Huh? Time to call your accountant to figure all of this out!

International Tax Considerations

An interesting phenomenon, almost a paradox, about taxes on stock options is that almost all of the reference material you will find is U.S.-centric — for U.S. residents working in the United States for a U.S. company. And in Chapters 13 through 15, I do the same thing, focusing on U.S. federal tax laws. However, consider the following situations, in which you may have a stock options package:

- You are a resident of another country (not the United States) working in the United States for a U.S. company.

- You are a U.S. resident working for a U.S. company, but live and work in some other country.

- You are a resident of another country working for a company from your native country, but you work in the United States.

- You are a U.S. resident working in another country but you work for a company from yet another country.

And so on. The point is that most of the material about taxes and stock options you will find is so U.S.-centric that if you fit into any type of multinational employment situation, then at best your situation will be more complicated than a U.S.-centric one; at worst, you could wind up with some very adverse tax consequences, especially if you don't fully understand what laws from what countries apply to you.

The most important rule for you to remember if you're a U.S. citizen, though: You will owe U.S. federal income taxes on your stock options at the appropriate times, which I discuss in Chapters 13 through 15, regardless of whether you're working for a U.S. company and regardless of whether you're working in the United States. Additionally, depending on the tax laws in the country in which you're working if you're working outside the United States, you might also owe taxes there as well; you'll need to determine that on a case-by-case basis.

And don't forget to check with your home state in the United States to find out whether you'll owe taxes there if you're out of the country for part or all of the year. For the other situations, complicated as they may be, there's help. On the Web site www.mystockoptions.com, in the Resource Center section, you'll find a Global Tax Guide that gives you some guidance to stock option-based tax situations in other countries.

Only use this information as a basic guide, though, because tax laws may change as frequently in other countries as they do in the United States, and you need to thoroughly understand your particular situation and the various scenarios that could occur from receiving and exercising options and then selling shares, and seek professional guidance from an accountant for complex situations. A sampler of tidbits from the myStockOptions.com Global Tax Guide follows.

Canada

Canada has two types of stock options: *tax-preferred* and *nontax-preferred*. For tax-preferred options, there is no tax on stock options at the time they are granted. Options are taxed at ordinary rates at the time of exercise on the difference between the market value and exercise price, but you are allowed to deduct 25 percent of that difference when computing taxes. You are then taxed on any additional gain at the time you resell shares.

For nontax-preferred options, no tax applies at the time they are granted, and then at exercise time, ordinary income tax rates apply to the difference between market value and exercise price, but no 25 percent deduction is permitted as with tax-preferred options. However, when shares are resold, the additional gain is taxed at capital gain rates rather than ordinary income rates.

Canada will also be implementing a new type of tax treatment for stock options similar to U.S. incentive stock options (taxes on ISOs are discussed in Chapter 14), but in early 2001, details were still being worked out.

England (U.K.)

England, like Canada, has two types of stock options: tax-preferred and nontax-preferred. For tax-preferred options, those granted under an "approved company share program" aren't taxed at the time of grant. At the time of exercise, options also aren't taxed as long as options aren't exercisable more frequently than every three years. Then, when shares are sold, capital gain rates apply.

For nontax-preferred options, if the term of an option is ten years or less, no tax applies at grant time. Then, when exercised, ordinary income rates apply to the difference between market value and exercise price, with capital gains rates applying to any further gains at the time shares are sold.

According to the myStockOptions.com Global Tax Guide, "in the U.K. the term is 'share options' instead of 'stock options,' and 'scheme' instead of 'plan.' Your employer may have gotten approval from the Inland Revenue for the share option scheme under which your option was granted. These approved company share option schemes, which may be considered 'tax-preferred,' offer significant tax advantages in the U.K."

Ireland

In most cases, no tax applies at the time options are granted, unless the option can be exercised more than seven years after the date of the grant. In that case, a tax charge is imposed the day the option is granted, based on the difference between the stock's value and the price paid for the stock. This tax charge may be set off against the tax imposed at the time the option is exercised.

At the time the option is exercised, tax will be imposed on the difference between market value of the stock and the option price at the exercise date. Then, normal capital gains tax rules apply when the shares are later resold.

Options granted between April 1986 and January 1992 under schemes approved by the Revenue Commissioners, also known as *Approved Share Option Schemes*, received more favorable tax treatment. Holders of these options were neither taxed at the time the option was granted nor upon exercise. However, the favorable tax treatment under Approved Share Option Schemes has since been terminated.

France

France also has both tax-preferred and nontax-preferred options. For the tax-preferred variety, no tax applies at grant time. At exercise time, "whether tax will be imposed at the time a tax qualified stock option is exercised depends on whether there is a discount between the shares' fair market value on the day the option is granted and the exercise price of the option. If there is no discount (or a discount less than 5 percent), then no tax is imposed when the option is exercised. But, if the discount exceeds 5 percent, the entire amount of the discount will be taxed as salary at the time the option is exercised." (Whew!)

At the time shares are sold, "if shares purchased upon exercise of a tax qualified option were held for at least five years, the spread between the fair market value of the shares at the exercise date over the exercise price (plus any discount up to 5 percent) is taxable at 40 percent upon resale of the shares. If the optioned shares are sold less than five years from the date of grant, the spread is taxable as salary, subject to averaging over the term of the option. If the discount exceeded 5 percent so that tax was imposed at the time of exercise, then capital gain rates will apply when the shares are later resold." (And I thought California income tax rules were complicated!)

Nontax-preferred options are much simpler. No tax applies at grant time, and at the time of exercise, the difference between market value and exercise price is taxed. Then, when the shares are sold, capital gains rates apply to the additional gain. That's more like it.

Chapter 13

Nonqualified Stock Options and Taxes

In This Chapter

▶ Understanding NQSOs

▶ Understanding taxes for cashless exercises

▶ Avoiding tax complications

▶ Taking the Section 83(b) election

▶ Figuring out tax withholdings when you exercise NQSOs

▶ Using the right tax forms

▶ Deciding when to exercise your NQSOs and other options

*I*t's time to shift from general discussion, strategy, and philosophy about stock options to the cold, hard numbers of taxes. I start with nonqualified stock options (NQSOs) in this chapter, because the tax rules and permutations are easier to understand than those of incentive stock options (ISOs), which I discuss in Chapter 14.

What Is a Nonqualified Stock Option (NQSO)?

A nonqualified stock option (NQSO) is a stock option that *does not* meet specific Internal Revenue Code rules that classify an option as an ISO. Or, to put it another way:

▶ A stock option is an ISO if it meets certain criteria, and if so, a certain set of tax laws apply.

▶ If all of the ISO criteria are *not* met, then the option is an NQSO, with a different set of tax laws applying.

Several other quick points to note about NQSOs:

- You will sometimes see the spelled-out wording as "non-qualified stock options" and other times as "nonqualified stock options" (without a hyphen). Either is correct, and for my purpose (primarily to avoid wordiness), I use the NQSO acronym.

- NQSOs may be held not only by employees of a company but also by nonemployees such as outside business partners and consultants; ISOs can only be held by employees. If you hold ISOs and leave the employment of your company but for some reason are allowed to retain your options, they will convert into NQSOs. This is because the options no longer meet the qualifications of an ISO — specifically, you're no longer an employee. Therefore, the set of tax laws that originally came with your options now change because the classification of the option has changed.

- You might also find other situations where you have ISOs that convert to NQSOs, such as if you exceed certain annual limits specified by the Internal Revenue Code (more on that in Chapter 14). So again, be aware that you may have certain assumptions about the tax laws that apply to your ISOs, but quite possibly those assumptions are invalidated because your options convert from ISOs to NQSOs.

One final point: Don't be concerned about the term *nonqualified* with regard to your stock options. As I previously note, the only disqualification is for consideration as an ISO. First-time stock option holders with little or no knowledge about options beyond the very basics (mostly, locking at today's stock prices for tomorrow's purchase) are sometimes concerned about what exactly their options aren't "qualified to be or do." So again: The only disqualification is for the tax laws and other characteristics of an ISO.

Understanding the Basics: NQSOs and Taxes

The good news about NQSOs and taxes is that, for *normal* situations, the tax rules are easy to understand, and I'd estimate that the vast majority of NQSOs can be considered *normal* situations. So before I talk about *abnormal* situations later, I'll focus on the easy part of this whole tax business.

Grant-time tax consequences

Rule number one for NQSOs: In almost all cases when you are granted an NQSO, you have no tax consequences at that moment. You don't owe any taxes, and if you wind up never doing anything with that stock option, you walk away with no tax considerations at all.

Why might you never do anything with an NQSO? Three situations mostly apply:

✔ The company never goes public, and therefore, the stock never has a market value because it's never traded on any market.

✔ The company already is public when you receive that grant, but the option goes underwater so you never exercise it.

✔ The company is privately held when you join it and does go public, but over time the option goes underwater, and you never exercise it.

Even if you have no tax consequences at the time an option is granted, the strike price of the shares on that option is formally established for future tax calculations.

Exercise-time tax implications when you hold your shares

Fast-forward from the time you are granted an NQSO to some point in the future when you decide to exercise your option. For now, assume that you decide to hold the shares, rather than sell them immediately in a cashless exercise — I cover that scenario in a moment.

Exercising an NQSO triggers *ordinary income taxes* but only on the shares you purchase when you exercise.

Example: Table 13-1 shows your stock option holdings on June 1, 2001, the day you decide to do an NQSO exercise, when your company's stock price is $15 per share. Assume that all of your option grants have traditional four-year vesting (for example, 25 percent of the shares on each option vest on each anniversary date of the option grant).

Table 13-1	Your Stock Option Holdings on June 1, 2001			
Date Granted	**Type**	**Total # Shares**	**# Shares Vested on June 1, 2001**	**Strike Price**
2/1/1999	NQSO	5,000	2,500	$10
12/1/1999	NQSO	2,000	500	$20
6/1/2000	NQSO	2,000	500	$15
12/15/2000	NQSO	2,000	0	$12

First, take a top-down look at your overall options picture. Only one of your option grants has shares that are vested *and* in-the-money — the first one you received on February 1, 1999. Your option grant from June 1, 2000 has, coincidentally, a strike price exactly equal to the current market price of the stock. And your most recent grant, on December 15, 2000, is in-the-money but currently doesn't have any vested shares.

Suppose, then, that you decide to exercise your first option received on February 1, 1999, for all 2,500 of the vested shares. Again, you are going to hold your shares, which means that:

- ✔ You will pay $25,000 for the stock you're purchasing ($10 per share × 2,500 shares).

- ✔ You will then own 2,500 shares of your company's stock, in addition to any shares you may already own.

- ✔ The *capital gains holding period* clock starts running on the day you exercise your option, fixing that date at June 1, 2001.

I previously mention that exercising an NQSO triggers ordinary income taxes. But this is true for only those shares you purchase. So even though you have options on 11,000 total shares from your four grants, the only ones that figure into your ordinary income tax calculation for this particular exercising event are the 2,500 that you purchase.

So for purposes of your tax calculations, you need to figure out taxes owed on 2,500 shares of stock.

This "selectiveness" of shares for tax consequences applies even if you're not purchasing all of the currently vested shares on an option. If you decide to purchase only 1,000 of the 2,500 vested shares from your February 1, 1999 grant, you only have to figure out taxes on those 1,000 shares.

The first step is for you to figure out how much of a gain you have to record as ordinary income. Fortunately, this is a relatively simple calculation:

```
# Shares Being Purchased × (Fair Market Value - Strike
        Price)
```

For purposes of the preceding calculation, fair market value is simply the current price of the stock at the time you exercise your option — in this case, $15 per share. So your calculation will look like:

```
2,500 × ($15 - $10) = $12,500
```

So, with your NQSO exercise, you are realizing $12,500 of ordinary income. That amount gets *added* to the rest of your ordinary income for the year — your salary if you're employed by a company, or your self-employed business income if you work for yourself — and is all "pooled together" for purposes of calculating your income taxes for the year. You treat the $12,500 just like income from a second job.

So if you were already in the highest federal tax bracket (currently 39.6 percent), you would add an additional $12,500 to all of your other income, meaning that 39.6 percent of that gain, or $4,950, would be your federal income tax bill from that particular NQSO exercise. If you were in some other tax bracket, then you would either owe a lower amount of taxes as determined by your tax bracket, or be pushed into a higher tax bracket if you had a significant gain from your NQSO exercise.

Don't worry too much about all of the tax bracket implications, though; they are what they are. Furthermore, as I previously mention, think of your gain from exercising as the equivalent to income from a second job or some other taxable activity, such as running a home business or writing.

And, like other sources of ordinary income, the gain from exercising your NQSO is also subject to the following:

- ✔ State income taxes
- ✔ Social security taxes
- ✔ Medicare tax

With regard to state taxes, pay careful attention to the cross-state tax implications I discuss in Chapter 12 (for example, the "Michael Jordan Law" that many states enforce for nonresidents).

For social security taxes, just like with other forms of ordinary income, you won't be subject to social security taxes above whatever cap the IRS sets in any given year. For example, suppose that for the year you exercise your NQSO, the maximum amount of earnings that is subject to social security taxes is $80,000. If your income from your salary is $100,000, you won't owe additional social security taxes on the gain from exercising your NQSO.

The maximum amount on which social security tax applies changes annually, so make sure you have the correct figures for determining whether or not you'll owe social security taxes.

Finally, under current tax law, the Medicare tax applies to all ordinary income, so you'll owe the Medicare tax on your gains (again, just as you would for income from a second job).

There is one big difference between ordinary income you realize from exercising an NQSO and holding the shares *and* income from a second job. You realize a taxable gain of $12,500, and will have to pay federal taxes (as much as $4,950), plus state taxes, Medicare tax, and maybe even social security tax, but you haven't actually received any money! Not only that, you've had to pay $25,000 to buy the shares of stock. So by the time the whole deal is over, you will likely have a cash outflow of more than $30,000 if you live in a high-tax state.

As I note in Chapter 12, one of the most unsettling aspects of stock options for many people is that they find themselves face-to-face with tax implications, even though they haven't actually received any money as part of some particular event, such as exercising an NQSO and holding the shares. That's why many people do *cashless exercises* on their NQSOs — the topic of the next section.

Exercise-time tax implications when you do a cashless exercise

You have two main reasons why you might do a cashless exercise rather than an exercise-and-hold with your NQSO:

- ✔ You don't have enough available cash to pay for the shares you purchase and pay the taxes on the ordinary income you realize.
- ✔ Even if you have the available cash to buy the shares and pay the taxes, you want to cash out, at least in part, and take some money off the table.

Sometimes, both situations occur: You don't have enough money, but even if you did, you still want the cash now rather than hold the stock you purchase.

When you do a cashless exercise, you are actually executing two different transactions that just appear to be one. First, you are exercising an NQSO to buy some number of shares at the preset strike price. Second, you are selling those shares immediately — technically a separate transaction that is equivalent to what happens when you sell shares you own after a buy-and-hold.

Using the same stock option holdings shown in Table 13-1, suppose you decide to do a cashless exercise on the vested, in-the-money shares from your February 1, 1999 grant. Assume that the market price of the stock is $15 per share, as in the earlier example.

Your tax calculation for the ordinary income you realize is the same as in the exercise-and-hold example:

```
2,500 × ($15 - $10) = $12,500
```

So when tax time comes, you would add $12,500 to all of your other ordinary income: salary, interest, side business income, and so on.

Assume that your company's stock isn't very volatile, or at least on the day of the cashless exercise, it isn't very volatile. Therefore, when your stockbroker turns around to sell your 2,500 shares, the price you receive is the same $15 per share. Therefore, the amount of cash you receive is $12,500 (minus any brokerage or administrative fees associated with doing the cashless exercise).

Even though you may not realize it, you have a *capital gain transaction* as part of your cashless exercise: the event of selling your shares. The good news, though, is that in the preceding example, the sale price is the same as your purchase price, so your capital gain transaction has neither a gain nor a loss, but it's still a transaction, as shown in Table 13-2.

Table 13-2	The Capital Gain Transaction Portion of an NQSO Cashless Exercise		
Transaction	**# Shares**	**Total Amount**	**Tax Consequences**
Purchase shares	2,500	$12,500	Already covered by ordinary income recognition
Sell shares	2,500	$12,500	Short-term capital gain of $0

The very act of selling shares is a capital gain transaction. The two important aspects are

✔ Because you held the shares for one year or less (actually, probably for less than an hour), the transaction is classified as short-term.

✔ Because your proceeds are the same as your *basis* — in this case, your cost — the amount of the "gain" is actually zero, meaning that you won't owe any additional taxes.

In some cases, a cashless exercise will have a small capital gain tax consequence when you sell your shares. Why? A cashless exercise is actually two transactions. In the first — the exercise and purchase of the shares — the purchase price is *marked* at the moment your stockbroker processes your exercise and purchases your shares. So putting a spin on my example, say that the opening price for your company's stock on June 1, 2001, is $15, and you call your stockbroker in the morning before the market opens to request the cashless exercise. The broker does the purchase side of the transaction shortly after the market opens, and the stock price at that moment is still $15 exactly. Then, a little while later after your broker sells the shares, the price increases slightly to $15.05.

In this situation, the ordinary income you realize would still be $12,500, because the purchase price you receive is $15. However, the capital gain side at the time of sale is *not* zero; you actually realize a five-cent short-term capital gain per share, or a total of $125 (2,500 shares × .05 per share).

Therefore, you have two taxable aspects of your cashless exercise: the ordinary income side and the capital gain side — admittedly a small amount, but still a taxable event.

If the share price were to dip slightly between the purchase price that you receive and the market price when your shares are sold, you may find a small short-term capital loss as part of your transaction. This capital loss can be used to offset other capital gains you have, up to (according to current tax law) $3,000 per year. Chances are, though, that unless you're doing a cashless exercise for hundreds of thousands of shares on a day when your company's stock is just about crashing with heavier-than-usual trading delays, a cashless exercise won't come anywhere near to $3,000 in a short-term capital loss.

Calculating taxes when you sell shares you acquire from exercising NQSOs

Suppose that on June 1, 2001, after exercising your NQSO that you had received on February 1, 1999, you now own 2,500 shares of your company's stock. Your *basis* has been established at $12,500 — your total purchase price for those shares, just as if you had bought those shares in the open market on June 1, 2001 for $15 per share, rather than exercising an NQSO.

From that point forward, whatever happens to those shares is, basically, unrelated to your stock options, and instead those shares are treated just like any other shares of stock you may own.

Say that on December 3, 2001, the stock doubles in price to $30 per share, and you decide that it's time to cash out. You sell all 2,500 shares that you had purchased for a short-term capital gain of *$15* per share, for a total of $37,500. Notice that I didn't say that your capital gain on each of those 2,500 shares was $20.

A common mistake when selling shares gained from having previously exercised an NQSO is to think that the basis price per share is the same as the original strike price of the option — $10 per share, in this case. But you have already paid taxes on the portion of your gain between $10 and $15 in the form of ordinary income you realized when you exercised the option on June 1, 2001.

Therefore, when you sell those shares, make sure you don't double-tax yourself when you calculate the amount of your capital gain, but instead start from the time of the *exercise*. If you look at the big picture for those 2,500 shares, you had purchased each share at $10 per share and sold at $30 per share, for a total gain of $50,000 (2,500 shares × $20 per share). However, the tax-related pieces of the big picture are split into two:

✔ $12,500 in ordinary income

✔ $37,500 in short-term capital gains

Table 13-3 illustrates the entire sequence of events for that particular NQSO. Note that for February 1, 1999, only the number of shares you're exercising — 2,500 — are listed, not the entire 5,000 shares from the grant.

Table 13-3	An Entire NQSO Tax Event Sequence with a Short-Term Capital Gain				
Date	**Event**	**# Shares**	**Price Per Share**	**Tax Conse-quences**	**Pre-Tax Gain**
February 1, 1999	NQSO grant	2,500	$10	None	None
June 1, 2001	NQSO exercise	2,500	$15	Ordinary income on $5 pershare	gain $12,500
December 3, 2001	Sell shares	2,500	$30	Short-term capital gain on $15 per share	gain $37,500

As I note in Chapter 12, under current tax law, short-term capital gain rates are the same as ordinary income rates. So if you are in the top tax bracket of 39.6 percent, the federal tax rate you pay on your $37,500 in short-term capital gains will be the same as you had paid on the $12,500 ordinary income six months earlier. (The actual amount of taxes will be different, of course, because the amount of gain subject to taxation is different.)

Your state may tax short-term capital gains as well. So far, the total amount of tax you will owe is the same as if you hadn't exercised the NQSO in June and, instead, had waited until December and done a cashless exercise.

But you will not have social security or Medicare tax consequences for your short-term capital gains, so you will save a little bit of money there by having part of your total gain classified as a short-term capital gain rather than ordinary income.

If you had waited to sell your shares until June 2, 2002 — one year and one day after you had purchased them — then your capital gain would be classified as a long-term gain, with a substantially lower tax rate (under current tax law). Assuming you're in the top 39.6 percent bracket, you would save just about half of the federal tax you'd pay since you'd only be taxed at 20 percent. (See Table 13-4.)

Table 13-4	An Entire NQSO Tax Event Sequence with a Long-Term Capital Gain				
Date	Event	# Shares	Price Per Share	Tax Conse-quences	Pre-Tax Gain
February 1, 1999	NQSO grant	2,500	$10	None	None
June 1, 2001	NQSO exercise	2,500	$15	Ordinary income on $5 per share	gain $12,500
June 3, 2002	Sell shares	2,500	$30	Long-term capital gain $15 per share	gain $37,500

If, therefore, your company's stock price were $30 on June 2, 2002, then on the next trading day, you could sell your shares, realize your $37,500 capital gain to give you the same total of $50,000 from the strike price, but pay less in federal capital gains tax.

The risk, though, is that while you're waiting for the long-term capital gain holding period to kick in, that the price could go down, perhaps even lower than your original strike price. The consequences, then, are that you may wind up eventually selling stock and taking a capital gain loss. Not only would you have laid out the cash you needed to purchase your shares on June 1, 2001 and then even more to pay the ordinary income taxes on those gains, but now you may wind up with only a token amount of cash when you sell your shares for a big loss. I discuss these kinds of decisions later in this chapter.

Complicating the Situation

This section discusses how the general guidelines of tax consequences along the NQSO road may vary from the norm.

Why you might owe taxes at grant time

In most cases, receiving an NQSO has no tax consequences for you because the option doesn't have any value above that specified by the terms of the grant. For a publicly traded company, an NQSO with a strike price equivalent to the market price of the stock is, basically, worth the same as the stock itself. Even if the option had no vesting schedule and all shares were immediately vested, the act of exercising your entire NQSO on the day you receive it and purchasing all of those shares would be the same as if you just bought those shares on the open market.

Or if your company is privately held, you can't readily trade in your company's stock, which means that your NQSO doesn't really have a fair market value at that point . . . because there is no "market" on which it trades.

But suppose you receive an NQSO with a strike price lower than the fair market value of the stock. According to tax law, you may have tax consequences from receiving an NQSO. Conceivably, even receiving an NQSO in a privately held company could have tax consequences if the strike price is low enough.

To be on the safe side, ask someone "in the know" at your company (preferably the stock plan administrator) if there are any grant-time consequences when you receive an NQSO (or, for that matter, an ISO). In almost all cases, the answer will be "no." But it's better to find out for certain before you find yourself socked with a tax bill that you weren't expecting.

Exercising and no taxes: Delayed income recognition

As I note earlier in this chapter, exercising an option usually results in your having to recognize ordinary income on the difference between the your strike price and the market price.

However, if you are allowed to exercise options in a privately held company, then sometimes the ordinary income tax is delayed. Specifically, if you exercise an option and the stock you acquire is subject to a substantial risk of forfeiture and not transferable, then you will not owe ordinary income taxes at the time you exercise an NQSO.

For more information on delayed income tax recognition at the time of exercise, I recommend consulting Robert Pastore's book *Stock Options: An Authoritative Guide to Incentive and Nonqualified Stock Options* (PCM Capital Publishing), which discusses pretty much every tax code permutation that you might run into for your stock options.

Understanding the Section 83 (b) Election

The Section 83(b) election is the point in which just about all of the "basics" of stock options get thrown out the window.

Consider two of the key fundamentals of stock options:

- ✔ You exercise a stock option to purchase shares that you will either resell immediately (that is, a cashless exercise) or perhaps hold and sell at some point in the future; but you will sell those shares.

- ✔ You are only allowed to exercise an option to purchase shares that have vested.

Many option holders' experiences are in concert with these guiding principles. However, sometimes you are allowed to exercise an option on *unvested shares*, even in a company that has yet to go public!

Welcome to the world of the Section 83(b) election.

Section 83(b) basics

The primary idea of the Section 83(b) election is to help you save taxes in the long run. However, as I discuss, you take on some risk when you go down this path.

When you make a Section 83(b) election on an NQSO, you exercise an option to purchase shares earlier than you normally would, because you want to realize the ordinary income consequences of the NQSO as early as possible. Doing so starts the clock running on the potential for long-term capital gains and the resultant tax savings

At the time you receive stock for which you decide to take a Section 83(b) election (more on the mechanics later), you would realize ordinary income just as with any other NQSO. Any subsequent gains would be classified as capital gains — possibly short-term capital gains but, more likely, long-term capital gains.

Earlier in this chapter, I mention that if you exercise an option to acquire shares that are subject to a substantial risk of forfeiture and also are not transferable, you don't owe ordinary income taxes at the moment. By filing the Section 83(b) election, you are, essentially, saying "Hey, wait a minute! I want to pay those ordinary income taxes now, even though I really don't have to, so I can start the capital gains clock running — even though it will cost me money to pay those ordinary taxes that I otherwise wouldn't have to pay."

The Section 83(b) election permits you to formally acquire and then own shares that you would otherwise not have access to, such as shares that aren't vested. The vesting restrictions still apply, though, but now to the stock itself. That is, you pay for the stock and own it, but you can't sell shares before you otherwise would have been able to acquire them from the original terms of your stock option.

For example, suppose that your company goes public after you take a Section 83(b) election and acquire unvested shares from your NQSO. You still can't dump all of those shares, even after the lockup period (see Chapter 8) expires. Instead, you need to wait until those shares vest, just as they would have under the "control" of the NQSO.

The main attraction, then: You get the ordinary income recognition out of the way on as many shares as possible and start the clock running on the capital gains determination.

Section 83(b) risks

Even though Section 83(b) gives you a vehicle through which you can try to minimize the taxes on your stock options over the long-term, the path toward lower taxes is also filled with many, many risks. Specifically:

- You are buying stock that you may never be able to sell at any price. Suppose the company never goes public, for example? Sure, your overall tax bill is reduced as compared to what that tax bill might have been, but in reality, since the options were basically worthless, you would never had had to pay any taxes at all.

- Unless you are absolutely certain that you have a long-term commitment to the company and will remain employed there for several years, going down the Section 83(b) path might not be the best idea. You could wind paying for shares that you own but can't sell — either at all, or perhaps according to vesting restrictions on those shares that will be in effect for several years.

- If you hold options on a large number of shares and your strike price "is not insigificant," then you could be putting out a large chunk of cash for, essentially, a bet. Example: You have an NQSO for 200,000 shares with a strike price of 50 cents per share. That's $100,000 you'll have to come up with for a stock that may never go public, just because you're trying to save taxes in the long run.

- Even if you work for a privately held company that does eventually go public, you probably don't have a good sense of how the company's stock will be valued in the public stock markets or how volatile the stock will be. Whereas, if you wait to exercise your NQSO until you either have gains "on the table" or at least have a sense of your company's stock's "behavior," you can better time your future actions with your options.

Section 83(b) mechanics

If you decide to take a Section 83(b) election, you need to send a letter to the Internal Revenue Service *within 30 days from the date you acquire the shares.*

There isn't any standard form or letter for the Section 83(b) election, so you should ask your stock plan administrator at your company for a standard letter that you can use as a template.

Beware, though: Don't miss the 30-day deadline; otherwise, you can't do a Section 83(b) election on those shares even if you want to!

Tax Withholding and Exercising NQSOs

When you exercise an NQSO and need to realize ordinary income, your company should come to your assistance by withholding appropriate federal, state (if applicable), social security (if applicable), and Medicare taxes from your proceeds.

If you are doing a cashless exercise, the withholding means that you will not receive the total amount of the proceeds from the exercise. Instead, 28 percent of the gain is typically withheld for federal tax. So if you live in a state with fairly high income tax rates and if you do a cashless exercise early enough in the year so that you haven't reached the maximum social security tax withholding, then close to half of your gain may be withheld.

You might also request that your company's accounting department withhold more than 28 percent of the proceeds from a cashless exercise, if you're running behind on tax withholdings for the year and want to get caught up. And with regard to any social security taxes that might be withheld, don't worry that you'll wind up owing more social security taxes than you otherwise would. You'll just wind up hitting the maximum amount sooner from your regular paychecks than you would have otherwise if you hadn't exercised an NQSO.

In general, the withholdings aren't really a problem because you'll owe that money anyway. But if you're doing a cashless exercise for the purpose of acquiring a certain amount of money for some specific need, then you should plan for the amount to be withheld to make sure you receive enough cash.

If you are doing an exercise-and-hold, then you need to file an estimated tax form with the IRS and, if applicable, with your state for the appropriate amounts.

If you've never filed estimated taxes before, get the appropriate forms and booklets from the IRS and your state so you meet all deadlines and file the appropriate forms.

NQSOs and Your Tax Forms

Make sure you file all the tax forms you are supposed to. But before even worrying about the tax forms you will file, you need to worry about the tax forms you will receive.

Your W-2 (and your pay stubs)

Your employer is supposed to include any gains you receive and the amounts of taxes withheld on your W-2 forms. So if your total salary for the year was $100,000 and if you receive a total gain on the exercise of an NQSO of $12,500, then your W-2 should show wages of $112,500.

Additionally, whatever taxes were withheld from those gains should likewise be included in the appropriate categories where applicable: federal, state, social security, and Medicare.

You can be sure that the numbers that show up on your W-2 will be correct before you receive the forms, though. The amount of ordinary income that you realize, along with the amounts of each type of tax, will show up in your paycheck stub at some point, usually within one or two pay periods after the date you exercise. Pay attention to the amounts shown for each pay period, plus the change from the previous period, to make sure that the numbers calculated by your company's accounting department match the correct amounts from your NQSO exercising event. If you find a discrepancy, or are unclear about anything dealing with the amounts, then ask someone in the accounting department as soon as possible, preferably long before the end of the year and the issuance of W-2 statements. If you do receive a W-2 statement that is wrong, you'll have to get the company to issue an amended W-2 to make sure the IRS has the correct information on file. Also, make sure your company gives you an amended W-2 in time for you to file your taxes!

Form 1040

If your company correctly applied all of the ordinary income and withheld taxes to your W-2, then you don't need to do anything more to the basic Form 1040, though you will need to file a Schedule D, as I discuss in a moment. If, however, the company omitted everything about your NQSO exercise from the W-2 (as contrasted with getting the data wrong, which needs to be corrected), then you need to include the calculated amount of ordinary income on the line for other income on Form 1040.

Don't forget that if you paid any estimated taxes, you should include them on the Form 1040 line that specifies taxes withheld and estimated tax payments — otherwise you may cheat yourself and have to double-pay federal taxes on the ordinary income you realize from exercising the NQSO!

Schedule D

All stock sales need to be reported on a Schedule D, even a stock sale that is a behind-the-scenes transaction as part of a cashless exercise.

Looking back at our cashless exercise example earlier in the chapter, I discuss two different scenarios: one in which the capital gain is zero and one with a small capital gain.

Looking at the first example (zero gain), you would show the following information on your Schedule D (see Table 13-5).

Table 13-5	Information About Your Cashless Exercise for Your Schedule D				
Date of Purchase	**Date of Sale**	**Number of Shares**	**Basis**	**Proceeds**	**Gain (or Loss)**
June 1, 2001	June 1, 2001	2,500	$12,500	$12,500	$0

That's pretty easy, right?

If you have a small variation between the purchase and sale prices that together comprise the cashless exercise, you would show that information on your Schedule D, as shown in Table 13-6.

Table 13-6	Information About Your Cashless Exercise for Your Schedule D (With a Variation Between Purchase and Sale Prices)				
Date of Purchase	**Date of Sale**	**Number of Shares**	**Basis**	**Proceeds**	**Gain (or Loss)**
June 1, 2001	June 1, 2001	2,500	$12,500	$12,625	$125

If you sell shares that you previously acquired from exercising an NQSO, then you would likewise fill in the appropriate information for purchase and sale dates, number of shares, basis, proceeds, and gain or loss.

The IRS tends to frequently change the structure of the Schedule D and how that information carries over to Form 1040, so carefully read the instructions each year to make sure you enter information in the correct places and correctly transfer information between forms and schedules. For an excellent guide to taxes, consider Eric Tyson's *Taxes For Dummies* (Hungry Minds, Inc.).

Timing Troubles: When Should You Exercise NQSOs?

You have a lot of factors to consider about when you should exercise the NQSOs that you hold. Some significant factors are the tax consequences from various points at which you can exercise, as well as whether you should hold shares you acquire after exercising an NQSO or whether you should just sell the shares, take your money, but pay higher taxes.

By no means, however, should tax consequences be the only factor you consider. And I know this is a matter of opinion, but given the volatility and downside in the stock market for most of 2000, I would even argue that tax consequences and scenarios should take a back seat to other factors — such as your company's outlook, if the stock price is overvalued, and all of the other items that I discuss in Chapter 17.

This section takes a look at several different strategies and how the tax consequences relate to other factors, such as the risk to which you're exposing yourself and your personal cash flow.

As soon as possible

One strategy for NQSOs is to exercise as soon as possible to limit the amount of ordinary income realized and then to start shifting future gains into the long-term capital gain bucket. Given what I've discussed in this chapter, this strategy requires you to hold shares after you exercise, rather than doing a cashless exercise. Additionally, you need to hold those shares for at least one year and one day to shift the capital gain status from short-term to long-term for the lower tax rates.

The primary advantage to this strategy is the preferred tax consequences. But you need to balance that quest for a lower tax bill with cash flow and risk.

Cash flow

The sooner you exercise, the sooner you have to commit cash that could be used for some other purpose or invested elsewhere. One of the advantages of stock options — both NQSOs and ISOs — is that you acquire the legal right to today's stock price as if you had actually bought the stock, but you don't have to pay the cash at that moment. By exercising as early as possible while you seek a lower tax bill, you negate much or all of the cash flow advantages of stock options.

Risk

Another key advantage of stock options in general, and NQSOs in particular, is that they give you the opportunity to "wait on the sidelines" before committing cash.

The reason I make a distinction between NQSOs and ISOs with regard to the level of commitment is that the tax laws related to ISOs (as I discuss in Chapter 14) are inherently geared toward holding the shares you acquire from exercising an ISO for at least long enough to qualify as a long-term capital gain. To do otherwise "disqualifies" the tax advantage and causes shares acquired from an ISO to be treated as NQSO shares.

With regard to NQSOs, the only way to acquire any kind of preferred tax treatment is to try to minimize the amount of ordinary income and hold your shares long enough so that your gains beyond the ordinary income qualify as long-term capital gains. Following that strategy, however, causes you not only to commit cash earlier than you might otherwise have done, but also greatly increases your risk.

That risk is magnified if you follow an early-exercising strategy along with a Section 83(b) election, as I discuss earlier in this chapter. You commit cash and own shares before you often have a good sense of how well the company and its stock will eventually do.

As late as possible

You could adopt a strategy for your NQSOs in which you wait as long as possible to exercise the options and buy shares. If you'll always do cashless exercises, then a late-as-possible strategy may be the way to go: Wait until the stock hits some desired price and buy and sell some or all of your vested shares in the blink of an eye.

The chief disadvantage to this approach, of course, is that all of the gains from your stock options will be categorized as ordinary income with a significantly higher total tax bill than if you attempt to shift part of those gains into the long-term. So if the stock price goes on a long-term upward trend with only a brief hiccup here and there, then in the long run you will have paid higher taxes by waiting to exercise your options than if you had exercised earlier in the life of those options.

At regular intervals

A balanced approach to managing your NQSOs is to exercise at more or less regular intervals during your employment tenure. You might exercise some portion as early as you can, even doing an 83(b) election if your company permits, but you still hold some of your options back in a wait-and-see mode.

Along the way, you do a mixture of cashless exercises and exercise-and-hold events, taking away some cash at various points and, at other times, building holdings of your company's stock into your overall portfolio.

One more consideration

If you have a number of different stock option grants, some of which are NQSOs and others that are ISOs, you may want to develop a combined strategy through which you do the following:

- Use your ISOs to purchase shares that you intend to hold, because ISOs are constructed to promote holding shares, along with the accompanying tax advantages.

- Use your NQSOs primarily for cashless exercises, at various intervals as you anticipate wanting to take cash away and diversify your portfolio.

Another Key Decision: Which Option (s) Should You Exercise?

Take a look back in Table 13-1, and notice that the option grant you received on June 1, 2000 had a strike price of $15 per share, which turns out to be the same exact stock price one year later on June 1, 2001.

As you can tell from the strike price on the December 15, 2000 grant, the stock price dipped to at least $12 — and perhaps went even lower before or on December 15, 2000 — but by June 1, 2001 had recovered to $15. Conceivably, the stock price might have even gone higher than $15 at some point. Say that on March 1, 2001, the stock price had increased to $20 before settling back to $15. However, for purposes of calculating the tax consequences of exercising NQSOs, the movement of the company's stock price is irrelevant. Only two prices matter when exercising an NQSO:

✔ The price on the day you received the grant, which becomes the strike price on your option grant; if the company is privately held when you receive the grant, the fair market value (FMV) of the stock becomes the "price" upon which your strike price is established.

✔ The price on the day you exercise the grant, which becomes the FMV for purposes of calculating your ordinary income.

No other day-to-day prices matter for your NQSOs.

Anyway, suppose you decide to exercise an option on June 1, 2001 and hold shares so you can start the long-term capital gain clock, but you want to minimize the amount of cash you have to spend. 500 shares from your June 1, 2000 grant have just vested, so you can exercise your June 1, 2000 option, giving you the following calculation for your ordinary income: # Shares Being Purchased × (Fair Market Value – Strike Price) or 500 × ($15 – $15) = $0.

Essentially, you will owe no ordinary income taxes from this exercise, because you have no gain: The fair market value is exactly the same as the strike price. Your total cash outflow is $7,500 — the price you pay for the stock — but you won't have to pay anything additional for any type of tax (federal, state, social security, or Medicare).

You might be looking at the preceding example and thinking to yourself, "So what would I need a stock option for in this case? Couldn't I just buy 500 shares of stock in the open market for that same $7,500?"

Absolutely! Think about what a stock option does, in the larger sense: It locks in the stock purchase price on the date of the grant, no matter how much higher the stock price goes. In this example, the stock price on June 1, 2001 is the same as it was on June 1, 2000, the date of the grant. So in effect, if you really wanted to own 500 shares of your company's stock and minimize the amount of cash outflow, you might very well be better off leaving that particular NQSO alone and just buying 500 shares of stock.

You could, of course, exercise your first option of February 1, 1999 for 500 shares and pay only $10 per share — or a total of $5,000, rather than $7,500. But then you would owe a greater amount of taxes on the ordinary income you realize.

Table 13-7 shows the tax consequences of the three different alternatives available to you for purchasing and holding 500 shares of your company's stock on June 1, 2001 at a price of $15 per share.

Table 13-7	Three Alternatives for Purchasing and Holding 500 Shares	
Alternative #	**Action**	**Tax Consequences**
1	Exercise February 1, 1999 option, purchase and hold 500 shares	Owe ordinary income taxes on gain of $2,500 (500 shares × $5 per share)
2	Exercise June 1, 2000 option, purchase and hold 500 shares	No ordinary income tax owed since market price = strike price
3	Buy 500 shares of stock through a broker	No tax consequences

Which alternative is right for you? The answer depends on what your primary objective is. If you're trying to start the capital gain holding clock as quickly as possible, then you should do either alternative 1 or 2.

Suppose, though, that you also want to spend as little cash as possible to acquire those shares. On the one hand, alternative 1 will only cost you $5,000 instead of $7,500 for those 500 shares (which is the same cost to you if you just purchase the shares in alternative 3), given the two different strike prices. However, with alternative 1, you will also owe ordinary income taxes on $2,500, which might cost you another $1,200 or $1,300 if you live in a high-tax state and if you're in a high federal and state income tax bracket. So the total difference between the two alternatives in terms of cash outflow isn't quite as large as if you were to only consider stock purchase prices.

If, for whatever reason, you want to leave as much of your options as possible intact, waiting on the sidelines, then you might want to just buy 500 shares of stock, paying a little more than with alternative 1.

A different perspective on buying stock versus exercising options

In Robert Pastore's book *Stock Options: An Authoritative Guide to Incentive and Nonqualified Stock Options*, the author presents an interesting discussion on the decision between buying stock in the marketplace versus exercising an option to buy and hold shares.

Mr. Pastore notes (on page 115) that "if the expectation is that the stock price will appreciate substantially, it naturally follows that retaining the nonqualified stock option, and buying the stock outright, is usually preferable to buying the stock and exercising the option."

The author then goes through a simple example based on the intrinsic value of the option (see Chapter 10). The key, though, is in the first part of the first sentence of that section: "The expectation is that the stock price will appreciate substantially. . . ."

Without getting into all of the mathematics, if you have, say, $10,000 set aside to purchase shares of your company's stock that you want to hold, and you also have in-the-money options with vested shares, then you should spend that $10,000 to buy shares on the stock market and leave your NQSO(s) intact. If, as you expect, the stock doubles or triples or goes even higher over the next few years, then the shares you purchase now will likewise increase, and you can then do a cashless exercise on your vested shares and pick up that substantial gain as well.

Keep in mind, though, this strategy and the decision to buy shares rather than exercise options is predicated on a high level of confidence that the stock's price will go way up. However, you need to keep the composition of your portfolio in mind as well. As I discuss in Chapter 11, you really should keep diversification of your portfolio in mind. If, as you might hope, your company's stock skyrockets and your options make you wealthy, then you would have been better off pouring most or all of your other investment funds into your company's stock as well, holding off exercising your options until they have substantial gains.

The catch, in my opinion, is the "expectation" of a substantial rise in your company's stock price. I assume that many dot-com or Internet consultancy option-holding employees, if asked in late 1999 or early 2000, would have said that they expected their company's stock price to rise substantially. However, you know what happened in that corner of the investment world.

My point is that when thinking about your investments in your employer's stock, try not to be overly optimistic or even greedy when it comes to deciding how to buy that stock.

Chapter 14

Incentive Stock Options and Taxes

. . . .

In This Chapter

▶ Understanding the basics of ISOs and taxes

▶ Looking at different types of ISO dispositions

▶ Previewing the Alternative Minimum Tax (AMT) and exercising your ISOs

▶ Understanding when multiple tax years apply to your ISOs

▶ Considering a wash sale

▶ Taking the Section 83(b) election

. . . .

To put a spin on the famous passage from George Orwell's *Animal Farm*, "All stock options are equal, but some options are more equal than others."

Whereas nonqualified stock options (NQSOs — see Chapter 13) are structured according to a relatively simple set of rules and tax laws, incentive stock options (ISOs) are much more complex.

True, ISOs might result in lower taxes for you than NQSOs in the long run, but the trip to "low taxville" might just have a lot of detours you have to navigate, and more than a few potholes. Here's your roadmap.

What Is an Incentive Stock Option (ISO)?

An *incentive stock option* (ISO) is a particular type of stock option that conforms to a tight set of Internal Revenue Code (IRC) guidelines. One restriction is that only employees of a company are permitted to own ISOs in that company; stock options conveyed to outsiders such as consultants or advertising agencies must be NQSOs.

In the context of ISOs, the word *incentive* is used in a sort-of-official way, referring to the particular IRC restrictions, rather than in a descriptive sense (such as "the stock options are an incentive for you to work very hard so the stock price goes up and you make money").

The tax laws that apply to ISOs are different than the tax laws that apply to NQSOs. As I discuss, though, sometimes the actions you take with your ISOs result in tax consequences that are nearly identical to those of NQSOs.

A fundamental principle of ISOs is that when exercised, the shares acquired from that exercise are intended to be held for at least two years from the date they were granted, *and* more than one year from the date of the exercise.

Note the use of *and*. To fully realize the tax advantages of an ISO, both conditions have to apply.

If you have a "normal" vesting schedule on your ISOs — that is, regardless of how long your vesting schedule is, the first batch of shares vests one year after the grant date — then the only date you really have to watch is the second date (one year from the date of exercise). Why? Because if you hold the shares you acquire from exercising an ISO for at least one year, then that date is automatically at least two years after the grant date, even if you exercise the first batch of those shares as soon as you are allowed to (specifically, on the first anniversary of the grant date).

Talking Taxes and ISOs: The Basics

I go through all kinds of ISO taxation scenarios later in this chapter. This section covers the basic guidelines of ISO taxation, including:

- ✔ Tax implications (or lack thereof) for various events, such as when you are granted an ISO and when you exercise an ISO
- ✔ The two different types of ISO "dispositions" and why the tax rules are very different for each scenario

Grant-time tax consequences

You have no tax consequences on the date you are granted an ISO. Certain key pieces of information are recorded for future use: the date of the grant and the strike price of the shares covered by the grant.

Exercise-time tax consequences

I have good news and bad news for you. The good news is that unlike an NQSO, exercising an ISO does not trigger recognition of ordinary income on the difference between what you pay for the stock you're acquiring (based on your strike price) and the fair market value of the stock (based on the then-current market price or fair market value). In fact, exercising an ISO does not trigger any ordinary income tax recognition at all, not even capital gains tax. As specified by the tax laws applicable to ISOs, exercising an ISO is a taxation "nonevent."

The bad news is that at the time you exercise an ISO, you do have some tax consequences.

No, the above two paragraphs are not contradictory to each other — I didn't make a big mistake that the copy editor didn't catch.

But how could that be, you ask? How could the same event — exercising an ISO — have no tax consequences and tax consequences at the same time?

The answer is simple, though not pleasant: According to "regular" tax calculations for ordinary income and capital gains, exercising an ISO truly is a non-event with regard to your taxes. However, the *alternative minimum tax* (AMT) does come into play when you exercise an ISO. And as I discuss shortly, one of the key tax benefits of an ISO — delaying taxation until you sell the shares you acquire from exercising an ISO — is just about totally negated by the AMT, which usually requires you to pay up.

Tax consequences when you sell ISO shares

When you finally sell shares you acquire from exercising an ISO, you will have tax consequences. The exact tax consequences will vary according to the time frame in which you sell those shares.

One of the key ISO principles is that you only realize the maximum tax benefits when you hold shares for more than one year after the date you acquire them (as well as for two years after the date you exercise the ISO grant). Consequently:

- If you do meet these holding period restrictions, then all of your gains are taxed as long-term capital gains.

- If you don't meet these holding period restrictions, then you will be taxed on your gains according to ordinary income rules.

Unfortunately, the above two statements are really a gross oversimplification of the real story with sale-time tax consequences. The next section digs into the details.

Pleasant disposition or nasty disposition?

When you sell shares that you purchased by exercising an ISO, the shares are categorized as either a *disqualifying disposition* or *nondisqualifying disposition* (also called a *qualifying disposition*), depending on whether they meet the holding period restrictions.

- ✔ Selling shares that have met the holding period restrictions of two years from the date of grant and more than one year from the date of purchase is considered a *nondisqualifying disposition*.

- ✔ Selling shares that have not met the holding period restrictions of two years from the date of grant and more than one year from the date of purchase is considered a *disqualifying disposition*.

Note: You might be wondering (as I have wondered) why the term nondisqualifying is used. The term nondisqualifying isn't exactly a double negative, but it's just as confusing. But for whatever reason, that term is often used rather than the simpler "qualifying disposition."

You might also see two totally different terms used:

- ✔ The term *sale of mature ISO stock* instead of nondisqualifying disposition

- ✔ The term *early disposition* instead of disqualifying disposition.

I stick with nondisqualifying disposition and disqualifying disposition for this chapter. Both types of dispositions, and their respective tax consequences, are discussed at length in the sidebar, "More disposition positions."

Disqualifying Disposition of an ISO

Even though the preferred course of action for your ISOs is to do a nondisqualifying disposition to realize lower taxes, I cover disqualifying dispositions first because the tax picture is most like what I discuss in Chapter 13 for NQSOs.

More dispositions positions

ISOs are a complicated enough subject, especially when you start factoring AMT considerations into the picture. So the examples in this chapter are all based on selling shares that you acquired from exercising an ISO.

Note that selling ISO shares is considered to be a disposition. However, there are other events that are considered to be a disposition as well. In addition, a disposition can be categorized as either a nonqualifying or qualifying disposition, depending on whether or not you have met your holding period requirements (see "Talking Taxes and ISOs: The Basics" earlier in this chapter).

In a legal sense, a disposition of shares occurs when you exchange those shares for other shares of stock, make a gift of those shares, or do some type of legal transfer of title. If, however, you pledge ISO shares as collateral for a margin loan from a brokerage, then you have not triggered a disposition unless the brokerage sells those shares to meet a margin call. Nondispositions also include transferring stock to your spouse, changing the registration of the stock to include your spouse if you live in a community property state, or possibly having ISO shares transferred to a bankruptcy trustee.

You can find additional information about various events and whether they are dispositions in the following books:

Robert Pastore's book *Stock Options: An Authoritative Guide to Incentive and Nonqualified Stock Options* (published by PCM Capital Publishing)

Kaye Thomas's book *Consider Your Options* (published by Fairmark Press)

In general, you should ask a knowledgeable financial advisor or financial planner for guidance on anything you plan to do with your ISO shares (other than selling the shares, which definitely is a disposition) to determine if that event would be considered a disposition and, if so, whether the disposition would be disqualifying or nondisqualifying.

A disqualifying disposition is one in which the ISO tax advantages are disqualified because you dispose of the stock before the holding periods have been met.

When you sell ISO shares in a disqualifying disposition, ordinary income tax rules apply, and one of two scenarios apply:

✔ You do a disqualifying disposition and make money on the deal.

✔ You do a disqualifying disposition and lose money on the deal.

Scenario #1: You make money on the deal

Suppose that you have received the two ISO grants shown in Table 14-1.

Table 14-1	Your Stock Option Holdings on February 1, 2002			
Date Granted	**Type**	**Total # Shares**	**# Shares Vested on June 1, 2001**	**Strike Price**
January 29, 2000	ISO	5,000	2,500	$30
January 29, 2001	ISO	2,000	500	$20

On February 1, 2002, you decide that you want to purchase 500 ISO shares and hold those shares for at least one year so they'll qualify for long-term capital gains rates. You decide to exercise the ISO granted to you on January 29, 2001, and pay $20 each for those 500 shares, rather than $30 — the price you'd have to pay if you exercised your January 29, 2000, option and purchased 500 of your 2,500 vested shares from that grant.

Why? Assume that the price of your company's stock on February 1, 2002, is $25 — higher than it was one year earlier, but lower than the price two years earlier. You want to exercise your in-the-money grant for those shares, thus paying $20 each, or a total of $10,000.

Suppose, though, that in mid-2002, your company's stock starts going higher and higher, echoing the glory days of 1999 when your company's stock quadrupled in value in only a few months. By September 2002, the price is $50 per share, having doubled in only seven months. You figure that sooner or later — probably sooner — the stock price will start to drop, and you want to take your $10,000 profits now rather than continue to hold the stock to try and meet the one-year holding period for the lower tax rates.

So on September 9, 2002, you sell your 500 shares for $50 each, realizing a gain of $30 per share, for a total of a $15,000 gain above what you paid for those shares. Three things have just happened:

✔ First, you have just done a *disqualifying disposition* of your 500 ISO shares since you did not hold the stock for more than one year after you had purchased those shares, or for two years after the date of the grant (January 29, 2001).

✔ Second, you have triggered tax consequences on your gains that are identical to those that would have been in effect if you had purchased the shares from exercising an NQSO. Specifically:

• You will owe *ordinary income taxes* on the difference between your purchase price ($20 per share) and the fair market value on the date you exercised the ISO ($25 per share on February 1, 2002). Since you had purchased and then subsequently sold 500 shares, you owe federal income taxes, state income taxes (if applicable), social security taxes (if the rest of your ordinary income doesn't meet the maximum amount subject to social security taxes), and medicare taxes on a total of $2,500 (500 shares × $5 ordinary income gain per share).

- You will owe *short-term capital gains taxes* on the rest of your gain above what was subject to ordinary income taxes ($2,500, as previously calculated). Specifically, you would owe short-term capital gains on $25 per share (your $50 sale price minus the $25 price on February 1, 2002, the date you had exercised the ISO). The total amount subject to short-term capital gains taxes: $12,500 (500 shares × $25 short-term capital gain per share).

✔ Third, the disqualifying disposition has just "negated" the AMT that had come into play back on February 1, 2002, the date you exercised your ISO. I know that I didn't mention the AMT yet, and I'll cover the basics shortly. But the key point to note is that because you have done a disqualifying disposition in the same year in which you exercised the ISO, the AMT "fades away." So stand by, I'll cover all of the AMT side of ISOs later.

Table 14-2 summarizes the different pieces of the preceding example transaction.

Table 14-2	Breaking Down the Tax Parts of a Disqualifying Disposition	
Type of Tax	*# Shares*	*Taxable Amount Per Share*
Ordinary income	500	$5 ($25 on exercise date – $20 purchase price)
Short-term capital gain	500	$25 ($50 sale price – $25 price on exercise date)

Before looking at the money-losing side of disqualifying dispositions, I want to put a slight spin on the making-money scenario. Suppose that you do a disqualifying disposition and make money — meaning that the price you receive for your shares is more than the price you paid — but the price you receive is now <u>less</u> than the price on the day you exercised (that is, the fair market value)?

Putting some numbers behind the premise, say that your worries about an end-of-year drop in your company's stock price were eerily insightful, but you decide not to sell the shares in September, hoping for the best. By November, the share price has dropped from $30 to $22. You decide that you'll sell then, because you fear the price may drop further, even below the $20 you paid.

Your ordinary income calculation will be different than it would have been had the stock's price remained at least at on the price of the exercise date. Instead of realizing the gain shown in Table 14-2 (that gain is $5 per share, for a total of $2,500), you realize less gain. Specifically, your ordinary income calculation will be based on a $2 per gain share (your sale price of $22 minus your purchase price of $20).

Basically, when you're calculating the amount you realize as ordinary income for a nondisqualifying disposition, you use the lower of your sale price or the price when you exercised.

Scenario #2: You lose money on the deal

If you do a disqualifying disposition but take a loss (that is, your sale price is less than the strike price you paid for those shares), the good news is that you don't have any ordinary income, since you really didn't have any income.

The bad news is that you do have a short-term capital loss. At this point, whatever rules governing offsetting capital losses and gains that are in effect that tax year will apply.

Traditionally, you can offset up to $3,000 of capital gains each year with capital losses, but check the rules and forms each year to figure out the best way to handle a capital loss situation.

More about disqualifying dispositions

Several points should be noted about disqualifying dispositions on ISOs:

- ✔ Some companies don't permit employees to execute disqualifying dispositions on ISOs. Check your stock option grant paperwork for any ISOs you receive to see if there is any language prohibiting the selling of ISO shares before the holding periods have been met.

- ✔ Some companies that do permit employees to execute disqualifying dispositions on ISOs (or, more accurately, they don't prohibit disqualifying dispositions) may also provide ISO holders with the means to do cashless exercises, just as with NQSOs. Other companies may not provide cashless exercise mechanisms for ISOs — only for NQSOs. However, you could still do a same-day sale of ISOs; you'll just have to set up a very short-term loan facility with your brokerage so it can buy the shares with money it obtains from your credit line, sell the shares, and repay the loan on your behalf from the proceeds.

Unlike when you exercise an NQSO, doing a disqualifying disposition of an ISO — even a same-day sale — does not trigger tax withholdings. Depending on your own particular situation (last year's tax bill, this year's withholdings from your paychecks, and so on), you may or may not need to pay estimated taxes on your early disposition gains. Be sure to check the estimated tax rules in effect in every year you do a disqualifying disposition to figure out whether or not you need to pay estimated taxes. If not, then you can park the money needed for the tax bill in some type of interest-bearing investment (bank CD, money market account, and so on) and earn interest before having to pay your taxes the following April.

Finally, the previous example is only one scenario of what might occur when you do a disqualifying disposition. I cover some other scenarios later in this chapter. For now, though, I want to talk about nondisqualifying dispositions.

Nondisqualifying Disposition of an ISO

A nondisqualifying disposition is one in which you sell shares you acquired from exercising an ISO and in which you've met the required holding periods from the date of grant and the date you bought those shares.

A nondisqualifying disposition of an ISO has no "real" tax consequences, but it causes the AMT calculations to kick in, which means you will probably have some tax liability.

For regular tax purposes (forgetting about the Alternative Minimum Tax), a nondisqualifying disposition of ISO stock is taxed just as any other stock purchase and sale that qualifies as a long-term capital holding. You realize a long-term capital gain on the difference between the sale price and the basis, if the sale price is higher than the basis (that is, you made a profit on the sale).

The basis is the price you paid for those shares. If you sell the shares for less than you paid for them, you would realize a long-term capital loss. Check the tax forms carefully for how you fill the numbers in on your Schedule D, because the IRS changes the forms on occasion.

Alternative minimum tax (AMT) considerations and exercising your ISOs: A preview

Think of the AMT as a parallel dimension to the taxation universe. Things in the two dimensions are mostly the same, yet there are a few twists in the AMT dimension that are different from our dimension in which "regular" tax laws apply.

In the dimension in which regular tax laws apply, you merrily fill out your Form 1040, take certain deductions that are permitted by the IRS, and use the tax tables or the tax rate schedules and figure out what your tax bill will be. In the AMT dimension, you follow the same steps, but the rules governing what is considered taxable and what deductions are permitted are different from the other dimension!

The key phenomenon to know is that through some kind of paradox, ISOs straddle both of these dimensions and thus are subject to the laws of both dimensions at the same time.

Chapter 15 covers AMTs in a little more detail; for this chapter, I just concentrate on the bare minimum so you can understand how the AMT applies to your ISOs. The key points to know are

- When the AMT kicks in
- The AMT calculation
- The importance of the December 31 deadline
- How your AMT tax obligation might vanish
- Multiple-year situations
- The dual basis situation
- The AMT credit

When the AMT kicks in

As mentioned earlier, the AMT kicks in when you exercise an ISO. This means that if you exercise an ISO in any year, then when you do that year's taxes you will have to do two sets of calculations: one according to regular tax rules and the other according to the AMT's "parallel dimension" set of rules.

The AMT calculation

Understanding AMT calculations is as simple as understanding the ordinary income portion of an NQSO, as discussed in Chapter 13. You take the difference between the price you pay and the stock price on the day you exercise an ISO, and — presto — you have the amount of gain that needs to be considered for AMT purposes.

Refer to the example earlier in the chapter relating to Table 14-1. On February 1, 2002, you purchase 500 shares from your January 29, 2001, grant at $20 per share, and the stock price that day is $25.

Recall that for regular tax purposes, the current stock price is irrelevant since exercising an ISO has no tax consequences.

For AMT purposes, though, you have a taxable amount of $2,500 — 500 shares × ($25 – $20).

Compare the amount subject to the AMT in this example — $2,500 — with the amount subject to ordinary income taxes if you were to do a disqualifying disposition, as shown in Table 14-2. You have the same amounts! Why? Because the calculation you do in each case is exactly the same: number of shares multiplied by your gain per share on the day of exercise.

Pay attention to December 31!

From the moment you exercise an ISO, an AMT clock starts running that expires on December 31 of that calendar year, as the clock strikes midnight and the ball drops in Times Square welcoming in the new year. Once that ball finishes dropping and the "Happy New Year" kissing begins, your AMT is "locked in" and must be considered when doing your taxes for the year.

If you do a disqualifying disposition before the New Year's ball finishes dropping, then the AMT calculations "vanish" as if they never existed. You have not only disqualified the ISO from being able to achieve the tax benefits of long-term capital gains, but you have also disqualified the AMT from applying to those particular ISO shares.

The AMT may still apply to you if you had exercised other ISO shares for which you did not do a disqualifying disposition. Or you might still be affected by the AMT for any one of many other reasons, such as having "too many deductions" that would substantially lower your taxes under regular tax calculation rules.

Crossing the December 31st boundary: Complications ahead

If you do a disqualifying disposition but not before the end of the calendar year, the AMT stays in effect, even though you have disqualified the ISOs from being eligible for long-term capital gain taxation. The key point: Even though the holding period for a non-disqualifying disposition is one year long (365 or 366 days, depending on whether you exercise in a leap year or not), the "wiping out the AMT clock" only runs to the end of the calendar year. So before the end of the year, you need to figure out how your company's stock is performing and what any changes in price mean to your gains and tax situation, and figure out what to do with regard to holding or selling your shares. I discuss your options later in the chapter.

The dual basis situation

If the AMT does stay in effect (that is, you don't do a disqualifying disposition on your ISO shares before the holding periods pass), then you need to determine the basis of your shares for tax purposes in two different ways: one for regular tax rules, the other for AMT.

For regular tax purposes, the basis of your ISO shares is the price you pay for those shares — that is, your strike price per share multiplied by the number of shares. Referring back to the example ISO grants in Table 14-1, suppose that you adhere to all holding period requirements for all shares you purchase from both grants; therefore, all sales will be nondisqualifying dispositions.

For the shares from the 1/29/2000 grant, the basis for each share will be $30, no matter:

- ✔ When you sell the shares (assuming you hold the shares for at least one year after exercise, thus making sure the sale is a nonqualifying distribution)

or

- ✔ How many times you exercise that option to purchase whatever number of shares you want; for example, if you do two exercise events, one for 2,500 shares in February 2002, and another for the remaining 2,500 shares sometime in 2005, every share will have a basis of $30.

The difference, then, between the price for which you sell those shares and the basis of $30 will be taxed as a long-term capital gain.

For AMT purposes, though, you have a different basis, formally calculated as follows:

```
Amount you pay for your stock + Amount subject to the AMT
```

Or, look at your AMT basis another way: the fair market value of those shares on the day you exercise, which is also the day that the AMT kicks in for those particular ISO shares you purchase.

Suppose again that on February 1, 2002, you exercise your January 29, 2000, grant with a strike price of $20 per share and a stock price that day of $25. Using the formal calculation, you pay $10,000 for the stock, and the amount subject to the AMT is $2,500, giving you an AMT basis of $12,500. Or doing the "shortcut" calculation, you purchase 500 shares from exercising an ISO when the market price per share is $25 (even though you're only paying $20 per share because you're exercising an option). But going by the stock price on February 1, 2002, the market value of those shares is $25 × 500 shares, or $12,500, which gives you the same number for your AMT basis.

The AMT basis becomes very important if you hold the shares long enough to do a nondisqualifying disposition. You will already pay taxes on your gains up to the AMT basis. Therefore, when it comes time to calculate the amount of your long-term capital gain and the taxes due, you would be double-taxed if that same amount of gains up to the AMT basis were taxed again. Therefore, you use the AMT basis to reset the basis on those shares and avoid being double-taxed on part of your profits.

The AMT credit

The AMT credit, which I discuss in Chapter 15, gives you a way to possibly lower taxes you'll have to pay in future years. The AMT credit is a byproduct of having to pay the AMT as a result of exercising an ISO and not doing a disqualifying disposition before the end of the year.

The Stock Option Titanic Scenario

2000 was the year in which many ISO holders found themselves facing the Stock Option Titanic Scenario.

Maybe you were one of them. You had enough foresight early in 2000 to exercise some of your ISOs and start the clock ticking on your long-term capital gains holding-period for those shares. Or your ISOs dramatically increased in value and you figured it was time to take some of your paper gains off the table.

Even if your company's stock kept increasing, you believed that the pace of those increases over the next few years would be much slower than in the late 1990s. Maybe the company's market value is gigantic — you might even say titanic — and maybe things are steaming along ahead of schedule according to the business plan, but these are rough waters you're in. Time to diversify, you wisely decide.

In late March, you're standing on the rooftop of your company's headquarters building, clutching your stock option grant paperwork in one hand, arms outstretched, yelling to people down on the sidewalk "I'm king of the world!" But before your company's CFO can say "Iceberg! Right Ahead!" your company's stock price drops 35 percent in only a few days.

The damage is far from over, though. Even as many of your co-workers cram the metaphorical lifeboats and call headhunters to find new jobs and bail out, the stock price keeps taking on water for the rest of the year, slowly sinking a bit more each week. By the end of the year, the only signs of life at the company are the remaining employees silently listening to the mournful string quartet playing at the small holiday party down in the building's lobby. But disaster is only minutes away, and you and all of the remaining survivors who didn't get to the lifeboats in time know it.

Finally, the layoff notices come, the company announces it's shutting down, and you and your co-workers are plunged into the icy waters of unemployment in a weakening economy.

Anyway, your second thought is along the lines of "Oh, no! I exercised my ISOs, and now the stock is almost worthless, but I still owe the AMT because when I exercised and bought the stock, it was before the price crashed!"

You have two very important considerations if your ISO shares have been clobbered after you exercised an option to purchase them.

The first — and most critical — is to avoid having to pay the AMT on gains that long since evaporated. Remember that if you do a disqualifying disposition on ISO shares before December 31st of the calendar year in which you exercised, you can "call off" the AMT.

Your second consideration is to avoid doing a disqualifying disposition after the December 31st date has passed. Once that date passes, your AMT is locked in, no matter how far your shares fall. You might then wind up with rather precarious circumstances that look like a no-win decision for you:

- ✔ If you really worry that the shares will continue to fall because the company is having lots of problems, then you could sell before the one-year holding period has arrived. However, since you now have done a disqualifying disposition, any gains you still have on those shares will be considered ordinary income and will be taxed at a higher rate than if you were able to hold on until the long-term capital gains rates kicked in at the one-year (after exercising) point.

- ✔ You may decide to continue to hold the shares until the one-year period has passed so you don't give up the chance for taxation at long-term capital gains rates. You are still stuck with the AMT — once December 31st comes and goes, there is no turning back — but while you're waiting, the stock price could drop even more, resulting in an even greater loss.

The earlier in the year you exercise an ISO, the closer the two key dates listed previously will align, giving you maximum flexibility to determining whether or not you will subject yourself to the AMT.

Suppose you exercise an ISO in early January 2002 and realize a nice gain of $95,000 on those shares, based on the market price the day you exercise as compared with your purchase price. As mid-December 2002 arrives, you have several important pieces of information at your disposal:

- ✔ What your AMT liability will be, based on the AMT calculations you should have made when you exercised your ISO (or shortly afterwards)

- ✔ How the stock has performed since the exercise date when you purchased the shares: Up a little or a lot? Down a little or a lot? About the same?

If, in mid-December 2002, the stock price is still around the same (or increased) as the market price on the day you exercised back in early January, then you're in pretty good shape. Even though you will need to pay close attention to the stock for the next couple of weeks until the end of the calendar year, unless something really unforeseen were to happen, the stock will probably finish the year near its current price. Then, most likely, the stock will stay around the current price for a few more days or a week or two until the anniversary of the date you exercised the ISO and purchased those shares.

At that point, you no longer have the option of doing a disqualifying disposition, so your long-term capital gain status has been locked in. You still have to watch the stock and periodically make hold-or-sell decisions for those shares, but you don't need to be quite as obsessed as during the first year.

Suppose, though, that by mid-December 2002, the Stock Option Titanic Scenario has taken hold and the stock has gotten clobbered, dropping way back to your purchase price. So in a matter of weeks (after December 31), you still owe the AMT on $95,000 even though you no longer have any gain at all on the shares you purchased.

You can still sell those shares as a disqualifying disposition because the one-year holding period for those shares is still three or four weeks away. You may not make much at all when you sell those shares — in fact, you may even lose money if the share price in mid-December has dropped below your strike price — but at least you won't still have a gigantic tax bill on a gain that has long since evaporated.

Suppose, though, that you had exercised that same ISO in late December 2001. And for the sake of this example, say that you had realized the same $95,000 gain for AMT purposes. After December 31, 2001, passed, your AMT liability became locked in, payable along with the rest of your taxes in April 2002. Meanwhile, the stock is going down a little bit almost every day, and by June 2002, half of your earlier gain has vanished.

Going by the earlier example, you know that you're probably still better off selling in June and salvaging at least a little bit of your gain, because by December 2002, even that will be gone. But in real life, you don't know for certain what will happen to the stock's price over the next six months or, for that matter, at any point in the future. So you're in a tough bind: Do you sell now, in June? Wait one more month? Until Labor Day? Selling on any of those days — or any other day up until late December 2002, the date of the one-year holding period — counts as a disqualifying disposition, meaning that any gain you salvage will be taxed as ordinary income. And meanwhile, you still have to pay the AMT, so that money is gone.

Try to avoid putting yourself in a no-win situation with your ISOs and the AMT. Here are a couple of tips:

- ✔ The earlier in the calendar year you exercise an ISO, the greater your chances of selling quickly and avoiding any AMT liability if you think the stock price is headed way down. By aligning the key dates for AMT liability and long-term capital gains decisions, you can mostly avoid having to do a "panic sale" and still owe the AMT anyway for gains you no longer have.

- ✔ If you decide to exercise an ISO late in the calendar year, you may be better off doing a same-day sale and making the transaction a disqualifying disposition. Even though you will subject the gains to ordinary income tax rates, you will wipe out the AMT liability and have the after-tax cash in your hands. In effect, you are surrendering the tax advantages of the ISO by treating it as if it were an NQSO. Ideally, if you hold in-the-money ISOs and NQSOs with vested shares, you should leave your ISOs alone and do the same-day sale with your NQSOs. If doing so isn't possible (for example, you don't have enough NQSO shares, or the NQSO strike price is way higher than your ISO strike price), then you may want to take the cash out of your ISO paper gains instead.

You can also play the middle ground with your ISO exercising. If you intend to hold your ISO shares for at least several years, no matter what happens to the price (and I'd only recommend taking this approach if you work for a very stable company with a long-term record of success), then you might exercise one or more ISOs sometime in late March or early April. You still have around nine months until the end of the year to do catastrophe avoidance if something totally unforeseen happens and the stock price drops far lower than anyone had envisioned. (Catastrophe avoidance would be selling those ISO shares and wiping out the AMT liability you incurred back when you exercised.)

Then, come the following April and tax season, you can safely sell some of those ISO-acquired shares after the one-year holding period has passed but before the mid-April tax day. Why would you sell some of the shares? If you need cash to pay the AMT liability you incurred the previous year when you exercised, you can sell enough shares to give you the necessary tax money, and the sale of those shares will themselves be taxed as long-term gains the following year.

Beware the Wash Sale Rules!

A *wash sale* is a set of related stock transactions in which you sell a stock — that you purchased either within the past 30 days, on the date of your sale, or 30 days after the date of your sale (a total of 61 days) — for a loss. The IRS disallows losses on wash sales because people might take losses just before the end of the tax year and then buy back the stock immediately after the new tax year began. If the stock went up, they'd eventually have to pay taxes on those gains from the price at which they purchased the stock, but the tax liability could be delayed for many years, and the IRS says "no way."

A confusing aspect to ISO shares and the AMT is whether or not the wash sale rules apply to AMT tax liability as contrasted with ordinary tax liability. If you do a "panic sell" on ISO shares at the end of the tax year to disqualify a large AMT liability from earlier in the year, and if you really want to hold the stock, you might be tempted to wait until right after New Year's and buy back those shares, which should cost just about what you received when you sold them only days earlier.

Some tax professionals advise that the wash sale rules in the Internal Revenue Code are written in such a way to cause the AMT to resurface if you don't wait at least 30 days to buy back the shares you had (in this example) sold in late December. In effect, even though you did a disqualifying disposition before the December 31st deadline, buying back the stock makes the situation the same as if you had done the disqualifying disposition after the December 31st date had passed, meaning that the earlier AMT liability is still in effect.

The rationale seems to be that even if you don't have a "real" loss on the shares you sell and then buy back, the parallel dimension situation of the regular tax laws and the AMT comes into play again. In the AMT dimension, your basis is higher than in the dimension where regular tax calculations apply. However, buying back the shares seems to cause the AMT basis to cross over into the regular tax dimension, meaning that when you sold those shares you would have realized a loss based on the AMT basis as compared to the price you received for those shares.

However, I've also seen written tax advice that claims that wash sale rules do not apply to the AMT, and other advice stating that the wash sale rules previously didn't relate to ISOs but now do. So what should you do?

In general, you should avoid wash sales — for ISO shares, other shares you own of your company's stock, or shares of other companies' stock — to keep from being caught in tricky situations. If you feel you absolutely must buy back ISO shares you had previously sold to keep the AMT at bay, get professional tax advice — two opinions, preferably — to give you guidance as to whether or not you will have to declare the AMT anyway when tax day rolls around.

There better be a very good reason for possibly subjecting yourself to an AMT wash sale situation, though. The only scenario I can think of is that things looked gloomy at the point you did the disqualifying disposition but turned around so quickly that you want to get back into the stock as soon as possible. However, I would argue that any surprise good news will likely get priced into the stock before you have a chance to buy, so you will probably miss out on most or all of the gains anyway if the stock price zooms back up.

You should probably just settle for the value increasing of the other ISOs and NQSOs that you still hold. Just chalk your panic sale up to a learning experience so you won't be so quick to do an unwise disqualifying disposition the next time around.

Can Section 83(b) Help with the AMT Situation?

Here is some good news about ISOs. Much of what has appeared in this chapter is how the AMT can really cast a dark cloud over an otherwise pretty nice aspect of your compensation and investments.

However, you do have one weapon that you might be able to use to keep the AMT at bay, but that weapon must be handled carefully.

In Chapter 13, I mention that doing a Section 83(b) election allows you to take an exercising event that otherwise would not be taxable and say, "Hey, wait a minute — I want to pay ordinary income taxes now, even though I really don't have to, because then I can start the long-term capital gains clock ticking and hopefully save taxes in the long run."

With NQSOs (as discussed in Chapter 13), you would typically use the Section 83(b) election for exercising privately held shares that aren't readily marketable and are subject to forfeiture.

You can also use the Section 83(b) election on ISO shares, if your company's stock plan permits you to do so. Because an ISO exercise is a nontaxable event for regular tax purposes but is a taxable event for AMT purposes, you essentially are saying, "Hey, wait a minute — I want to pay the AMT now, even though I really don't have to, while the spread is still low, so I can just get that out of the way."

As with NQSOs, the risk to an early exercise and doing the Section 83(b) election is that you may be purchasing shares that you may never be able to sell. So make sure you have enough confidence in the future of your company, plus be fairly certain that you'll want to stay employed by the company for a while, before laying out the cash. Because, after all, you're giving up the "waiting on the sidelines" aspect to stock options if you do an early exercise.

You must file a letter indicating your intention to do the Section 83(b) election within 30 days after the date of the exercise. Don't miss the deadline!

Part V
Changes and Special Circumstances

The 5th Wave   By Rich Tennant

"I've never been good at this part of the job which is why I've asked 'Buddy' to join us. As you know, business has been bad lately, and, well, Buddy has some bad news for you..."

In this part . . .

You must stay on top of changes that happen with your job or your company to make sure you maximize the gains from your stock options. This part discusses what happens to your stock options in several different situations: if your company is acquired or if you leave your job. You'll also see how to pick up hints and clues that may foretell the fate of your stock options. You'll also take a look at special circumstances that you may encounter with your stock options, which will prepare you for any of those out-of-the-ordinary situations.

Chapter 15

The Alternative Minimum Tax and Stock Options

In This Chapter

▶ Reviewing the AMT (Alternative Minimum Tax) basics
▶ Finding out about AMT calculations and rates
▶ Recovering some of the AMT you paid on your ISOs
▶ Considering state AMT issues

The Alternative Minimum Tax (AMT) is one of the least known aspects of the United States tax code. Originally enacted to close tax shelter "loopholes" that helped wealthy and high-income individuals dramatically lower their tax bills, the AMT has, over time, come to affect more and more American taxpayers.

The AMT became much more widely known at the end of 2000 and in early 2001, for two reasons. First, many holders of incentive stock options (ISOs) who exercised options early in 2000 before the free fall in Internet stock prices found themselves facing the AMT on stock gains they no longer had. To prevent getting clobbered with a tax bill for more than their shares were worth at the end of 2000, they needed to get very smart about the AMT very quickly, and decide if a disqualifying disposition (see Chapter 14) on their ISOs was the way to go.

The second reason is that President Bush's proposed tax cut doesn't, at the time of this writing, include any provisions for modifying the AMT. Thus, many taxpayers who would otherwise receive a tax cut if the President's bill is passed would have some, or perhaps all, of that tax cut negated by the AMT.

For these two reasons, many people who previously had no knowledge of nor interest in the AMT suddenly are wondering: Just what is this AMT business, and how does it affect me?

In this chapter, I build on the discussion in Chapter 14 and provide more information about the AMT to help you understand how the AMT might affect you.

Understanding the AMT

Chapter 14 introduces the following points with regard to ISOs and the AMT:

- The AMT kicks in at the point you exercise an ISO.

- If you don't do a disqualifying disposition by December 31 of the year in which you exercised the ISO, the AMT is locked in.

- If you do a disqualifying disposition by December 31 of the year in which you did the ISO exercise, you can wipe out the AMT for those ISOs.

- If you do a disqualifying disposition for ISO shares after December 31 of the year in which you did the ISO exercise, the AMT still applies, and calculations get very complicated.

- Because of the AMT, certain assets — such as your ISO shares — will have a dual basis, and you need to keep track of the difference so you don't double-tax yourself.

Fortunately, the above points are fairly easy to comprehend, after you go through them a couple of times. So now it's time to move into more about the AMT.

Calculating AMT

For specific numbers and rates that apply to the AMT, go straight to the Internal Revenue Service. The IRS has an AMT primer available online at www.irs.ustreas.gov/tax_edu/teletax/tc556.html. But I give you the highlights with regard to calculations and rates in this section.

AMT rates

Two tax rates apply for ordinary income: 26 percent and 28 percent. For capital gains rates, the maximum rate (currently 20 percent) applies. So forget the 15 percent tax bracket and the 39.6 percent tax bracket and all of the other "regular tax" ordinary income brackets. Just remember 26 percent and 28 percent. The first $175,000 of your AMT income is taxed at the 26 percent rate, anything more at 28 percent.

AMT exemptions

Three different exemption numbers apply, depending on your filing status:

  ✔ $45,000 if you are married filing jointly or are a qualifying widow or widower

  ✔ $33,750 if you are single or head of household

  ✔ $22,500 if you are married filing separately

Wow! Those are some hefty exemption numbers! So what's the problem with the AMT? First, whatever exemption applies to your filing status may be phased out as your income increases. So the higher your income — and the more you need the exemption — the less of the exemption you'll probably be able to use.

Check the most recent IRS booklets and forms for phasing-out rules and amounts.

AMT deductions

Another offsetting factor to the seemingly large (but quickly shrinking) exemption amounts are that many of the itemized deductions you would claim on a normal Form 1040 Schedule A cannot be subtracted from your AMT income. In general, home mortgages and charitable deductions are still permitted, but most taxes — state and local income, real estate, personal property, and so on — are not. Check the most recent booklets and forms each year to make sure you're operating from the most current set of rules.

Combining the basic calculations and rates

Table 15-1 illustrates a side-by-side comparison for the regular tax calculations and the AMT tax calculations of a high-income individual.

Table 15-1	The Regular Tax and the AMT, Side by Side	
Item	*Regular Tax*	*AMT*
Salary	All of it counts	All of it counts
Exercising an ISO	Doesn't count	The gain in value on the date of exercise applies
Exemptions	Moderate personal exemptions for individual and dependents, but may be phased out at high-income levels	Sizable exemptions, but are phased out at higher income levels

(continued)

Table 15-1 *(continued)*

Item	Regular Tax	AMT
Deductions	Everything on Schedule A is deductible	Only some of the Schedule A items are deductible
Tax rates	Brackets from 15% to 39.6%	26% and 28%

Looking at the contents of Table 15-1, for the average person without an ISO exercise event, the AMT might increase the taxes by a little bit, but in general, that person shouldn't see a huge increase in taxes.

For an ISO holder, though, the exercise event is the big difference. A modest ISO gain subject to the AMT will probably result in a modest increase in AMT-based taxes over the regular tax calculations. However, realizing a substantial gain in the value of the ISOs at the time of exercising can result in a doozy of a tax bill, much larger than would otherwise be the case with regular tax calculations.

If you have an extremely high salary with only a modest amount of ISO gains, and very few deductions (no mortgage interest because your home is paid off or you rent, for example), you might be looking at the side-by-side comparison in Table 15-1 and thinking that maybe you would be better off with the AMT than the regular tax calculations. If the majority of your income is taxed at the 39.6 percent tax bracket, wouldn't you be better off taxed at 28 percent?

Sorry! The rules for the AMT calculations specify that you pay the higher of the regular tax amount or AMT amount. If you would benefit from the AMT, then sorry, it's not for you!

Getting Some of Your AMT Payments Back

Suppose that because you exercise ISOs you do wind up having to pay the AMT. Believe it or not, there is some sort-of-good news for you. Some of the additional tax you pay — perhaps even all of it — might find its way back to you in a future year, courtesy of the *AMT credit*.

In years in which you don't have to pay the AMT, you might be able to take advantage of the AMT credit. As the IRS puts it: "If you are not liable for alternative minimum tax this year, but you paid alternative minimum tax in one or more previous years, you may be eligible to take a special minimum tax credit against your regular tax this year. If eligible, you should report this credit on line 47 of Form 1040 and check Box C. Also, use *Form 8801, Credit for Prior Year Minimum Tax — Individuals, Estates and Trusts.*"

So if you do have to pay the AMT because you exercised an ISO (or for any other reason), forget about the credit for now; don't even waste your time trying to do any calculations. A very important and complicated point to note is that when you eventually do a nondisqualifying disposition of your ISO shares, you can then create a "negative AMT adjustment."

Carefully follow the instructions on the AMT form to make sure that you correctly calculate and then apply the negative AMT adjustment. Also, if you have a loss on your shares rather than a gain, you might also be subject to limitations on capital losses. Again, be absolutely certain about your calculations and how you fill out the forms. I'd recommend getting professional assistance unless you've previously sold ISO shares and calculated your negative AMT adjustment. And, even then, you should at least use a PC-based tax program to do your taxes that year.

State Taxes and AMT Considerations

Some states have their own version of the AMT. If you exercise an ISO then you absolutely need to pay careful attention to your home state's rules, if any, for AMT-like calculations of your state taxes.

Additionally, be careful if your company complies with the "Michael Jordan Law" (see Chapter 12) regarding cross-state tax liability. Quite possibly, you could even find yourself subject to some other state's AMT calculations for your tax liability in that state. Make sure you do your research, and you'll probably need professional tax advice, too!

Chapter 16

Acquiring or Being Acquired: Dealing with Corporate Change

In This Chapter

▶ Understanding the reasons your company's ownership might change

▶ Discovering the differences and similarities in how private and public companies are acquired

▶ Understanding how an acquisition impacts your stock options

▶ Figuring out your stock option strategies during and after an acquisition

*I*f your company is acquired by another company, your stock options will be affected. Almost all company stock option plans make provisions for a *change in control* of the company's ownership. Sometimes, the change in control itself and its effect on your stock options can be very beneficial to you, perhaps even more beneficial than an IPO. Other times, though, working for a company that is acquired can cause your worst stock options nightmares to catalyze and, before you know it, the value of your stock options has gone down the drain.

In this chapter, I look at the many facets of changes in a company's ownership and control and how *your* stock options might be affected.

Understanding Why Companies Sell Out

Companies sell out for many different reasons. Before listing those reasons, though, I do want to mention that when I say "sell out" I don't necessarily use that phrase in a negative manner. (Or, as the saying goes, "you say that like it's a bad thing.")

Selling out is exactly that: Selling all or part of a business to someone else, usually another business or a group of investors. You shouldn't read too much into finding out that your company is in negotiations, or has reached an agreement, to sell out and change its ownership.

So why would a company sell out to someone else? The reasons include:

✔ Achieving greater growth than they would likely have achieved on their own

✔ Your company's principals want to do something else.

✔ Your company's management fielded an unsolicited, yet attractive offer.

✔ A company sale was part of the original business plan's end game.

Seeking growth

Companies — especially smaller, younger, privately held ones — continually need capital to grow. Two of the primary ways of raising capital are to take on debt (or more debt) or to seek additional rounds of investment from a venture capital firm or other investors.

Quite possibly, neither of these approaches is attractive to the company's owners and management team. Perhaps the company already has substantial debt on its books. Or perhaps accepting additional venture investment will require giving up too much of the company's ownership and control to outsiders, harming the company's culture and long-term prospects.

An option available to the company's growth-seeking management team is to sell the company to another company, usually a large market-leader with substantial financial resources. The company's management consciously makes a decision to trade off its independence for the synergies and financial resources that will be available after the acquisition deal is completed. If all goes according to plan, the company will be better able to grow and prosper under its new ownership than if it had remained independent.

Time to do something else

Many owners of small companies are really entrepreneurs at heart rather than managers and administrators. That is, they love the challenge of starting and growing a company and taking it to a certain stage of growth, but are much less interested in growing the company to its next levels.

One option for a company's founder or founders is to turn the company's management reins over to someone from the internal management ranks who may be more suited to fostering the next stage of the company's growth. Alternatively, the company may seek to bring in an outside "executive management professional" with a proven track record of successfully growing similar companies at similar stages.

However, a third option for the current entrepreneurially focused management team is to do neither of the previously mentioned options, but rather to sell the company to another company and, effectively, cash out of their investment and role within the company. In effect, they are bringing in outside professional management, but doing so through selling out rather than continuing to hold a significant management and ownership presence.

Receiving an unsolicited offer

Sometimes a company's management has no intentions of selling out, but it receives an unsolicited offer from another company or group of investors, and the offer is attractive enough (or becomes attractive enough after negotiations) that a change of control is suddenly in the works.

Selling out was the plan all along

In some situations, a privately held company's original business plan and all of the company's activities along the way have been oriented to lead to a sale to an outside party rather than an IPO.

Hopefully, you and your fellow employees have known that direction instead of being misled by company management. When joining a privately held company, especially one in which you are granted stock options, you should always ask if there is a specific future ownership strategy — acquisition, IPO, or staying privately held — or if any of those three possibilities has an equal chance of occurring.

Dissecting the Deal

You may find yourself in one of several kinds of change of control situations, such as an acquisition, a merger, or a divestiture. The following sections discuss each in detail. Some deals involve a sale for cash, while others use stock as the financial medium of exchange, as the following sections illustrate.

Acquisitions

An acquisition is, in most cases, a takeover. One company — the acquirer — is purchasing all of (or at least some of) the company assets of the acquiree, including buildings, equipment, future revenue that is already contracted, and employees. (Yes, in the acquisition world, you and your fellow employees are assets that are being sold by your company to another company.) Almost always, the acquiring company pays a premium on top of the current market value of the acquired company to be able to secure the deal.

If the acquired company is publicly held, the premium is usually some price above its current stock price. (For example, the acquired company is trading at $20.00 per share the day before the acquisition occurs, and the acquisition price may be $30.00 per share.) However, if the acquired company is privately held, arriving at that company's value — and the premium that the acquirer will pay — is a job for the financial pros with MBAs from an Ivy League school or other top-notch business program who work on Wall Street, drive fancy cars, and all that. The Mergers and Acquisitions business from both sides — advising acquirers and target acquirees — can be very lucrative because of the skill and expertise that is required to try to ensure that the acquired company's owners are getting a fair deal and, at the same time, the acquirer isn't grossly overpaying.

In many cases, the top-level management team of the acquired company bails out following the completion of the deal, courtesy of the *golden parachute* provisions in their respective employee agreements. They may receive large severance packages: usually at least several million dollars for even a medium-sized company, often in the tens or even hundreds of millions of dollars for a large Fortune 100-sized company.

What are left behind after their departure are the remaining assets that the acquiring company set out to purchase in the first place. If all goes as planned, the acquired company's operations will be smoothly integrated into those of the acquirer within a reasonable period of time (typically 6 to 18 months), and wonderful synergies will occur.

However, most acquisitions are anything but a coming together of equals. Organizational politics and other unfortunate occurrences (such as incompetent management) often doom an acquisition to failure before the ink on the deal is dry. In the case of organizational politics, the "us" camp from one of the companies often assumes a hostile stance toward the "them" camp from the other company, even though the respective CEOs were all smiles when they were on CNBC touting the amazing synergies of the deal.

In the case of the employees of the acquired company, the change of control triggers the change of control conditions of that company's stock plan and the clauses in employees' stock option agreements. As I discuss later in this chapter, those conditions might be very advantageous to you and your stock options.

In the case of employees of the acquiring company, an acquisition usually doesn't trigger the change of control conditions in that company's stock plan because from their perspective, a change of control has not occurred. The executive management of that company is still in charge, possibly augmented by new executives brought in from the acquired company (those who don't bail out, that is). The ownership of the post-acquisition company looks identical, or nearly identical, to that of the acquiring company before the acquisition took place. So for employees of the acquirer, none of the change of control events that I describe later in this chapter will typically occur.

In a financial and economic sense, however, employees of the acquirer may see a change in their respective stock options, in terms of their value. If an acquisition is *dilutive* — meaning that when all the money or stock (or both) changes hands, the earnings per share (EPS) of the post-acquisition combined company is lower than the acquirer's pre-acquisition (EPS) — then the acquirer's stock price may drop (sometimes significantly) as a result of the deal. Consequently, stock option holders (as well as stockholders themselves) of the acquiring company may, for a little while at least, see the value of their holdings depressed as a result of the deal.

Mergers

Mergers are very similar to acquisitions, except that at least in theory, two companies come together as equals (or near-equals) rather than one company taking over the other. What remains after a merger is a single company comprised of the assets of each of the pre-merger companies. But, as with an acquisition, a change of control has occurred, which triggers the change of control conditions of stock option agreements.

In the case of a merger, unlike an acquisition, the option holders of both companies might be subject to a change of control, meaning that the conditions and clauses of their respective plans and agreements will kick in. Depending on the terms of the merger deal and depending on the language in each company's stock option plan and agreements, a change of control may or may not have occurred.

Assume, for the purposes of this chapter, that in the case of a merger, a change of control has occurred for both companies and their employees (and, of course, their stock options). However, make sure you find out from your company's management as to whether or not a change of control has occurred.

Divestitures

A divestiture occurs when a company sells or otherwise "spins off" some part of the company into a separate legal entity (basically, a separate company). In most divestitures, the original company will retain an ownership stake (often a significant stake) in its spin-off.

When a divestiture occurs, the employees who work in the division or group that is being divested usually have a change of control event occur. However, employees who work in other divisions or groups usually don't have the same change of control event because from their perspective, their company's ownership has not changed.

Additional outside investment

Very often in the pre-IPO life of a company, additional outside investment will come from venture capital firms or other sources. The company will likely issue new stock, and if the investor has not had a prior ownership stake, then the overall company ownership picture will change somewhat.

However, additional investment does not constitute a change of control, at least in accordance to the usual language in stock option agreements. So don't expect a windfall in terms of accelerated vesting or other benefits, as I discuss later in this chapter, just because additional money comes into the company.

Cash versus stock deals

A change of control deal might be structured around cash, stock, or both as the purchase medium. I talk about cash deals first, because those are the easiest to understand.

Cash deals

Suppose that Company A is acquiring Company B, and both companies are publicly traded. Company B's stock price just before the deal is announced is $20.00, and for the past few months its trading range has been between $17.00 and $22.00.

The deal that the two companies strike is for Company A to purchase all outstanding shares of Company B at $30.00 per share cash, or a 50 percent premium over Company B's current price. (Keep in mind that during the negotiations for the deal, Company B's stock price was bouncing around a bit, both a little higher and lower than $20.00 at times, so the premium wasn't always exactly a nice round 50 percent.)

In an all-cash deal, Company A will pay each of Company B's shareholders $30 in cash for each share of Company B stock they own. The deal could still conceivably fall through before it closes for reasons such as government intervention, but unless that were to happen, Company A pays cash for all of the Company B shares and presto, the deal is done.

Stock deals

Many acquisitions are not done for cash, however, but rather for stock, and therefore become more complicated. Assume the same parameters as the preceding example — Company B's current stock price is $20.00 per share, and Company A strikes a deal for a $30.00 per share buyout. But instead of cash, Company A wants to do an all-stock deal, and Company B agrees.

So now, Company A's stock price comes into the picture as well. Assume that on the day of the announcement, Company A's current stock price is $60.00 per share. In an all-stock deal for a $30.00 per share buyout, Company A gives each Company B shareholder one share of Company A stock for every two shares of Company B stock. The reason: At the moment of the deal, each share of Company A stock is, basically, the same as a $60.00 bill (if one existed), and therefore Company A can use that "$60.00 bill" to purchase 2 shares of Company B stock ($30.00 × 2).

So far, things are fairly straightforward. But an acquisition may take anywhere from several weeks (at the very minimum) to almost a year to close. (An example of a deal that took almost a year: AOL and Time-Warner, announced in January 2000, and still going at the time of this writing, though almost approved and finalized by the end of 2000.) Along the way, both companies' stock prices may fluctuate, which could change the terms of the acquisition deal.

(**Note:** Don't worry, your stock options do come into the discussion, so please don't think I'm going off on an M&A tangent. I just want to establish what happens in an all-stock deal because, if an acquisition could ever turn sour and turn into a loser for you and your fellow stock options holders, it will be a prolonged, all-stock deal that will do it to you!)

Suppose that the investment community isn't very impressed with the acquisition, and the stock of the acquiring company (Company A) drops a little bit after the deal is announced and continues to stay weak, settling in at $50.00 per share while the acquisition is being finalized. Assume that you're a Company B stockholder, expecting that "$60.00 bill" — one share of Company A stock — in exchange for two of your Company B shares. But now, that "$60.00 bill" is really a $50.00 bill (which actually exists!) because Company A's stock price has dropped. So now you should be getting more than one share of Company A stock for your two shares of Company B stock, right?

Maybe, but probably not, at least if most 1990s-era stock deals are any indication. The answer depends on how the terms of the deal were expressed.

If the acquisition was expressed in fixed-price terms even though the deal was being done using stock, then you would receive exactly $60.00 worth of Company A stock at the time the deal is finalized, regardless of whether Company A's stock price:

- ✔ Jumps back up to $60.00
- ✔ Stays at $50.00
- ✔ Drops below $50.00
- ✔ Rises above $60.00

If Company A's stock price somehow dropped down to $30.00 per share, you would have to surrender only one share of your Company B stock for that Company A share, because Company A's stock price is the same as the per-share acquisition price being paid for each share of Company B. Or, at the other extreme, if Company A's stock price recovers and somehow zooms upward to $90.00 per share, then you would receive one Company A share — now a "90.00 bill" — for every three of your Company B shares.

Either way, you still receive exactly $30.00 worth of Company A stock for each share of your Company B stock. Depending on the price of Company A's stock at the moment the deal is finalized, maybe $30.00 worth is exactly one share, less than one share, or more than one share. You, the seller, are price-protected.

However, the more common situation in a stock-based acquisition is for the deal to be expressed in terms of some *exchange ratio* rather than in fixed price terms. That is, the acquisition will be formally structured (using the previous example prices) as an exchange of one share of Company A stock for two shares of Company B stock. The exchange ratio will stay the same regardless of the changes in Company A's stock price and Company B's stock price from the time the deal was announced to when it's finalized.

So assume that Company A's stock price really does drop to $30.00 per share after the deal is announced. Assume also that Company B stock jumps from $20.00 to $30.00 per share because of the impending acquisition.

With a fixed exchange ratio, you would still be giving up two shares of your Company B stock — $60.00 worth — and receiving one share of Company A stock in exchange. However, that one share of Company A stock is now worth only $30.00 per share, meaning that you will receive only half as much in value as the deal was originally set.

On the other side — the better side — if Company A's stock price goes up to $90.00 per share and Company B's stock price jumps to $30.00 per share and stays there, you will now be getting $90.00 worth of Company A stock (the one share you will receive) in exchange for $60.00 worth of Company B stock (the two shares you will be giving up). Not bad, huh?

Stock price fluctuations also occur on the acquiree side (Company B in this case). Say that Company A's stock price stays at $60.00, but Company B's stock price drops from $20.00 to $10.00 per share, perhaps because of a bad earnings report while the deal is being finalized. With the 2-for-1 exchange ratio still in effect, Company A will be paying $60.00 for only $20.00 worth of Company B stock (two shares at $10.00 each), meaning that there will be a whole lot of very upset Company A shareholders!

In reality, the stock prices of both the acquiring and to-be-acquired companies will start to move somewhat in tandem after a deal is announced. In the preceding example, if Company B's stock price in an all-stock exchange ratio-style deal were to drop to $10.00 per share, Company A's stock price will likely get hammered and drop way down. This is not necessarily because of any bad news out of Company A or a bad stock market in general, but because of the terms of the acquisition and how the drop in Company B's stock price will affect Company A's financial picture.

Sometimes an all-stock exchange ratio-style acquisition will feature price protection in the form of a *collar* — basically, an agreed-to price range for the deal. If the acquiree's stock price drops below some specified price or the acquiring company's stock price rises above some specified price — or some combination of both — that takes the terms of the deal outside the collar. At that point, either party has the option of backing out of the deal or perhaps renegotiating the terms.

Private and Public Companies: The Mix-and-Match Combinations

One last general topic about changes of company control has to do with the various combinations of private and public companies that can be involved in a transaction. The four main combinations are discussed in this section.

Don't worry about strange variations of one of the four combinations, such as "a public company buys another public company but then divests it into a privately held company for a short time then takes it public again using a tracking stock." (Whew!) You and your stock options are most likely to be affected, acquisition-wise, by one of the situations discussed in this section.

Public company acquired by another public company

I start with the most straightforward situation first. As with the examples in the previous section, the valuation of each party in an acquisition is well established because each company's stock is publicly traded. You could argue that the stock market is overvaluing one company in the transaction and undervaluing the other, or vice versa, or some other combination, but regardless, either a cash acquisition or a stock acquisition can be valued and completed in a straightforward manner.

Following a public-public acquisition, the acquired company's stock no longer exists. That is, however, unless the acquiring company sets up the acquired company as a publicly held subsidiary company with its own traded stock. But even in those situations, the resulting stock may be a different financial entity than originally existed before the acquisition.

Private company acquired by a public company

Suppose that you work for a privately held company that is acquired by a company whose stock is publicly traded. Following the completion of the acquisition, any actual shares of stock you held in your company (assuming you work for the acquired privately held company) will cease to exist. You will either have received cash for your shares if the deal was cash-based, or you will now own publicly traded stock in the acquiree if the deal was for stock.

As with a public-public acquisition, your pre-acquisition stock ceases to exist. And, in the case of your stock options in the acquired company, they will typically be exchanged for options in the acquiree, as I discuss shortly.

Typically, the biggest wildcard in acquiring a privately held company is the valuation of that company, both before the acquisition commences as well as the acquisition price itself. After both parties in the transaction (and their advisors) agree on the overall valuation of the acquisition target, a price per share can be established not only for outstanding shares of stock but also for options in the to-be-acquired company's stock.

Private company acquired by another private company

A private-private acquisition is very similar to a public-private acquisition, except that the question of valuation applies to both the acquiree and the acquirer. Both companies need to agree on each other's value, in an aggregate (company) sense as well as on a per-share basis.

The good news about a private-private transaction, however, is that stock-based acquisitions aren't subject to the valuation fluctuation in exchange rate deals that I discussed earlier. Basically, the acquisition price that both parties agree to will stay in effect from the time the deal is announced to when it's finalized.

The bad news, however, is that unless the combined company eventually goes public, or itself is acquired by a publicly traded company, then the stock's value is still "up in the air" with regard to employees from either company being able to eventually cash in from either stock or stock options.

Public company acquired by a private company

The strangest acquisition combination is when a publicly traded company is acquired by a privately held company. Quite possibly, holders of stock options in the acquired company that are within shouting distance of having shares become vested (and thus exercisable and salable) could suddenly wind up having their options exchanged for those in the acquiring company — options that may wind up with inaccessible shares if the acquiring company never goes public.

What Happens to Your Options After a Change of Control?

How are your options affected if your company is acquired? You may see an impact in the following:

- ✔ The structure and number of your stock options, in relation to the exchange rate of the deal
- ✔ Your vesting schedule(s)
- ✔ Prohibitions on exercising options for some period of time
- ✔ Additional options coming your way

I discuss each in this section.

The exchange rate means you get a new number of shares

Earlier in this chapter, I discussed how a stock-based acquisition is built around an exchange rate between the shares of the two companies in the deal. Typically, that same exchange rate is used to determine how many shares you have in your options package in the new company.

Referring to one of the earlier examples in this chapter, suppose that Company A with a stock price of $60.00 per share is acquiring Company B for $30.00 per share in a stock-based transaction. So every Company B stockholder will receive one Company A share in exchange for every two Company B shares. Further, assume that the 1-for-2 exchange ratio is firm, regardless of fluctuations in either company's stock price while the acquisition is finalized.

If you work for Company B and have options on 10,000 shares, then you will wind up with options on 5,000 Company A shares after the change of control because of the deal's exchange rate for the companies' shares.

Accelerated vesting (maybe)

Many company stock option plans and the option agreements of their employees specify that in the case of a change of control, some or all of the unvested shares on each agreement will be subject to accelerated vesting. Accelerated vesting may take one of the following forms:

- All unvested shares automatically vest upon the change of control.

- Some percentage of unvested shares will automatically vest upon the change of control (Example: 30 percent of each employee's unvested shares, regardless of the number).

- A fixed number of shares will automatically vest upon the change of control (example: 1,000 shares, whether an employee has 1,000 or 100,000 unvested shares).

- All unvested shares will have some fixed period of time, such as 12 months, added to the vesting schedule, meaning that not only will some shares automatically vest, but all other unvested shares will vest one year earlier than they would have before the acquisition.

However, your stock options may have no accelerated vesting at all. Be sure to read your stock option agreements (each one you have), plus the company's stock option plan, to find out if some form of accelerated vesting is part of the change of control picture if your company is acquired.

Post-acquisition lockups

Accelerated vesting (which I discuss in the preceding section) can be very beneficial to you; your company is, essentially, giving you a bit of a "bonus" for riding out an acquisition. However, that "bonus" might be accompanied by a *lockup*, a period of time in which you cannot exercise options. (I discuss lockups in Chapter 8.)

For example, you may be prohibited from exercising any of your new options for six months. The company may want to prevent a mass exodus of employees following an acquisition, and by instituting a lockup on your options, you would have to forego those options should you decide to leave the company during the first few months after the change of control.

Check your stock option agreements to find out if a post-acquisition lockup period is in the picture for you and your options. If so, and if you work for a publicly traded company, you may wish to do a cashless exercise (see Chapter 6) on some or all of your vested shares before the official change of control if you want to cash out some of your optionable shares.

Why? If you don't have a very good feeling about the upcoming acquisition and the combined company's prospects, or if you are worried about your job security, you may want to stash away some cash just in case, courtesy of your options. Chances are that your company's stock price is close to or at the proposed acquisition price because of the upcoming deal. You may be giving up some potential gains (the difference between the agreed-to acquisition price per share and the current market price, if the latter is lower) plus the tax benefits from holding shares rather than selling immediately, but sometimes cashing out early may be your most prudent and risk-averse strategy.

You could also find yourself subject to a post-acquisition lockup even if you didn't receive any accelerated vesting on your options. So if you have any shares that were scheduled to vest during the six months (or however long the lockup period is) after the change of control, you will have to wait until the lockup period expires to exercise options on those shares that otherwise would have been accessible to you.

Sweetening the pot (or the golden goodbye)

Occasionally, you may receive an option on new shares as part of an acquisition, in addition to your current options package. You may receive these options for one of two reasons (one good, the other not so good).

The good reason: The acquiring company is sweetening the pot for some or all of the employees coming onboard as a result of the acquisition. The rationale: Give the newcomers even more of a potential equity stake in the fate of the future combined company, and help make up for the concern that often accompanies an acquisition.

The not so good reason: The acquiring company wants to shed some portion of the acquired company's employees. Instead of a cash severance plan, or in addition to a very modest cash plan, they may choose to grant to-be-eliminated employees options with an extended period beyond the typical 90 days after termination date in which those options may be exercised. The rationale: Cheap severance, and don't let the door hit you in the butt on your way out, thank you!

Understanding the Tax Implications of a Change of Control

In most change of control situations, you will not find yourself facing tax implications as a result of your old options being transitioned to the new options of the acquiring company.

However, you could conceivably find yourself in such a complicated acquisition scenario that tax implications might be a result of the change of control, such as realizing ordinary income from vested options that are canceled and exchanged for cash as part of the deal. At the first official word you receive of an impending change of control, you need to find out if there will be tax implications based on the details of the deal that is being finalized. Ask your manager, someone in the HR department, someone in corporate finance, your stock plan administrator, and everyone else who you think may be able to give you knowledgeable, correct guidance.

A Final Word: It's a Whole New Ballgame After a Change of Control

After a change of control, you need to go back the drawing board when you become part of a new company.

Do you enjoy working for your new employer? What is your stock option philosophy (see Chapter 3) for this new company? What are your co-workers doing — staying or leaving? What does "The Street" (the investment community) say about the combined company? What is *your* analysis of the combined company's future?

An acquisition could be great for you if you become part of a great company such as Microsoft, Cisco, or General Electric. However, if the acquisition was purely a financial play for the big guys to cash out — a true sellout, in every negative sense of that phrase — then chances are you're in for trouble even if the initial indications (make that propaganda) about the acquisition seem positive.

So keep your eyes and ears open, and be prepared for anything!

Chapter 17

Trying to Predict What Will Happen to Your Stock Options

*W*ouldn't it be wonderful if you had a crystal ball that would reveal the fate of your stock options to you? (Not to mention all kinds of other secrets of the future, but that's another story.) Should you exercise stock options now, or wait until next year or even the following year? If you exercise now, should you do so for all of your vested shares, or only some of them? After you exercise a batch of stock options, should you sell those shares immediately or hold them for a while to try and lessen your tax burden? Decisions, decisions, decisions.

Alas, no such crystal ball or any other kind of fortune-telling device exists that will guide you with absolute certainty through the many decisions you face in handling your stock options. However, by keeping your eyes open (literally) and your ear to the ground (figuratively), you can pick up a large number of hints and clues that will help you make informed decisions about handling your stock options, rather than having to simply "hope for the best."

First and foremost, you must acquire a sixth sense about what's really going on inside your company. (Remember the Bruce Willis movie *Sixth Sense*? Think about turning to a trusted co-worker and saying, "I see dead stock options!" as you e-mail your résumé to a couple of headhunters, looking for a new job as quickly as possible because of impending doom at the company.) I provide you with a long list of items to watch for and the significance of each — both good and bad — on the future value of your stock options.

Additionally, you also need to look at external factors such as the economy as a whole and what outsiders such as stock analysts are saying about your company. I go through a long list of these items as well.

Looking at What's Going on Inside Your Company

Sure, you should keep your nose to the grindstone (figuratively, of course, even if you do work in a mill or some other place that actually has a grindstone) and concentrate on doing the best job you can day after day. After all, your company's fate — and the fate of your company's stock price, and therefore the fate of your stock options — is largely influenced by you and all of your co-workers working hard, working smart, and helping to build a great company.

At the same time, though, you are bombarded day after day with hundreds or thousands of little pieces of information, all of which eventually ooze together into something of substance, just like in a science fiction film (remember the bad terminator in *Terminator 2*?). And once these pieces of information come together, you often have an "ah-hah!" effect as some previously hidden secret of what's really going on inside your company is revealed to you, if you're paying attention. Here's what should you be watching and listening for:

- Your co-workers — who's coming and who's leaving, and why?

- An early warning about whether your company's sales are slowing, or (on the better side) good news that the sales are turning out better than previously expected

- What the big guys are doing with their own stock and stock options holdings, and what their actions might mean

- Signs that your company's management is out of touch with what's going on in "the real world"

- Cronyism — friends of the CEO and other company leaders suddenly joining the company as executives, and what that might mean for the company's future (you might be surprised at the real significance of cronyism)

The sections that follow explain each item in detail.

The retention and turnover picture

Watching the comings and goings of employees at all levels of your company — your peers, even the company's executive management team — is often a very accurate barometer for your company's health. Are lots of people joining the company and very few are leaving? If so, chances are that your company is doing well and has a fairly bright outlook, at least for the near-term and intermediate future. Conversely, if you suddenly find many of your co-workers heading out the door for greener employment pastures elsewhere, you've just hit upon an early warning indicator that something is amiss and problems are probably just around the corner.

You need to keep retention and turnover statistics in context, however. As you probably know, the days of career-long employment with a single company have just about faded from existence in American business and in most other countries around the world. Societies have become highly mobile, and that mobility most certainly stretches into professional lives.

Therefore, you need to understand how your own company's retention and turnover are benchmarked against similar companies, such as those within your industry. For example, a consulting company may have an annual employee turnover rate of 15 percent — and that's pretty good! Since the late 1990s, many consulting companies have had to deal with employee turnover that typically tops 20 percent, sometimes creeping up into 30 percent or even 40 percent in those companies who aren't quite as successful as they once were. Therefore, assuming you work for and hold stock options in a consulting company, you want to gauge whether your company's turnover is higher, lower, or about the same as the average of companies across the industry.

If you find that 30 percent of your company's employees have left in the past year and the industry average is, say, 20 percent, then something is probably amiss. People have various reasons for leaving a company — personal reasons, family reasons, or work-related reasons such as a personality conflict with an immediate supervisor — so you'll never find a company where nobody is leaving. But if lots of people are walking out the door and cashing in as much of their own stock option holdings as they can, then you need to try and figure out what's up.

You also need to see how the most recent turnover statistics compare to those in the past. If your company's turnover is only 15 percent and the industry average is 20 percent, then that's probably a good sign, unless that 15 percent statistic is a dramatic jump from the previous two years where less than 5 percent of the company's employees left each year. Watch the trend line, too!

Watch out for involuntary turnover (layoffs and firings). *Restructuring* is a favorite term used by executives to describe that something isn't quite right with the way the company is currently operating. Often, the investment community perversely cheers a company's restructuring and layoff announcements by bidding up the company's stock price — the theory being that cost-cutting is a good thing. Sometimes, the investment community is right, and better days for the company are ahead; other times, though, the investment community leaves something to be desired and restructuring-driven layoffs are only the first step in a long, downward spiral for the company, it's stock price, and the value of your stock options. So beware!

Listen to what people are saying! The answers you seek aren't found only in raw turnover and retention statistics, but rather in the meaning behind those statistics. If your co-workers are leaving on bad terms — and believe me, they'll let others know if they're leaving because they're disgusted! — then be advised that the company's outlook might be dimming, even though executive management might still be issuing rosy statements about the company's bright future.

Or perhaps newcomers to your company rave, "Things are so much better here than where I came from! I love it here!" If you hear that enough, then chances are that, at the very least, your company's workforce will be fairly stable and turnover well within desired limits. That's not a 100 percent guaranteed sign that the company will be successful and its stock price is headed up, but it's better than hearing many of your co-workers say, "This place is horrible! I'm so sorry I took this job!"

Pay special attention to the comings and goings at the executive level. Does your CEO's resignation mean that the company is doomed? Not necessarily. For example, a company's founder may be stepping down to let a more experienced manager take the company's reins to drive the next stage of growth. The willingness of a founding CEO to move aside may well portend a great future for the company.

But you should watch for a large number of resignations from the executive ranks within a relatively short period of time. Keep in mind that these folks usually have very large stock options packages with a large number of unvested shares at any given time. A large number of departures may be a signal that these people in the know see a brighter future for themselves elsewhere, and tough times may be ahead for the company and its stock price.

What's the latest buzz on the company's sales picture?

You can pick up little tidbits in the course of day-to-day work that can give you a hint about how your company's sales are doing and possibly spur you into deciding that you had better exercise your stock options now and sell those shares, taking whatever profit you can while there's still time to do so (before the stock heads downward). Note that I am not advocating illegal insider trading; doing so is wrong, wrong, wrong, and the penalties for illegal insider stock trading are very severe! For example, if you stumble across a copy of the company's consolidated quarter-to-date sales statistics on the internal network, read the file and see that sales are down all across the board and that the forecast for the remainder of the quarter is grim, and then exercise options on all of your vested shares and immediately sell those shares, this is illegal insider trading.

Suppose, though, that you work in a consulting company and in the past month, about half of the people in your office are "on the bench" (that is, not assigned to a billable client project). You have a clue right there! In your office, at least, sales are soft. Does the same situation exist in other offices as well? If the on-the-bench situation lasts for more than just a few short weeks, you can likely assume that difficult times might be ahead.

My favorite story about picking up hints and clues for what is happening with the company's sales picture happened several years ago, and every time I think about this story, I can kick myself for not realizing at the time the significance of what I was hearing. I was listening in on a company-wide conference call with our company's CEO, who was going on and on about how the company's most recent reorganization was so wonderful and how the company's future was so bright, and how all of our stock options would one day be very valuable to us. Yet about two-thirds of the way through his speech, he made a remark along the lines of "you all need to keep your eyes open for sales opportunities, and if you hear of anything at a client where you're currently at or anywhere else, contact an account manager immediately." Ding-ding-ding-ding! Alert! Alert! Alert! The translation of the CEO's comments, as I figured it out later: "we're half-way through the quarter, sales are soft and not looking all that good for the rest of the quarter . . . help!"

Again, don't do anything that could possibly be considered illegal insider trading. But you absolutely should continually try and figure out the significance of what you're seeing and hearing with regard to whether your company is selling to its full potential — no matter what industry your company is in — and then figure out what the impact of good news or bad news might be on your company's stock price and the value of your stock options.

Watching the big guys and their (legal) insider trading activity

You probably assume that no executive in your company would engage in illegal *insider trading activity* — that is, buying or selling your company's stock (or exercising stock options) based on knowledge that he or she has that isn't available to the general public.

Executives and other insiders (such as members of the Board of Directors) do, however, buy and sell stock at various times, and even when everything is on the "up and up" (no illegal activity), you can still pick up lots of clues as to what's really going on inside your company.

When insiders actually buy stock on the open market, that's usually a good sign because they're signaling their faith that the cash investment they're making in those shares will be worth more than they're paying for the stock. After all, would someone deliberately buy shares of stock thinking there's a good chance the price will drop?

Executives and other insiders who buy stock aren't infallible! Sometimes, they guess wrong, and their investments turn out to be losers. But overall, significant insider buying activity is a good sign. Of course, insiders also sell stock in their company. Just because an insider — say, your company's CEO — is selling some of his or her stock holdings doesn't mean the sky is falling and your company is collapsing. People — and insiders — sell shares of stock for all kinds of reasons, such as diversifying their assets so their holdings aren't overly concentrated in a single investment vehicle. (Check out Chapter 11 for a discussion of your own portfolio and the major factors you need to consider for your own stock options.)

Suppose, though, that you find a long list of Form 144 filings indicating that insiders are lining up and basically shoving each other out of the way to unload stock they own. (An insider who plans to sell shares must file a Form 144 before doing so. Chapter 4 discusses Form 144 filings and where you can find this information.) The underlying significance: most likely, bad news. You can read between the lines and assume that a whole bunch of "in the know" people all think that the stock is most likely headed down, down, down, and they want to unload some portion of their own holdings (perhaps a substantial portion) before the stock price declines.

Pay special attention to "early insiders" with very inexpensive stock options exercising those options and selling those shares after your company's stock price has already declined substantially. You may have seen this happening during 2000, as many Internet company stocks collapsed.

Is company management out of touch with the real world?

If day-to-day life in your company resembles something out of *Dilbert* then your company's management might not only be poor managers and executives, they could also be out of touch with the real world. Do you continually receive absurd product deadlines that everyone — including the person making the assignment — knows cannot possibly be met? Do the product specifications for what you're working on resemble what your company's closest competitor introduced three years earlier and have since introduced two new product versions?

If you've seen the movie *Animal House*, you might recall the parade scene near the end of the movie when Kevin Bacon's character, dressed in his Army uniform, is standing in the middle of the pandemonium all around him, waving his arms and screaming, "All is well!" just before he is run over and flattened by the Delta House float. If your company's CEO or some executive is doing the corporate equivalent — saying, "Don't worry, everything is great!" on internal company-wide conference calls and also to the outside world, while the company is actually teetering on the brink of disaster — then you need to think about the eventual impact on your company's stock price and the value of your stock options when reality overcomes corporate delusion.

Cronyism

Cronyism occurs when you suddenly find former colleagues and buddies of your company's chairman or CEO (or maybe both) joining your company in senior executive positions, even though those newcomers might have little or no direct experience in your company's industry or otherwise possess somewhat suspect qualifications for their new jobs.

Cronyism is often a two-way indicator. On the positive side, you could infer that the current insiders are saying to their friends, "Hey! We've got something good going on here that you want in on." The cronies join the company, get very generous stock options packages, and if all goes according to plan, the company's stock price heads skyward, and they all cash in and make lots of money. And, even though the number of shares for which you have stock options are probably a pittance compared to those of the big guys, by "piggy-backing" on the underlying meaning for bringing cronies on board you can probably share in the gains through your own stock options.

On the negative side, cronyism rarely leads to long-term success and growth for a company. In many cases, the newcomer cronies — as well as those insiders who brought them in — intend to reap short-term benefits and then move on to someplace else once the company has been "played out." It's even conceivable that the gains these people intend to take out of your company might not even be from their own stock options, but rather from excessive salaries, bonuses, and perks (such as that generous $1 million housing allowance). Most likely, they intend to hedge their bets — stock gains if possible, but if not, cash compensation.

So be sure to monitor the compensation packages of all executives in your company, and especially newcomers who appear to be cronies of the executives already there. Excessive salaries and bonuses might be a leading indicator that the company's stock may not really be going anywhere. Alternatively, "normal" salaries and bonuses accompanied by behemoth stock option grants are a hint that the insiders think the stock is headed way up, and they're getting their buddies in on it. If your company is publicly traded, you can find information about executive compensation packages in several locations online, such as on Yahoo! Finance (biz.yahoo.com) under Company Profiles, or through SEC filings available through www.edgar-online.com or www.freeedgar.com — see Chapter 9.

What's Going on Outside Your Company?

Sometimes, the most professionally managed company with world-class products sees its stock price go into a free-fall because of factors beyond the control of company management, such as the economy sinking into recession. On the other hand, some other company with totally incompetent management, and a business plan so faulty it would have received an "F" in a business school class, might see its stock price go up 1,000 percent the first year after its IPO, simply because the stock market as a whole is skyrocketing.

Therefore, you need to pay attention to not only what's going on inside your company — the good and the bad — but also what's going on outside your company. You need to watch:

- The overall economy and how ups and downs might affect your company

- Where your company sits among your competition within your industry (Hint: #1 or #2 is usually a good sign!)

- Whether your industry on the upswing or heading down, down, down

- What professionals like stock analysts and CNBC commentators are saying about your company

- What amateurs like Internet bulletin board and chat room participants are saying about your company

It's the economy, stupid!

(*Note:* just so you don't take offense at this section's title, it comes directly from the rallying cry of Bill Clinton's 1992 Presidential campaign, as coined by campaign strategist James Carville. And it worked for him, didn't it?)

The relationship between the economy and stock prices isn't quite as straightforward as you might think it would be. In general, strong economic times should be accompanied by rising overall stock prices, while weaker economic times @slowing growth, even recession — should likewise see an environment of weak stock prices, anywhere from sluggish overall performance to dramatic decreases.

If you've invested in, or at least followed, the stock market for any period of time, you know that the economy-stock price equation often gets "out of whack." The economy may be booming, yet stock prices start weakening because of fears of interest rate increases, which in turn might eventually lead to a slowing of the economy. Correspondingly, you occasionally find periods like the early 1980s with the economy still facing high inflation and recession, yet the stock market finally roars to life in August of 1982, anticipating better times ahead.

Stock prices are often a leading indicator (that is, a predictor) of future economic direction. If investors believe that better economic times area ahead, they'll bid stock prices up in anticipation of improved corporate profits. Conversely, an outlook for poorer economic performance and reduced corporate profits will usually see dropping stock prices many months before any actual economic weakness. The secret, then, is to pay attention to what the collective opinions of the investing public are indicating about not only the current economic picture but also the economic outlook.

Paying attention to the economy does not mean that if the stock market begins weakening because of down-the-road economic concerns that you should automatically (and mindlessly) exercise all of your stock options and immediately sell all of those shares. A common investing witticism is that "the stock market has correctly predicted 14 of the past 3 recessions," meaning that oftentimes stock market prices dip in anticipation of economic weakness that never appears. So you don't want to be too quick on the trigger with regards to your own stock options; exercising and selling too soon can dramatically reduce your gains from your options.

Paying attention to the economy is most beneficial if you have specific plans to use some portion of the on-paper gains from vested but unexercised options over the next 9 to 12 months. If you see economic storm clouds gathering in the distance, then you may be better off exercising some of your options now, selling those shares, and tucking away the profits for whatever you have planned.

But don't panic! If you work for a solid company that exhibits many of the positive characteristics that I discuss earlier in this chapter — low turnover, solid management, steadily increasing sales — then even if your company's stock price drops in concert with the overall stock market as a result of economic weakening, you will most likely see a recovery in the stock price (and the value of your stock options) when the economy strengthens.

Is your company in the buggy whip industry?

A fairly standard business school cliché when I was in college in the late 1970s went something like this: "The best company in the buggy whip industry still went out of business if it didn't transform itself in time." The example dealt with companies in the late 1800s and early 1900s as the automobile was being introduced into society, and the primary mode of transportation for most people was still by some type of horse-drawn vehicle, like a buggy or carriage. Drivers of horse-drawn vehicles would use a buggy whip, along with reins, to help control the speed of the horse or horses pulling that vehicle (and also to get reluctant horses to move at all).

As the automobile took hold, though, fewer and fewer buggy whips were needed, and the companies that made buggy whips found their sales declining. The story goes that some companies went into other lines of business and survived; others that stuck too long with their "old technology" wound up going out of business. And so the employees of many buggy whip companies watched their stock options go underwater and eventually become worthless. (Just kidding, of course . . . I'm talking about the early 1900s, not the early 2000s, and I can't imagine finding a whole lot of stock options-holding employees in the days when wages were probably a few dollars a day at best!)

The moral of the story: No matter how well your company is doing today, failure to adapt to changing market conditions can be fatal!

Does the buggy whip story apply to today? Of course! In Chapter 2, I briefly discuss the decline and fall and eventual disappearance of one of my former employers, Digital Equipment Corporation. In the late 1980s and early 1990s, Digital did the technological equivalent of sticking with manufacturing and distributing buggy whips even though its customers were switching to automobiles. The company either missed or jumped in too late in the following areas:

- ✔ The rise of UNIX
- ✔ The switch from centralized computing to client/server architecture
- ✔ The growth of the personal computer marketplace (the company did make PCs, but they were woefully inadequate compared to those manufactured by IBM and other competitors)
- ✔ RISC (reduced instruction set computing) hardware architecture

And so the once-number two computer manufacturer in the world headed down, down, down.

Don't think, either, that Digital Equipment is an isolated example or an artifact of the early 1990s. Many software companies not only missed the dramatic growth of the Internet, but weren't as smart as Microsoft when the company (Microsoft) dramatically reengineered its entire company structure to get caught up as quickly as possible in the Internet market.

If, therefore, your company is in the 21st century equivalent of the buggy whip industry – that is, an ever-shrinking marketplace with an ever-shrinking client base because of dramatic changes — and your company isn't quickly adapting to those market forces, watch out!

What the professionals are saying about your company

You'll never have a lack of opinions about your company's future prospects in the post-2000 investment world. From analysts at investment banks and stock brokerages to cable television financial news channels like CNBC to financially oriented Web sites, you'll probably find dozens, if not hundreds, of "professionals" willing to tell you that your company's stock is a "strong buy" or that "sales should increase 35 percent in the next 12 months."

How accurate is the information you receive from these seemingly authoritative sources? How do you reconcile the fact that three stock brokerages have your company's stock rated at their respective highest grades, while three others rank your company's stock a grade or even two grades lower?

The answer: In most cases, you should ignore bits of information such as stock analyst upgrades and downgrades, for the simple fact that few analysts issue upgrades and downgrades in time for even the most trigger-happy, short-term-focused investors to do anything with that information. Stock market activity during 2000 exposed the futility of trying to act upon analyst recommendations, when you would commonly see a formerly high-flying Internet company's stock price drop anywhere between 60 percent and 90 percent, and then an analyst or two would downgrade the stock. Gee, thanks!

Many stock analyst rating systems are somewhat perverse anyway, if not downright misleading. You need to sort through terms such as "market perform," "market outperform," and "hold" in the various ratings schemes and try and figure out things like "if a stock has been downgraded from 'strong buy' to 'buy,' does that mean I should still buy shares, or is the downgrade itself really saying that investors should sell despite the terminology used? Further confusing the landscape is that analysts almost never actually issue an actual "sell" recommendation, even if they could do so with a high degree of accuracy before a precarious stock price drop.

Your time in watching and listening to investment professionals can be far better spent focusing not on stock rankings, but discussions of your company's operations, financial position, and other "raw data" — and then coming to your own conclusions about what you should do with your stock options. For example, an apparently knowledgeable asset manager who appears on CNBC and spends five or ten minutes analyzing how a company's sales have broadened over the past year from a relatively narrow customer base to now include customers in new and fast-growing market segments, and how by doing so the company has positioned itself very well for its next stage of growth, can provide you with far more valuable information than buy-or-hold recommendations.

Pay attention to what guests on various financial news outlets disclose about their own holdings in stock they discuss. On the one hand, disclosing that they own shares in your company's stock while they're touting its prospects might be an example of them "putting their money where their mouths are." Alternatively, an investment professional who is ethically challenged might be engaging in a "pump and dump" scheme whereby that person speaks glowingly of the prospects of a stock holding, and after the price goes up, the stock is "dumped" for the quick profit. Over time, you'll learn which public investment analysis figures have solid reputations over a long period of time and whether the analysis you hear is truly unbiased.

What the amateurs are saying about your company (and whether it matters what they're saying)

One of more interesting and often entertaining developments of the Internet era has been in the era of financial bulletin boards and chat rooms. Sites such as Yahoo! (biz.yahoo.com), Silicon Investor (www.siliconinvestor.com), and Raging Bull (www.ragingbull.com) all provide vehicles through which anyone — even you — can offer your own seemingly authoritative opinions about the merits (or lack thereof) of any publicly traded company.

If you can sift through the noise such as *flame wars* (nasty messages and postings flying back and forth decrying someone else's intelligence or maybe even that person's right to exist), and even occasional public online flirting and sexual innuendo, among those who seem to spend all of their waking hours posting on these sites, you might be able to pick up a valuable nugget or two of information about your company. For the most part, though, postings on these Web sites — even those postings coming from "insiders" like your co-workers — are often little more than rants and venting.

My advice: Check out these Web site bulletin boards and chat rooms occasionally for entertainment value, but don't depend on them to provide any authoritative direction into what you should do with your stock options.

Chapter 18

Leaving Your Job: What Happens to Your Stock Options?

In This Chapter

▶ Leaving your job — no matter what reason

▶ Digging out your stock option agreement paperwork

▶ Avoiding the clawback!

▶ Knowing how long you have to exercise options on your vested shares after you leave

▶ Understanding any relationship between the stock option package you're leaving behind and compensation at a new employer

▶ Switching to part-time employment or contractor status

*P*arting is such sweet sorrow . . . .

Breaking up is hard to do . . . (Apologies to Neil Sedaka.)

So long, farewell, *auf wiedersehen*, goodbye. . . . (Apologies not to the cast of *The Sound of Music*, but rather to you readers!)

Maybe you love your job, or maybe you hate it. Perhaps your stock options have made you wealthy (or you're on your way to options-driven wealth), or possibly your options package has turned out to be absolutely worthless. Regardless of your personal situation and feelings, one thing you can absolutely be certain of is that someday, you will no longer be an employee of the company where you're working right now.

You might resign and move on to another opportunity elsewhere, or maybe your departure will be your company's idea rather than yours as the result of layoffs. Or maybe you'll retire (yes, people actually still do retire from their employer, and some of them even still receive old-fashioned pension plans). Or, more ominously, your employment could come to an abrupt end because of an illness or your death.

Whatever the reason, at some point your employment will end, and you — or your estate, if something very unfortunate has happened to you — will need to make some very important decisions about your stock options, usually during a very short period of time.

So the time to prepare for that eventuality (and to prepare others as well) is now. In this chapter, I'll cover a multitude of issues and situations with which you'll eventually have to deal, and (in your best interests) you should start considering this very moment.

Does the Reason You're Leaving Matter?

For the most part, the reason you're leaving your job will have little impact on what happens to your stock options. Whether leaving is your idea (that is, you've handed in your resignation, usually because of another opportunity elsewhere) or your employer's idea (you've been fired for some reason — more on that in a moment — or you've been caught in a company layoff), three very important factors govern what happens to your stock options:

1. The provisions specified in each stock option grant agreement that you've received regarding "condition of employment" or an equivalent phrase (see Chapter 5) immediately kick in upon the termination of your employment.

2. On the last day of your employment, the vested or unvested status of all option shares governed by all of your stock option grants is immediately frozen. That is, no more shares will vest, and all unvested shares will remain unvested for all eternity (except in a few out-of-the-ordinary circumstances, as I discuss later in this chapter).

3. On the last day of your employment, the clock starts running for how long you have to exercise any of your vested shares, and except for circumstances of your death or disability (discussed later in this chapter), this clock's battery is running pretty low. (Translation: You only have a few short months to exercise any vested shares, so don't procrastinate!)

Tick, Tock, Tick, Tock . . . The Clock Is Running

Three months — that's the amount of time you almost always will have (after your last official day of employment) to exercise options on shares that have vested as of that date. In the case of incentive stock options (ISOs), the time frame is specified by the Internal Revenue Code that governs the terms of ISOs. The rules specify that if your employer does permit you longer than three months after your departure to exercise options on vested shares, you are no longer eligible for the preferred tax treatment of ISOs (see Chapter 14), and your ISOs convert to nonqualified status with the applicable tax rules for NQSOs.

In the case of NQSOs, the three-month period is customary on the part of employers if you resign, or you are laid off or fired for some reason other than cause. If your employment is ending for some reason other than resignation or layoff/firing, chances are that you'll have a different time frame apply to your options and vested shares. Specifically:

- If you're disabled or otherwise having serious health problems that cause you to leave your position of employment, the time you have to exercise will be extended, perhaps by several years. Note, though, that your stock option grant must also specify in the "Cancellation" clause that the option does not expire upon your termination as it would with a "normal" resignation or company-specified termination. Basically, you need to make sure that in the case of disability you have an extended period in which to exercise because the option is not cancelled as it otherwise would.

- If you die while an employee, your estate may also have one year — or, in some cases, several years — to exercise options on vested shares. As with a disability situation, both the cancellation terms and the vesting period must reflect the extension because of your death.

- If you retire in accordance with your employer's retirement plans (typically, you work there for at least some specified number of years), you may have an extended period after your retirement to exercise vested shares, perhaps even several years. Unlike situations of disability or death, extended post-employment exercise periods in cases of retirement are independent of option expiration dates and terms. That is, even if your company's stock option plan allows retirees, say, four years to exercise options on shares vested at the time of retirement, you wouldn't be able to exercise vested shares three years after your retirement date if the option covering those shares has since expired. So make sure you pay attention to both the extended vesting period and the option expiration date! (Note that in cases of death or disability, you also must watch the option expiration date.)

Sometimes, a company that has been forced to lay off an entire group of employees may offer those affected by the layoff additional time to exercise options on vested shares, perhaps doubling their plan's 90-day period for NQSOs to 180 days. Another "benefit" (if you want to put a positive spin on being laid off) you may receive is that your employer will accelerate the vesting on some of your shares that otherwise would still be unvested — and therefore lost — on your last day of employment.

Don't automatically expect such generosity — companies usually have accounting implications from changes such as those previously described. But if you are laid off and your termination package includes extended post-termination option exercising, accelerated vesting, or maybe both, be grateful and pay attention. You might just be able to squeak out some stock gains from an unfortunate job situation!

If you decide to be a "good corporate citizen" and give your employer two weeks (or even more) notice of your departure when you resign, you need to be aware of any imminent vesting dates. If, for example, you submit your resignation on May 1, effective May 15, and you have a vesting date coming up on May 8, your employer might decide to terminate you immediately on May 1, perhaps pay you two weeks of salary as if you had worked until May 15. And, since you are no longer an employee of the company on May 8, your shares will not vest. So make sure you submit your resignation after a significant vesting date, even if doing so means you have to put up with a horrible job situation for a couple of weeks longer.

Should You Sign a Termination Agreement?

Many companies try to force employees whom they fire or lay off, and even some who resign, to sign a termination agreement. My suggested response: Laugh hysterically!

Seriously, you know that a termination agreement thrust in front of you will be overwhelmingly slanted toward the favor of your soon-to-be-former employer. And you already have a termination agreement (of sorts) in effect: your original employment agreement, which almost always clearly states terms and conditions of termination, restrictions on your postemployment activities (not recruiting the company's employees to leave and not competing against your now-former employer, typically), and so on. Why sign something else?

Sometimes, however, you may have a few carrots dangled in front of you in exchange for signing an agreement: a cash severance package, or perhaps a new batch of stock options or changes in terms on your existing options. The catch: You will most likely be asked to agree in writing to increased noncompete terms or to forego your rights to file suit against the company after you leave. So make sure you read everything very carefully before signing, and if you have any uncertainties or questions, consult a lawyer.

Exercising Stock Options After You've Already Left

After you've left your now-former employer and perhaps moved on to a new job (or are waiting to do so), exercising options *should* be done in the same way as when you were an employee. You call your plan's administrator, identify the shares you wish to exercise, decide if you're going to do a cashless exercise or an exercise-and-hold, and then take the steps I discuss in Chapter 6.

If you were an executive at the company you're leaving and were subject to *blackout periods* (see Chapter 8) that prohibited you from exercising options or selling shares during certain times (such as around the reporting of earnings), beware! You are probably still considered an *insider* for options and securities purposes, meaning that you need to be aware of blackout periods during the brief time you have after your termination of employment to exercise options. Make sure that if, for example, a blackout period covers the final 6 weeks of your 90-day post-termination exercise period that you exercise any options that you want to before the blackout period begins, otherwise you will probably lose those shares! Also, find out if you need to file any SEC forms (such as a Form 4 or 5 — see Chapter 4) for selling shares if you're considered an insider.

Read Your Stock Option Agreements Now!

Somewhere in every stock option agreement that you've received, probably buried somewhere in the middle of the document, you'll find the clause or clauses that spell out exactly what happens to your stock options if you leave your job.

Make sure you read each stock option agreement that you've received during the time of your employment. Chances are that all of the agreements read alike with regard to details such as no more shares vesting after your last day of work, or the time frame you have to exercise options on vested shares before they're lost forever. However, you could find some differences from one agreement to another if the company's stock option plan has changed over time. Additionally, options you receive under special circumstances such as repricing, special bonuses, or replacement options for those that are underwater (I discuss all of these special circumstances in Chapter 19) may very well have out-of-the-ordinary restrictions. So again, make sure you find and thoroughly read each piece of paperwork you've received regarding your stock options.

What Happens to Pre-IPO Options If You Leave?

If you leave a company in which you are holding pre-IPO options — on a small number of stock shares or a large number, it doesn't really matter — and the company is still privately held, then realize that in most circumstances, you'll be leaving your entire options package (including all grants you've received) behind, with no chance to ever profit from the company's stock in the future. Your options grants will all be canceled at the end of the post-termination exercising period, and because the company is not yet public, you will be shut out from exercising and selling shares. There is no market for those shares because the company is still privately owned.

But how about exercising and holding shares? Depending on the terms of your stock option agreement, you may be able to exercise options while your employer is still privately held. Or you may not be able to exercise options. You need to read your grant agreements to see exactly what you can and can't do with regard to exercising.

If you are permitted to exercise options before the company goes public, you could do so, but you need to understand that you might be buying stock in a company that may never go public. As such, your stock may not be marketable, and you may never be able to sell those shares. If you are confident that the company may someday go public after you leave, then you might want to take a chance and exercise options, holding those shares until some time in the future. However, you need to understand that not only do you have to deal with all of the regular risks of investing in equities (specifically, that stock prices go down as well as up, and there's no guarantee that falling stock prices will ever recover), you are assuming additional risk by buying stock that you may never be able to sell to anyone, at any price.

If your stock option agreements prohibit you from exercising options until the company has gone public, or for many years down the road past when you are thinking about leaving, then you are pretty much out of luck. Wave goodbye to your options, don't look back, and get ready for your next employment opportunity and hope it turns out better than this one did.

What About Underwater Stock Options?

Suppose that on your last day of employment, you are holding stock option grants with 5,000 vested shares, half of which have a strike price of $7.50 and the other half with a strike price of $10.00. The bad news, however, is that your company's stock price is $3.25 per share, and hasn't been above $5.00 per share for the past year. Therefore, all of your options are underwater.

Remember, the clock is running. If your now-former employer's stock somehow rises above $7.50 during the 90 days after your last day of work (or whatever time-to-exercise period is in effect for your options), then you will be able to salvage at least a small gain from half of your vested shares. If the stock price were to pop even higher — above $10.00 per share — during that same period, then you will be able to salvage at least a $2.50 per share gain from 2,500 shares and a smaller gain from the other 2,500 shares.

Hey, it's not exactly lottery winnings, but if you really can salvage even a small profit during the few short months after you leave your job, then congratulate yourself. For most people, options that are underwater at the time they leave will still be underwater when the options are canceled, and no further exercising is permitted.

If your options have an extended post-employment exercise period because of disability, death, or retirement, then there is a chance that underwater options could once again be in-the-money if the company's performance improves and the investing public rewards it with an increase in its stock price. Therefore, you or — if you're not around or are incapacitated because of disability — whoever is managing your estate or affairs — needs to consistently monitor the company's stock price to see if shares ever do recover and the options can once again be exercised for a gain.

Also, don't look back! Even if you succumb to the temptation to follow your former employer's stock price movements (perhaps because you still own shares), avoid the temptation to *think* about the gains you might have made from your stock options if you had remained employed at the company. You've moved on; concentrate on managing the stock options that are within your control, not those you no longer own.

Read Your Overall Employment Agreement

You should also read through your employment agreement that you signed at some point, probably on the first day of your employment or soon thereafter. Why? Because quite possibly, your employee agreement has clauses related to what happens after you leave your job that could affect your stock options.

Of particular interest — make that concern — to you are portions of your employment agreement that detail the various reasons that you or your employer may decide to terminate your employment. For example, your employment agreement probably has a "Terminated for Cause" portion that basically says if you violate any one of a number of company policies, from stealing company secrets to alcohol or drug abuse, you forfeit all kinds of rights, including the right to further exercise any vested stock options.

Under most circumstances, though, "terminated for cause" conditions and restrictions shouldn't be a problem. Mostly, you want to look for any possible conflicts or contradictions between your stock option agreements and your employment agreement to make sure you don't have any problems while trying to maximize the value of your options during your last days of employment or during the few months after you leave the company.

As I discuss in Chapter 5, though, you should have already thoroughly read your employment agreement and compared it against the wording in your stock option agreement long before you even get close to leaving your job. Ideally, you should read through every official document you receive from your employer as soon as the paper gets into your hands, especially if you are required to sign that document!

In most cases, the terms specified in your employment agreement categorize your employment as "at will," meaning that you can resign your position at any time or your employer can fire you or lay you off at any time without any type of "consideration," such as a severance payment or other post-employment benefits. If, however, you are one of the big guys at your company (see Chapter 4), it's possible that you not only have a basic employment agreement between you and your employer but also some type of employment contract that does include sizable severance payments and benefits such as accelerated pension vesting and payments or some other form of postemployment compensation like a minimum-hours consulting contract with the company.

If you have a big guy employment contract, you need to look through that contract — just as with any ordinary "at will" employment agreement — for any terms and conditions that affect your stock options, such as accelerated vesting (which I discuss later in this chapter) or, as I discuss next, a clawback provision.

Beware the Dreaded Clawback Provision!

Okay, I know the title of this section sounds like an old gypsy curse from a bad 1950s movie, and the mention of "claw" probably makes you think of some cheaply constructed Hollywood-style monster from the precomputerized special effects days. But in today's world of stock options, *clawbacks* are a real monster that, if you resign and join a new company, could conceivably eat up gains you've already realized from your stock options!

A *clawback* is a provision in your stock option agreement(s) that specifies the following: If you go to work for a competitor of your employer or otherwise engage in what your employer specifies as "detrimental" behavior, you not only lose rights to vested but unexercised shares from your stock options, but you are also required to surrender gains you've already realized from your options (that is, you actually have to write your company a check for the amount of your gains!) typically during the six months prior to the termination of your employment.

Whereas stock option agreements and employment agreements have long specified that you are subject to losing some of your post-employment rights if you "do something the company doesn't like," clawback provisions take these restrictions to a whole new level by attempting to force you to give back gains that you have acquired through a key component of your compensation: your stock options.

The least onerous form of clawback provisions are, basically, noncompete provisions that take away the post-employment time frame you would otherwise have to exercise options on vested shares. If, for example, your stock option agreement specifies that you have 90 days to exercise all vested shares, the least problematic form of a clawback would take away your exercise rights, in effect stripping you of all vested shares that you have not yet acquired by exercising your stock option(s).

From that point, clawback provisions get worse — much worse! The perfect wording to describe horrendous clawbacks is found in an article titled "The Money Manager: Beware the Clawback" by Carolyn T. Geer for *Fortune*, available online at www.fortune.com/fortune/investor/moneymanager/2000/04/17/index.html. Ms. Geer notes that some companies' clawback provisions "require you to disgorge option profits if you exercise and then join a competitor within a certain period of time . . . you are forced to pay the company the difference between what it cost you to exercise your options (the strike price) and the market value of the stock at the time of exercise."

What a word: disgorge. It has just the right tone to indicate that any way you look at it, if you find yourself subject to the type of clawback provision described in the preceding paragraph, you're looking at boatloads of trouble.

Ms. Geer also notes later in the article that "if you were forced out of your job and land at a competitor, your former employer is unlikely to enforce a clawback provision." However, unless your stock option agreements explicitly state that a clawback provision is not applicable if you are laid off or fired, then you have no guarantee that your company won't still try to get you to (I have to say it) disgorge your gains from your stock options, as if you had resigned to go to work at a competitor.

Remember that in almost all cases, you receive stock options not out of the goodness of your CEO's or CFO's heart but rather because you are consciously making a tradeoff between cash compensation today — salary and bonus — and the potential for a higher amount of cash compensation tomorrow through stock option gains. Therefore, I find the idea of clawback provisions particularly troubling, for several reasons:

- Clawback provisions "change the rules" by, in effect, going back in time and converting actions you took while you were an employee in good standing and had every right to take — in particular, exercising stock options and perhaps selling some or all of those shares — into punishable actions. Your former employer interprets your actions as an intention to injure the company, so therefore, you must be punished financially.

- Clawback provisions usually don't take the reasons for your leaving into consideration. Even if leaving to go to a new employer is your idea, you may be doing so because you have a new manager who is totally incompetent and hates you and has made every workday absolutely miserable. Or, on the less extreme side, you may simply have a better employment opportunity elsewhere, and your current employer has refused to give you more responsibility or to increase your salary, and in the interests of you and your family, you decide to move on.

- The situations that could trigger a clawback provision may be very vaguely stated. If, for example, your employer requires you to repay stock option gains if you go to work for "a competitor," what is the precise definition of a competitor? Is it another company in the exact same business with the exact same services (for example, another consulting company that specializes in Web site development)? Or is a competitor any computer consulting company, regardless of the services provided? How about any consulting company at all, such as a management consulting company that doesn't do systems integration or hands-on work at all? Okay, how about a software company with a small technical support consulting organization? You hopefully see my point: Your now-former employer could conceivably make all kinds of claims that trigger the clawback provisions of your stock option agreements, and before you know it, you have more points of disagreement than a Presidential election.

- Even if you concede that perhaps there are merits to the concept of a clawback provision (I don't), the fact remains that those who are subject to a clawback may very well find themselves facing financial hardship if their former or soon-to-be-former employer claims that the provisions should be enforced. Why? Say that you are leaving your job and six months ago (the time frame of your agreement's clawback language), you performed a cashless exercise on a large number of options for a sizable gain, paid your taxes, and used the money for a downpayment on a house. What are you supposed to do — sell your house so you can give money back to your former employer? Or suppose you used the money to pay medical bills for a family member that weren't covered by your employer's health plan, and the reason you're changing jobs is so you can stop traveling and stay closer to home to help care for that family member. Give your gains back? Give me a break!

- If you are required to pay back stock option gains, your tax situation will become very complicated, especially if you had a taxable event in one year and are being forced to surrender profits in another year. And, to make matters worse, I can just about guarantee that your company's human resources and financial organizations will get the calculations and tax forms wrong, leaving you not only poorer but also with a big mess to straighten out.

✔ You have made sacrifices in terms of compensation in exchange for those stock options and you've been a good employee and done your job, so the idea of clawbacks is fundamentally unfair, unjust, and un-American.

You should be very hesitant to join a company whose stock option plan contains the most financially punitive form of a clawback provision, especially one with very vague language indicating when it would kick in. However, if you still really want to take the job, then be sure that you are always aware of the time frame specified by the clawback provision. If, for example, your stock option specifies that you will be required to surrender any gains from your stock options in the six months prior to your date of termination and you know that you're probably going to move on to a new job, do your best to exercise your options and sell your shares outside the window specified by the clawback provision. You will likely still find yourself on the short end of the deal with optionable shares that vest during your last six months of employment, but at least you can salvage something from the gains you earned.

Finally, as I note earlier in the chapter, make sure you carefully read each stock option agreement that you've received. If you've been with a company for more than a few years, chances are that your earlier stock option grants did not contain clawback provisions and unless you've signed something along the way agreeing to add a clawback provision to those older grants, you are on firm ground that vested but unexercised shares at the time of your departure are not subject to any type of clawback. Make sure you know exactly what your situation is for each of your option grants!

How Does Your Soon-to-be-Former Stock Option Package Affect Your New Job's Compensation?

"Get your new employer to make you whole." In job-searching terminology, *making you whole* means that when you accept a new job, your compensation package will contain aspects that will make up for what you've left behind at your former employer. Some common "left behind" items include a bonus that you were anticipating but now won't get because you have accepted a new job; a salary increase that would have taken affect in several more months; or stock option gains from unvested shares

According to Jay Klapper, an executive recruiter based in northern New Jersey, getting a new employer to make you whole on stock options is often a hit-or-miss proposition. Several very important factors are at work as you negotiate a new position, including:

- Employers increasingly are taking a position of a "fresh start" for you, meaning that your stock options package at your former employer is not really that much of a factor when establishing your new compensation package (or negotiating with you).

- If you've left behind underwater stock options, companies with which you're negotiating not only know that your options were underwater but they will overtly (and sometimes gleefully!) tell you that just because you have, say, 20,000 options, "worthless is worthless."

- Just because you might currently have options on tens of thousands of shares at a pre-IPO startup that is going under, don't expect an established company to even try and match your current stock options package in an equivalent numbers of shares.

Your prospective new employer may very well meet you part-way (notice I didn't say halfway) as you negotiate over compensation terms. If, say, the company's standard options package for someone at your level calls for 5,000 shares, and you're sitting on a decent-sized gain in your options at your current employer — but your shares aren't yet vested — they may increase the number of shares in your offer by a few thousand. Whether they would choose to "make you whole," however, is more a factor of your skills and accomplishments and the type of role you're being offered rather than simply being a holder of stock options at a company you're considering leaving.

The key is to treat your negotiations with prospective employers as you would if you had no options at all: Try to get as much as you can, but going in, have a pretty good idea of the ranges you can expect to receive for salary, signing bonus, annual bonus, and stock options package.

Special Job Change Circumstances and What Happens to Your Stock Options

Most of what's been discussed so far in this chapter deals with common circumstances regarding your leaving a company — no longer being employed at or affiliated with a company — where you had held stock options. However, you need to be aware of other situations that may apply to you some day, such as switching from full-time to part-time employment status, switching to contractor status, or taking a leave of absence.

Switching to part-time employment status

Interestingly, most stock option plans and agreements make no explicit mention of what happens to your stock options should you decide to switch from full-time to part-time status. What typically happens, then, is . . . nothing (at least to your currently held options).

Because you are not leaving the company, you are protected from regulations-driven factors such as no longer being able to hold ISOs. You still are an employee of the company, and therefore eligible to hold ISOs. Likewise, nothing usually happens to your nonqualified stock options (NQSOs).

Check your stock option agreement, though. As employers increasingly are permitting part-time workers in their workforce, you will likely find a few option-granting companies that will adjust facets of your stock option holdings if you do leave full-time status. Typically, you won't have to worry about shares being taken away from you; what might happen, though, is that the vesting schedule will be adjusted, prolonging a four-year schedule to perhaps six years or eight years for shares that have yet to vest. As I keep saying, read your stock option agreements!

What may happen, though, will be changes with newly granted options. If your next option grant would likely have been for 2,000 shares if you were on full-time status, then very likely the company may grant you an option on only 1,000 shares if you are on 50 percent status, or some other number of shares proportional to the "full order" of what you would receive as a full-time employee.

Switching to contractor status

Companies increasingly grant stock options to nonemployee contractors who are members of their "extended family." For example, a software vendor may augment its workforce with independent consultants for functions such as software development, testing, or customer support.

Suppose that you decide that you no longer want to work full-time for your company as an employee, and part-time work isn't of interest to you. Instead, you want to set up shop as an independent contractor and work for your now-former employer, as well as for other companies, according to your own schedule.

If you're holding ISOs, then all of the regulation-driven holding requirements for employees apply, and you will either have to exercise those options within the three months after your last day of employment or wave goodbye to them. However, your former employer — now client — may create a stock option package for you, allowing you to retain your nonqualified stock options with continued vesting, in addition to allowing your ISOs to be converted to NQSOs (or granting you new options as a replacement for ISOs you have to surrender).

Basically, everything is negotiable. Assuming that you have a fairly good relationship with the company you're leaving — the company probably wouldn't be a client of yours if you didn't have a good relationship established — then you can set up the terms of your contract to explicitly state what happens with your stock options.

Remember, though, that just like with decisions you have to make about salary versus options, you'll probably have to make decisions about how much your consulting fees will be reduced from your "regular rate" in exchange for keeping your stock options and even being granted new options as a contractor.

Taking a leave of absence

If you take a leave of absence from your employer — either a paid or unpaid leave — you need to see what your stock option agreements say about the effect on your options. As long as you remain an employee of the company, even one who is neither getting paid nor receiving any benefits, your stock options should remain intact.

However, your vesting schedules may be suspended for the duration of your leave of absence. For example, if you decide to take a year off from work with permission from your employer, when you return to work one year later, your options will resume vesting from the point at which you took your leave of absence.

One major caveat, however: Every state has its own particular labor laws that govern employer and employee rights. Quite possibly, an unpaid leave of absence may put you into a nonemployee status, even if you will resume your job or an equivalent one when you return. Therefore, there might be an impact on any ISOs you're holding, depending on the particulars of how your state interprets a leave of absence. Be sure to ask your stock plan administrator for a definitive, authoritative ruling on what happens to all of your stock options — particularly your ISOs — if you take a leave of absence.

Likewise, if you need to take a medical leave of absence, then the terms of your absence, including benefits and other aspects of compensation, may also be governed by state law. Make sure that you fully understand not only your benefits but also any state laws or regulations governing stock options in case of medical leave.

If your leave of absence is for paternity or maternity reasons or part of a company-sponsored sabbatical, the vesting schedules of your options should not be suspended or affected in any way.

Get the Lawyers! Lost Stock Options and Lawsuits

Suppose you are fired or laid off, and in addition to being out of a job, you find yourself anguishing because you are leaving a whole lot of unvested options behind. Maybe your employer is privately held, or maybe it is a publicly traded company. Maybe — in the case of a privately held employer — you aren't really sure exactly what your options are worth because you can't easily reference the stock price, but you know the options are worth something because your company isn't going out of business or anything. You were just unfortunate enough to get caught in a layoff, that's all.

Sometimes more agonizingly, however, you might find yourself laid off from a publicly held company and you know absolutely how much gain you're being forced to surrender from those unvested, in-the-money options, because that big old stock price is just staring you right in the face.

Guess what? Increasingly, people who have been fired or laid off and who have been forced to leave behind unvested options are turning to lawyers and the courts to try and recover gains they believe they are entitled to. As noted in a CNET News.com story (Dawn Kawamoto's "Stock Options May Trigger More Wrongful Termination Suits," available at http://news.cnet.com/news/0-1003-200-2576435.html), wrongful termination lawsuits driven by former employees feeling that they have been cheated out of their stock options are fighting back via the legal system and increasingly winning.

Even in the case of options in privately held companies, laid-off employees and their attorneys are building cases based not on speculation, but on sound mathematics. How? In Chapter 10, I discuss the Black-Scholes Model for valuing stock options, noting that the complex mathematical model goes far beyond the simple calculations of [# of shares × (current price – strike price)]. Even though I mention that for most of your purposes a simple arithmetic calculation would be satisfactory for figuring out what your options are worth, I did mention that Black-Scholes (or any other complex valuation model) does have its uses.

Suing your former employer over stock options is one of those uses. As noted in Dawn Kawamoto's CNET News.com article, "Although employees must normally stay on the job a year or more to turn their stock options into cash, accounting experts insist that stock options have a monetary value unto themselves. The Black-Scholes method is the most widely used tool for valuing unvested stock options."

So if you find yourself in a being-fired or laid-off situation, you may want to at least consider seeking a legal resolution if you feel that you've been blatantly cheated by your former employer over your stock options — even the unvested ones. If the company is going or has gone down the tubes and is headed into oblivion, you're probably wasting your time. However, if the company is fairly successful and is just engaging in a cutting-employees-to-make-quarterly-numbers-look-good-and-make-Wall-Street-happy move (whew!), or if it's still privately held but its future prospects are bright — but management has just decided they no longer want you around, for reasons that have nothing to do with your performance — then you should at least check out your legal options.

Part VI
The Part of Tens

The 5th Wave   By Rich Tennant

"And just how long did you think you could keep that pot o' gold at the end of the rainbow a secret from us, Mr. O'Shea?"

In this part . . .

This part contains several concise, easy-to-remember lists to help your decision-making process for your stock options. You'll see why your stock options might be worth a lot . . . or maybe worth nothing, ever! You'll also see a list of items to double-check and triple-check in your stock option agreement paperwork before signing on the dotted line. Then there's the "bad stock option experience recovery program" — how to get back on your feet and learn from that job with the great stock option package (or so you thought) that didn't turn as you had hoped. You'll also find the every-six-month checklist to help you stay on track with your job and your stock options.

Chapter 19

Special Stock Option Circumstances

In This Chapter

▶ Repricing

▶ Reissuing

▶ Reloading

▶ Using stock options as a form of currency

What do your stock options have to do with gambling in a casino, The Riddler (Batman's nemesis), and *Star Trek's* Captain Kirk?

For most employees, stock options mostly have a routine life cycle. They are granted options, exercise them at some point, and hopefully walk away with some profits.

You could, however, face some "special circumstances" with your stock options that are outside the normal life cycle discussed in other chapters in this book. This chapter discusses different types of special circumstances. Stay tuned for the answer — same Bat-time, same Bat-channel!

Understanding the Three R's: Repricing, Reissue, and Reload Options

Maybe in elementary school, your "three R's" were reading, writing, and 'rithmetic. (They certainly didn't include spelling, that's for sure.) But in stock option-land, the three R's that might be of importance to you are

✔ Repriced options

✔ Reissued options

✔ Reload options

Repriced options

Imagine that you take a trip to Las Vegas and go down to the casino in the hotel where you're staying, clutching the gambling stake that you've set aside (let's say $100), and then sit down at a 25-cent slot machine. You methodically feed your quarters into the machine, which on occasion gives you a small win of a dollar or two, but within an hour, your $100 is gone.

Now imagine that as soon as your money is gone, a casino representative walks up to you, smiling, and says, "We apologize for our machine taking all of your money, but don't worry about it. Just go up to the cashier's window over there, and we'll give you another $100 if you'll agree to come right back to this same machine — we'll hold your seat for you so nobody takes it — and you can keep playing."

"I must be in a casino in Bizzaro World," you think to yourself incredulously. (Readers of Superman comic books and *Seinfeld* fans will understand the Bizzaro World reference: A universe where everything is the opposite of how it is in the normal world.) "A casino that takes all of my money and then wants to give me more? How could that be?"

Sensing your puzzlement, the casino representative explains that he has enjoyed having you around; he wants you to stay in that casino and, in fact, stay right at that same machine, rather than check out of the hotel and go gamble in another casino.

Welcome to the world of repriced stock options. Unfortunately, it's a world bordering on extinction. And here's how that world works.

The basics of repricing

Suppose that you go to work for NeverShouldHaveGonePublic.com, an Internet consulting firm that built its business model around constructing Web sites and business-to-consumer capabilities for dot-com companies. Not a bad idea, back in the 1998–1999 timeframe; not such a great idea, though, by the time late 2000 rolled around when so many dot-com companies crashed, taking the stock prices of most Internet consulting companies along for the free-fall.

Unlike some of your co-workers, you didn't begin working at NeverShouldHaveGonePublic.com in the pre-IPO days when you would have received very inexpensive stock options — many with a strike price of less than a dollar per share. You were hired after the company went public at $7.50 per share and saw its stock price skyrocket past $60 per share within the first six months of being publicly traded. Your initial stock option package for 10,000 shares had an exercise price of $14.75 per share — not too bad when the stock price was sitting in the $60s, but not that great at the moment, considering that the stock price right now is $4.50 per share. Eleven months after going to work there, all of your shares from your stock option grant are underwater, big time!

Just as you start touching up your résumé, the word comes down from the company's CEO: All of the company's underwater stock options are going to be repriced, at today's closing stock price, which turns out to be $4.50 per share.

What has happened here? Basically, the company has issued the following proclamation. "Hey, all of you employees with underwater stock options: We know you're probably looking at moving on to another job because your options are worthless, so we have an offer that you can't refuse. Forget what your old strike prices were on your respective option grants; from this day forward, we issue a proclamation that all of you have a new strike price, and that strike price will be $4.50 per share."

But wait, there is more good news.

"Furthermore, we issue a proclamation that the other key aspects of every stock option grant for every employee — specifically, the number of shares and, most important, the vesting schedule — shall remain just as they were. So come out, come out, wherever you are, and see the young lady who fell from a star."

(Oh wait, that's *The Wizard of Oz*. I guess I confused Munchkinland and all of the proclamations there with Bizzaro World casinos and companies giving employees do-overs on their stock options.)

Anyway, close the word processing program with your updated résumé and think about what just happened:

- ✔ You still have an option on 10,000 shares of NeverShouldHaveGonePublic.com.

- ✔ The vesting schedule on that stock option grant remains intact, meaning that next month (you've worked there for 11 months, remember), the first 25 percent of your shares will vest (assume a four-year vesting schedule for this example).

- ✔ Best of all, the strike price on your options is $4.50 instead of $14.75!

The catch

Now before you start singing "Ding dong, the bear market is dead," you find out that the company has put a catch on the repriced stock options. Remember our Bizzaro World casino example? The condition given to you by the casino representative was that he'd give you another $100, but only if you agreed to come back to that same slot machine. Well, repriced stock options usually come with a similar catch: Your vesting schedule will continue, but you must agree to stay with the company for some designated period of time, otherwise you will have to forfeit your repriced options, even if the shares are vested!

Companies usually enforce the stay-at-the-company condition through a *blackout period* (see Chapter 8) to the stock option grant you'll receive and have to sign as part of the repricing event. The new grant document will specify all of the details — the original vesting schedule and number of shares, the new strike price, and all of the other terms and conditions that were in your original stock option grant document — but with an additional clause that will specify the following: If you leave the company within the specified period (often six months from the date of the repricing, possibly as much as one year from that date) the whole deal is off.

Worse, if you do resign during that blackout period, none of your shares will be exercisable, even if the stock price has climbed back above the original strike price that you had! For example, suppose that two months after the repricing, the company's stock price skyrocketed to $30 per share because of favorable overall stock market conditions as well as a couple of gigantic new consulting contracts the company has won. However, you receive a job offer from another company for a much higher salary than you're receiving right now, and with far more responsibility than you currently have.

Suppose, then, you resign to accept this new job. You can't turn around and say, "OK, let's forget about this repricing business. I'll go back to my original strike price of $14.75. And because 2,500 of my shares vested last month, I'll take my gains of $38,125 (the $30 market price minus your $14.75 strike price, times 2,500 shares) as a nice farewell present. I'll even buy dinner for everyone at my going-away party!"

Sorry, it doesn't work that way! Your old stock option agreement has been voided; it no longer exists as a legal document. Your new stock option agreement — the one you signed as a condition of receiving the repriced options — clearly stated that you needed to remain employed by the firm for at least six months, otherwise you would not be able to exercise any part of your option, even for vested shares.

(For another example, see Chapter 5 where I discuss what once happened to me with repriced options and how the expiration clause in a stock option agreement can really come back to clobber you if you leave before the repricing-related blackout period is over.)

Repricing and the "big picture"

Leaving aside the "thou shalt remain an employee" catch, repriced options are a pretty good deal, right? After all, everyone wins — the employees who had previously held underwater options, plus the company that entices those employees to hang around rather than go work elsewhere. Nobody loses, right?

Well, not quite. As I note in several other places in this book, the concept of employee stock options is often criticized by stock market experts who focus on company valuation because a significant portion of employee-related costs are "hidden" from the official company accounting. Repricing stock options only complicates the accounting picture. The accounting basis for figuring out future employee costs that will have to be recognized when stock options are exercised becomes even more difficult and imprecise.

Even aside from the accounting issues, repriced stock options come under fire for violating a key principle of equity-based compensation: Employees should be rewarded along with the shareholders of the company when the company's stock price rises, and likewise should be "punished" when the company's stock price falls.

With the options repricing scenario previously described, employees are actually rewarded when the company's stock price falls. The company's stockholders don't get that do-over, though: Someone who bought 100 shares of the company's stock at $59 isn't able to turn those shares in, get his or her $5,900 back, and then pay $450 for that same ownership stake ($4.50 per share × 100 shares), with $5,450 left over that can be invested elsewhere!

True, a company's sinking stock price may simply be from overall stock market conditions or the company's stock price "getting ahead of itself" and going much higher than it should have in a runaway bull market. But whatever the reason, the criticism of stock option repricing has nothing to do with assigning blame. Critics note that the interests of the company's shareholders are compromised when employees get a do-over.

Appalled at the freewheeling and cavalier use of stock option pricing, the powers-that-be changed the accounting rules in the late 1990s with regard to repriced stock options. Without going into all kinds of complicated details, the upshot was that companies that repriced options had to take an accounting charge for doing so, thus affecting their earnings. The objective: To drastically reduce, or even eliminate, the amount of options repricing that was going on.

Keep in mind, though, that repricing still occurs. A company whose stock price has fallen into the penny stock range (around $1 or less) and is still showing significant losses may figure it has nothing to really lose by repricing options, *if* the company's management really feels it can turn the company around. Keeping the workforce intact is a key to the turnaround.

The important thing for you to remember, though, is that even if stock option repricing sounds like a pretty good deal because of the do-over aspects, repricing will only occur after your employer's stock has dropped so significantly that an overwhelming majority of employee stock option grants are very underwater. So even forgetting about the big picture implications, if you find yourself in a repricing situation, then things aren't very pretty at your company, at least at the moment.

Reissued options

A variation on the options repricing theme is when companies don't formally reprice options, but instead reissue new options to employees. However, the existing underwater stock option grants remain intact. *Reissued options* — sometimes referred to as *exchange options* — are a way to get around the accounting conditions of repricing.

The basics

For example, suppose the management at NeverShouldHaveGonePublic.com decides that because of the accounting impact, repricing employees' underwater options is not a viable alternative. Yet, managers are concerned about the escalating employee attrition as their key workers seek greener stock option pastures elsewhere.

The management decides to issue new options to every employee that has underwater options. But unlike repricing, these new option grants are brand new, with a whole new set of terms:

- The strike price will be $4.50 (assuming $4.50 is the current fair market value of the company's stock price).

- Vesting starts from the day these new options are granted rather than picking up an old vesting schedule from previously issued grants.

Reissued options may or may not be done on a share-for-share basis. For example, following the example from the repricing section, if you have an underwater stock option for 10,000 shares, you might receive a new reissued grant for 10,000 shares; or alternatively, you might receive a new reissued grant for a number of shares might be less than your total number of underwater shares (for example, you receive a new grant for 7,500 shares rather than 10,000 shares).

Suppose, though that you do receive a new grant as part of a reissuing event by NeverShouldHaveGonePublic.com for 10,000 shares. As shown in Figure 19-1, you now have options on 20,000 shares!

Table 19-1 Total Stock Option Holdings After a Reissuing Event		
Date of Grant	**# Shares**	**Strike Price**
January 5, 2000	10,000	$14.75
December 5, 2000	10,000	$4.50

Typically, a reissued stock option grant will have the same vesting percentages that your original grant did; only the actual vesting dates will be different. So if your at-hire grant for 10,000 shares was effective January 5, 2000, you will still have (assuming 4-year vesting) 2,500 shares vested on January 5, 2001. For your reissued grant — say that happened on December 5, 2000 — your first 2,500 shares (again, assuming the same 4-year vesting) from that grant will occur on December 5, 2001. Table 19-2 shows what your consolidated vesting schedule will look like.

Table 19-2	Consolidated Vesting Schedule			
Date of Vesting	# Shares Vested	Strike Price	Which Grant?	Total Shares Vested
January 5, 2001	2,500	$14.75	Original at hire	2,500
December 5, 2001	2,500	$4.50	Reissue event	5,000
January 5, 2002	2,500	$14.75	Original at hire	7,500
December 5, 2002	2,500	$4.50	Reissue event	10,000
January 5, 2003	2,500	$14.75	Original at hire	12,500
December 5, 2003	2,500	$4.50	Reissue event	15,000
January 5, 2004	2,500	$14.75	Original at hire	17,500
December 5, 2004	2,500	$4.50	Reissue event	20,000

Not a bad deal, right? Suppose that on July 1, 2002, the company's stock price has recovered to $30 per share, and you decide to do a cashless exercise on all of your vested shares. Under the original grant you received when you started the job, you would have had 5,000 shares vested on that date, which you could then have exercised and sold for a gain of $15.25 per share, or a total of $76,250.

Now, however, you not only have those 5,000 shares vested but you also have an additional 2,500 from your reissue grant (the first 25 percent that vested on December 5, 2001). And those shares have a strike price of only $4.50. So you do a cashless exercise on those also, for a gain of $25.50 per share, or additional $63,750!

The catch

You're probably thinking that there has to be a catch, and you're right — actually, two catches.

First, many companies that reissue options cancel your old grant that is being "replaced," especially if they're doing a share-for-share reissuance (in the preceding example, giving you an option for 10,000 new shares to replace 10,000 underwater shares). In these cases, a reissuing event is very much like a repricing, except that you don't get to retain your original vesting schedule and you don't get a chance to double the number of shares covered by your option.

The other catch is a bit more subtle. Even if the company does let you keep your original shares when doing a reissuance, those original shares may never ever be in-the-money again. Consider the Internet and technology companies whose stocks crashed 90 percent in a matter of months during 2000. Many employees joined those companies at or near the time when the respective stock prices had peaked. A stock that want from more than $200 per share to under $10 per share is not likely to ever recover to those heights. Or at the very least, it will take many, many years of flawless business execution to ever have the investing public place a valuation of more than $200 per share on that company's stock.

So even if a former high-flying company (in terms of their stock price, that is) still lets you retain your option for, say, 3,000 shares with a strike price of $195 per share when they reissue you a new grant for 3,000 shares at the new low price of $2.75 per share, the chances of your original option expiring after 10 years without ever being in-the-money are just about 100 percent.

Sometimes, though, you do find a variation on the reissuance theme that does resemble the scenario shown in Table 19-2 and your ability to benefit from reissued options in the long run. Suppose you work for a "real" company whose stock went on a "ride to the stars" just as the shares of Dell, Intel, Microsoft, Oracle, Cisco, General Electric, and many other companies did during the 1990s. Now suppose you have a stock market environment like the latter half of 2000, when even well-managed, profitable companies saw their shares get clobbered along with the shares of the dot-coms and other "shooting star" companies that came and went in a blink of an eye.

Concerned about employee stability, management of a "real" company may decide to use a period of stock price weakness to accelerate the granting of new stock options to employees — sort of like a reissuing event, but not necessarily on a 1-for-1 basis.

For example, suppose you had just received a stock option grant for 3,000 shares right when the company's stock price was peaking at $75 per share in March 2000, but by the end of the year, the stock price was sitting in the low $40s. You are next scheduled to receive an annual grant in March 2001 for an expected 3,000 shares. The company may decide to accelerate part or all of your grant to late 2000 or January 2001, to give you the advantage of what is hopefully only a temporary weakness in the company's stock price.

Basically, the company is helping you to average down with your stock options just as an investor might average down with actual shares of stock he or she owns.

(*Averaging down* means that if you own 5,000 shares of stock that cost you $100 per share and you then buy another 5,000 shares after the stock price drops to $50, your average cost per share is $75 for your total holdings.)

You have no guarantees that accelerated grants will work in your favor. If, for example, you receive an accelerated grant in December 2000 but the company's stock price keeps dropping for the next three to four months, then you would have been better off (at least in terms of strike price) if the company waited until March 2001 for your regularly scheduled annual grant. But, just like with buying stock, nobody knows with certainty whether a company's stock price will go up or down, or by how much, so those are the chances you and the company take when trying to "catch a dip" in the company's stock price.

A company that does reissue all underwater stock options but still lets employees hang onto their original grants may very well be compromising its future financial picture and stock price if all of those shares wind up in-the-money and are exercised. Basically, the company's earnings per share will be significantly lower simply because there will be so many more shares outstanding after a reissuing event if the company does not cancel the option grants being superseded by the new grants.

On the other hand, though, a company that is accelerating grants by a few months or as much as a year to help employees try to catch a dip isn't radically violating its own predetermined guidelines for how many options will be outstanding at various times. The primary impact is that a small group of options — those that are granted on an accelerated basis as part of a "quasi-reissuance" — will vest earlier than they might have otherwise done had they been granted when originally anticipated. But, in the long run, the company's overall model for outstanding shares of stock won't be disrupted too significantly.

Reload Options

Imagine Batman's nemesis The Riddler sneering and saying, "Riddle me this, Batman: If you have a stock option for 100 shares and you exercise that option, how could you end up with 100 shares of stock and still have a stock option for 100 shares?"

Batman and Robin figure that The Riddler flunked Stock Options 101, so they subdue him (Pow! Zap!) and send him off to share a jail cell with The Joker. (I'm sure The Riddler would have preferred to be sharing a cell with Catwoman, but that's another story.)

But wait one Bat-minute! The Riddler isn't crazy! It is possible for The Riddler's scenario to actually occur! And this brings me to my discussion about reload options.

(*Note:* Reload options are sometimes called *restoration options* or *replacement options* — gotta stay with those R's!)

Reload option basics

A reload option works just like the term implies: As you exercise shares on an option, the option reloads itself with new shares.

The trick: You use stock, rather than cash, to pay for the shares when you exercise the option, thus enabling the reloading process.

The option needs to be set up as a reload option; that is, language describing a reload feature must appear somewhere in your stock option agreement.

For example, suppose you have a single option for 2,000 shares, all of which are vested. Your strike price is $10 per share, and the company's current stock price is $20 per share. In a "normal" (nonreloading) situation, you would pay $20,000 (2,000 × $10 per share) and, should you decide to hold your stock rather than do a cashless exercise, own 2,000 shares of your company's stock.

With a reload option, however, you could pay the total exercise price of $20,000 with 1,000 shares of company stock (remember that, currently, each share is valued at $20). You receive the 2,000 shares as you would have anyway, but the option reloads itself and now is for 1,000 shares — the number of shares you used to pay for the stock.

The catch: You must own at least 1,000 shares of company stock in order to be able to pay for your shares with the necessary 1,000 shares.

As football announcer John Madden might say, "let's look at this again in slow motion," because the mechanics of reload options are sometimes difficult to understand, let alone the benefits.

1. Suppose that you own exactly 1,000 shares (the amount you'll need to exercise the option), plus you have your option for 2,000 shares. Your stock is worth $20,000 (1,000 shares × $20 per share), and the paper gains on your option total another $20,000 [2,000 shares × ($20 − $10)].

2. If you do a "normal" exercise without the reload, you would have had to come up with $20,000 in cash if you wanted to hold onto the shares you acquire from the exercise. Assuming that you do, you'll have a total of 3,000 shares — your original 1,000 shares plus the 2,000 you acquire — worth a total of $60,000.

3. Alternative Version: If you use shares you currently own to pay for new shares you acquire when you exercise your option, you don't have to come up with $20,000 in cash; you will own 2,000 shares of stock, worth $40,000; and you will have an option on 1,000 shares at $20 per share, which is also the current market price.

Table 19-3 shows the various points and the value of your different assets. For the sake of this example, assume that at the beginning, you have a total of $30,000 in cash in your bank account.

Table 19-3	The Value of Your Assets			
Step	**Your Cash**	**Value of Your Stock**	**Unrealized Gain on Your Stock Options**	**Total Assets**
Step 1: Before Exercising	$30,000	$20,000	$20,000	$70,000
Step 2: After Normal Exercising	$10,000	$60,000	$0	$70,000
Step 3: Alternate Reload Exercise	$30,000	$40,000	$0	$70,000

So, according to Table 19-3, before you do either kind of exercise, your total assets (including any unrealized gain on your stock options) is $70,000; after you do either type of exercise, you still have total assets of $70,000, just with a different allocation. So what's the deal here?

Benefits of using a reload feature

The primary advantage to using a reload feature, according to the answer to a frequently asked question (FAQ) that appears on www.mystockoptions.com (see Chapter 9), is that it "allows you to exercise the original options earlier than you otherwise might have . . . you start your capital gain holding period sooner." So basically, you can do an exercise-and-hold on vested, in-the-money shares covered by your stock option(s) to start the long-term capital gain clock (see Chapter 12), but without having to spend cash to do so.

You have another tax benefit, though. Internal Revenue Code (IRC) Section 1036 specifies that exchanging shares of stock in a corporation for shares of stock in the same corporation, as is the case here, qualifies as a *tax-deferred exchange*. So going back to Step 3 where you take advantage of a reload feature, say that you had previously purchased the 1,000 shares of stock for $7 per share. According to the IRS, you aren't selling those 1,000 shares — which would cause you to realize a taxable gain of $13 per share ($20 – $7) — but instead are taking advantage of the tax-deferred exchange.

After you exercise an option with a reload feature, even though the number of optionable shares may change (as in the preceding example), the expiration date of the option stays the same as it originally was (most likely, 10 years after the date of the original grant).

I review the key points of reloads, because believe me, they get much more complicated:

- ✔ Using a reload feature does not create value — your total assets (including unrealized stock option gains) are the same whether you use a reload feature or not when exercising. You'll just have a different mix between different investments (cash, stock, and stock options).

- ✔ A key advantage of using a reload feature: Being able to exercise and start the long-term capital gains holding period without having to spend a whole bunch of cash to do so.

- ✔ Because you can take advantage of provisions for a tax-deferred exchange, you don't have to pay taxes on the shares you exercise your option because you're not considered to be selling those shares.

Reload option cautions

If you have a nonqualified stock option (NQSO) with a reload feature, then you need to remember that like any NQSO, you will owe ordinary income taxes at the time of exercise on your gains (see Chapter 13). So you need to sit down with a spreadsheet or paper and pen — and I'd also recommend a second set of eyes to double-check your calculations and to help you work through various scenarios — and figure out the tax implications of the exercise.

You should figure into your calculations considerations such as:

- ✔ Interest you can earn on the money you "save" by not having to use your saved cash to pay for your options

- ✔ Other uses you may have for that cash if you need it for personal, business, or other needs

- ✔ All of the factors discussed in other chapters in this book with regard to your decision as to whether you should just take the money and run by doing a cashless exercise versus exercising and holding your shares (for example, company and stock price stability, overall stock market conditions, gains you already have, and so on.)

Complicating factors

Reload features can be even more complicated than the examples and discussion presented above. There is no such thing as a "standard reload feature," as plans can vary from one company to another. Additionally, you have a number of ways in which you are permitted by the IRS to actually use stock you own to pay for your optionable shares and reload the option, some of which are specified by IRS private letter rulings.

If your stock options don't have a reload feature — or if you're considering taking a job that comes with stock options that don't have a reload feature — my advice is not to worry about the whole subject, given how complicated it can be. However, if reload options are part of your stock option picture, then you need to do extensive research. I'd recommend the online sites discussed in Chapter 9, as well as Robert Pastore's book *Stock Options: An Authoritative Guide to Incentive and Nonqualified Stock Options* (PCM Capital Publishing), which discusses in detail IRS private letter rulings and the specifics of various Internal Revenue Code (IRC) sections that apply to reload options, such as Section 1036 for tax-deferred exchanges.

Using Stock Options as Currency

Blame it all on Captain Kirk.

Pretty much anyone who watched television or listened to the radio between 1998 and 2000 saw William Shatner's commercials for Priceline.com, in which he appears as a lounge singer and (ahem) "sings" pop and rock standards such as *Two Tickets to Paradise*.

But aside from being an official spokesman for Priceline.com, Mr. Shatner also inadvertently became an unofficial spokesman for using stock options as a form of currency. In March 1998, Mr. Shatner received options on 125,000 shares of Priceline.com stock in exchange for his spokesmanship role. As the fates would have it, Priceline.com's stock price skyrocketed along with so many other dot-com and Internet-related companies, and the value of Mr. Shatner's options increased like Tribbles.

(For non-Trekkies, Tribbles were little furry creatures in a classic episode of the original Star Trek series. Tribbles multiplied out of control, causing no end of problems for the Enterprise's crew.)

Before you could say "Looks like we got us a convoy," people in all walks of life were trying to emulate Mr. Shatner's good fortunes, requesting — no, make that demanding — pre-IPO stock options as compensation for goods and services. For example:

- ✔ Landlords, especially in the Silicon Valley area of California, wanted pre-IPO stock options in companies to which they leased office space in exchange for cutting their lessees a break on the sky-high Bay Area lease rates.

- ✔ Consulting companies and independent consultants who built Web sites or put in customer relationship management (CRM) systems for dot-coms gleefully accepted stock options as partial payment for services rendered, often cutting the cash part of their total bill by as much as 50 percent. Receiving pre-IPO options was preferrable but if the client had already gone public — what the heck — post-IPO options were almost as good!

> ✔ Advertising agencies increasingly told their dot-com clients, "Forget the cash! How about some of those pre-IPO stock options? We'll help you get all of those 'eyeballs' (Internet-speak for number of people who view a Web site) and page-view counts that will make your stock skyrocket, and we'll all get rich!"

Don't worry, I won't get into yet another diatribe about how the dot-coms and Internet companies came crashing down in 2000; hopefully, you've picked up on that point by now, even if you were on a desert island for most of 2000 and didn't watch the day-by-day deterioration of much of the U.S. stock markets.

The point, though, is this: For one brief shining moment (just like the fictional Camelot, which makes this an appropriate analogy), stock options were the most valued currency in the land — better than cash, better than gold, better than anything. Those who controlled stock options could selectively disburse them as payment for real goods and services without the recipients complaining that (apologies to The Beatles and their *Abbey Road* album) "You never give me your money; you only give me your funny paper."

What happened? Take a look at the boom-and-bust of stock options currency through Mr. Shatner's experiences with his Priceline.com options.

In early 2000, according to SEC filings, Mr. Shatner exercised options on 35,000 of his 125,000 shares at around $95 per share, yielding proceeds of more than $3 million. Not too bad, considering that if he had originally been paid in cash back in 1998 rather than stock options, his fees and royalties probably wouldn't have come anywhere near to $3 million. After all, Priceline.com was a startup, not a long-established company like Nike with its mammoth endorsement contracts for Tiger Woods, Michael Jordan, and other athletes over the years. So by using stock options as a means of currency, everyone seemed to be a winner: Priceline.com got a marquee spokesman, and Mr. Shatner wound up receiving big bucks anyway.

But jump ahead to late 2000, after Priceline.com's stock price tumbled to low single digits. How about Mr. Shatner's remaining 90,000 shares? They were now valued much less than they had been only eight or nine months earlier. Imagine the dialog:

Kirk: "Engine Room! Scotty, we've got to get the stock price higher . . . right now!"

Mr. Scott (in his Scottish accent): "I'm giving her all I can, Capt'n, she's already redlining, and I don't think she can take any more!"

Kirk, turning to Dr. McCoy: "Bones! Can't you do something?"

Dr. McCoy: "Damn it, Jim! I'm only one man!"

Mr. Spock, sighing: "Captain, you're just not being logical."

But whereas Mr. Shatner had the good fortune to hold options that did sky-rocket in value and had the foresight to cash in at least a portion of his gains, there are a whole lot of landlords, advertising agencies, consultancies, and other businesses that basically wound up with very little — and often nothing — in exchange for the goods and/or services they provided. Maybe they accepted pre-IPO options from a company that never wound up going public; or perhaps options were granted in a company that did go public (or was already public), but the stock price never went anywhere. Or maybe the stock price rose and fell before anyone had an inkling that maybe cashing in on some of those options might not be a bad idea.

The key point to remember is that stock options actually are a form of currency, in that they can be exchanged for goods or services if both parties agree to the transaction. However, for a few brief years, recipients of stock options didn't even think about determining the true value of those options. The equations were immutable; they thought that pre-IPO options would quickly become post-IPO options, and the post-IPO stock price would go higher and higher.

My favorite pop culture example of stock options as a means of currency is from a *Doonesbury* cartoon strip in early 2000, in which cartoonist Gary Trudeau satirized the mania. In the strip, a college dean is chastizing a college student for his grades, noting that the student is once again on academic probation. The student replies that the reason for his horrible grades is that he's been spending his time working on his business plan, to which the dean replies that "a few stock options make this go away" ("this" being the student's academic probation).

How appropriate: stock options as the preferred currency through which a bribe is solicited!

As pretty much everyone knows by now, reality reared its head in the world of stock options, giving pause to the ridiculous expectations, at least for a little while. But you could still conceivably find yourself considering a stock option situation that is not related to your employment, which is the focus of almost all of this book. Perhaps you're an expert in your particular field and you're asked to sit on the Board of Directors of a startup software or consulting company. Or maybe you leave your job to become an independent consultant, and a prospective client proposes "paying" you with a combination of cash and stock options.

Whatever the scenario, the same guidelines and emphasis on sensibility and reality that I emphasize with regard to employee stock options should likewise guide whether you accept stock options as a means of exchange for goods or services you provide. If a stable company in which you have a high sense of confidence extends that offer to you and accepting less cash will not cause you any personal or business hardship, then by all means consider the offer.

Or if you're being offered a Board of Directors position that won't take too much of your time, rather than insist on a token cash payment for your services, you may very well benefit from receiving stock options in exchange for your services. If it doesn't work out and the value of the options goes nowhere, then basically you're no worse off for the experience.

If, however, you have office space to rent in a building you own and have a choice between two tenants — a stable company willing to pay cash or a brand-new startup company whose owners are demanding that you accept stock options in their company as a large portion of the lease payment — you should let your instincts guide you. If you have little confidence that the brand-new startup will ever grow into a "real" company, you should look elsewhere for a tenant, especially if the amount of cash you would have to forego will cause a significant financial hardship for you.

The degree to which stock options will be used as a form of currency will rise and fall over time. In times of rising stock markets, especially those that are favorable for IPOs, then increased usage of stock options will be the order of the day. In days of declining markets, people and businesses are more likely to say, "Forget that stock option nonsense! Show me the money!"

Chapter 20

Ten Signs That Your Stock Options Will Be Worth *a Lot*!

In This Chapter

▶ Working at a growing company

▶ Investing in a high-quality management team

▶ Supporting an active Board of Directors

▶ Retaining employees

▶ Emerging as a market leader

▶ Returning customers

▶ Providing good internal systems

▶ Empowering employees

*I*f you're looking for clues that your stock options will someday be very good to you, take a look at this chapter. Notice, though, that not one single item has anything to do with stock market analysts saying that they love your company, or with your company's stock price having skyrocketed in recent months. Instead, take your clues from how well your company is performing, and the stock price will take care of itself.

A Steadily Growing Company

Study your company's financial performance. If your company is privately held and doesn't publish its quarterly numbers, that's no excuse! Ask your manager or the company CEO or *someone* to tell you how the company is doing.

You should see at least three years of steady growth in both the *top line* (company revenue) and *bottom line* (company profits, or at least steadily shrinking losses). None of that late 1990s "voodoo company analysis," like "profits don't matter, only the number of customers visiting your Web site does" for you. You want to regularly hear your company's management tell the employees that sales are increasing, profits are increasing, and everything is on track for that growth to continue.

A Stable and Highly Qualified Management Team

Your company's CEO is well-respected within the company, within your industry, and within the financial and investment community. The company's executive management is battle-tested with varied backgrounds, and they complement each other very well in their respective roles. And you know what? They all seem to really like their jobs!

And then, when you get down a level, you find division and functional managers that are also respected within the company — nobody makes fun of these folks behind their backs! And as the clincher, the management team has stayed around — even those who may have already made a lot of money from their getting-in-early stock options. Bingo! You have just hit the stock option jackpot (or at least you've stacked the deck in your favor).

A Very Active Board of Directors

The role of your company's Board of Directors is to do exactly what the name implies: provide a sense of direction to the company's management team. Even though the Board of Directors doesn't have day-to-day responsibilities like the management team does (aside from executives who also sit on the Board, like your company's CEO), the board is an important part of the overall company leadership. They provide financial guidance.

They provide a broad set of perspectives about what's going on in the marketplace and what opportunities — and dangers — are waiting just ahead. They provide the corporate governance to ensure that your company's management team stays on the right path and doesn't fall prey to temptations. If your Board of Directors does what it's supposed to do, then your company's management team has that extra boost to help sail through any bumps on the road to stock price (and stock option value) growth.

Relatively Low Turnover Among Employees

If your company's roster doesn't resemble a revolving door, that's another good sign! A good company has stability, not only in its managerial ranks but also among the "rank and file." If the faces around you stay the same year after year — except for newcomers, who also stay there year after year — then your company will likely create the critical mass and momentum it needs to do well in its marketplace . . . and increase revenues and profits.

A relatively stable workforce in a great company is very much like a winning sports team in the midst of its glory years. Employees, like a football player or a tennis player's long-time doubles partner, develop a sort of sixth sense about other employees' strengths and weaknesses, and automatically fill in gaps to head off problems. Long-time co-workers also require less management time explaining basic work processes; they (and their managers) can spend more of their time focusing on their primary jobs.

All of these characteristics of a stable workforce often point to long-term, year-after-year success in the marketplace and on the stock market.

Market-leading Products or Services

Jack Welch, the legendary CEO of General Electric, puts it best: Your company has to be number one or number two in its industry. Industry leaders build a loyal customer base through leading-edge products and superior customer service, all of which leads to marketplace dominance. And marketplace dominance leads to steadily increasing revenues and profits, which then leads to the stock price going up, up, and away.

Even though GE has since relaxed that tight number-one-or-two-only restriction when contemplating whether or not to enter new businesses, the concept of marketplace dominance remains a sound one — and a "leading indicator" of sorts in foretelling whether or not your employer will recover from a stock price slump.

Newcomers can and often do shake up a particular pecking order in a given industry. Leading companies occasionally fall from grace, replaced by an upstart. But for the most part, leading companies tend to dominate their respective industries for years: examples include General Electric, Oracle, Microsoft, and Exxon (now ExxonMobil).

Returning Customers

Not only are customers satisfied, but they come back again and again. And each time, they buy more and more!

It doesn't matter whether your company sells consumer goods or business-oriented products or services, such as consulting or financial advice. The pieces of the puzzle all fit together very neatly: Happy customers = repeat customers = increasing revenues and profits = a happy and stable workforce = a good chance for your stock options to increase in value. And if your company's leadership in the executive ranks and on the Board of Directors is watching over all of this as they should, the chances of everything all falling apart are greatly reduced.

Good Internal Systems and Infrastructure

An often overlooked sign of a good company is one with very good internal systems and infrastructure (computers, networks, voice communications, and so on). I've worked for several companies that, on the surface, put a positive spin on how great they were. (Hey, anyone can produce glossy brochures saying they're great.) But as the companies failed, it was interesting to note how out of date their respective systems and infrastructures were.

Without early warning systems that problems were afoot and without a management team that was smart enough to invest in the company's infrastructure (and was just out for a quick buck), the companies went down the tubes. So there's a strong cause-and-effect between systems and infrastructure, and how a company will do in the future.

Employee Empowerment

If your company empowers its employees, chances are that you're working at a winner. By empower, I don't mean the ineffective half-truths that many fly-by-night companies tell recruits — like, "We want employees to be innovative, and we'll fund your ideas," when in reality, all you are is a cog in a wheel.

When your company truly tells you that it will support you if you have a good idea and are willing to go out on a limb and work hard, then you have a company that will continually reinvent itself in the face of ever-changing market conditions. And you know what? Out of those efforts by empowered employees, a winner or two will help the company's stock price — and the value of every employee's stock options.

Thorough New-Employee Training Programs

You and all of your co-workers — and the company's management and Board of Directors — are all part of a team. Yeah, I know that sounds pretty trite, but it's true. And a company that is willing to formally train its new employees to be highly effective members of the team will have far less problems than other companies with a minimal "sign all of this paperwork and then get to work!" kind of employee orientation.

The more thorough your company's training programs are for new employees, the quicker those folks will become productive rather than counterproductive — which will likely help your company's stock price and the value of your stock options.

Chapter 21

Ten Signs That Your Stock Options Will Probably Be *Worthless*!

● ●

In This Chapter

▶ Self-serving management team

▶ Uncaring Board of Directors

▶ Senior managers and other employees leaving

▶ Wearing rose-colored glasses

▶ Finding out about high customer dissatisfaction

▶ Having poor internal systems and infrastructure

▶ Receiving inconsistent internal communications from management

▶ Giving into panic

● ●

*B*eware! If your company exhibits more than one or two of the characteristics discussed in this chapter, then it's highly doubtful that your stock options will ever make you wealthy. In fact, your stock options will probably wind up worthless.

The Serial-Entrepreneur Management Team

Check out the backgrounds of the top executives in your company, particularly the chief executive officer (CEO) and chief financial officer (CFO). If their work history shows that most of them have gone from one startup to another, never lasting at any one company for more than three to four years, watch out. You're very likely working in company that has been founded with the single objective of getting large enough to either be acquired by another company, or to go public with a stock price that stays high enough long enough for those "serial entrepreneurs" to make a lot of money and then move on to their next company.

Please understand that I'm not knocking the entire concept of entrepreneurship. I have great admiration for risk-takers who start and build companies like Dell, Microsoft, and Oracle — companies that have been around for many years and that grow to become leaders in their respective markets. However, you will find a great deal of difference between these start-and-grow entrepreneurs and other entrepreneurs who start companies solely (or at least primarily) to make a quick buck and cash out as quickly as possible, leaving behind the wreckage when the façade they created finally collapses.

If you are working at a startup where the leadership is only interested in sustaining companies long enough to cash out, then the odds are that you and your co-workers will be left out in the cold while those serial entrepreneurs laugh all the way to their next startup.

A Disinterested Friends and Investors–Dominated Board of Directors

In Chapter 20, I mention that an active Board of Directors not only provides a sense of direction to the company's management team but also provides the necessary oversight and corporate governance to help a company grow and prosper.

However, many startup companies' Boards of Directors are little more than another conduit for venture capitalists and other investors, plus friends (read: cronies) of the company's executives, who want to pick up additional stock or stock options by going to a couple of Board meetings each year. Cool travel, good meals; who can beat that?

A disinterested, friends-and-investors dominated Board usually does very little — if anything at all — in the area of corporate governance and guidance. So check out who's on your company's Board of Directors and what their backgrounds are. If the Board is too heavily dominated by cronies and investors, then chances are your company won't be there for the long run, and your stock options will sink in value.

A Revolving Door of Managers

Executives come and go in a company; that's the way the business world works. But if you see too many executives, especially those with large stock option packages, heading out the door for new opportunities, pay attention: They probably have a good idea that, at least for them, there are far greener pastures elsewhere.

When you see late-comer executives — not just the serial entrepreneurs — coming into the company and leaving only a few months later — as was common with many Internet companies in late 2000 and early 2001 — watch out!

Last One Out, Please Turn Out the Lights!

Check out the employee turnover numbers in your company, and watch for these danger signs:

- ✔ A big jump in turnover in the most recent quarter as compared to the previous quarter
- ✔ A big jump in turnover as compared to the same quarter in the previous year
- ✔ A continued upward trend in turnover (that is, one bad quarter wasn't just an anomaly)
- ✔ Much higher turnover than comparatively sized companies in the same industry (you can find out other companies' turnover statistics from Internet financial sites, public companies' SEC filings, and other sources)

If the employee retention (or lack thereof) picture in your company exhibits two or more of the above characteristics, then chances are your company's stability will be affected with corresponding adverse effects on revenues, earnings, and stock price.

Rose-Colored Glasses Syndrome

People in your company, including you, really know what's going on "out there." Are your company's products good ones or are they sad imitators of your competitors' products? Has the skill level among employees been steadily deteriorating?

If you look around and don't like what you see, but the company's management still insists that "all is well!" then the value of your stock options is in serious danger. Every company faces problems and challenges at one time or another. The great companies face those challenges and overcome them — or at least hang in there until external factors such as a poor economy improve.

However, when a company's management refuses to acknowledge problems and challenges, then correcting those deficiencies usually isn't even possible, and things will probably continue to get even worse. And for your stock options: Look out below!

High Levels of Customer Dissatisfaction

As your customers go, so goes your company. (Or something like that.) If your customers are extremely dissatisfied — almost everyone hates your latest products because they're defective, or your company's call center has the lowest problem-resolution rankings in the history of call centers — then before long, those customer problems will filter into your company's sales, earnings, and stock price.

Poor Internal Systems and Infrastructure

A sign of a company that will go nowhere is one with very poor internal systems and infrastructure. You'll usually find a high correlation between a company founded by serial entrepreneurs (discussed earlier in this chapter) and the lack of adequate systems and infrastructure. If they're just in the company for a quick buck, why spend money on computer systems and all of that, right? And it will all eventually tie into a company's financial performance, which will, in turn, reflect in a falling stock price.

Open Talk Among Employees About Leaving

Not only are employees leaving, but the ones who are still working by your side (their numbers dwindling by the day, however) openly talk about the interviews they're going on, really cool opportunities you should check out, or how they can't wait to move on to a real company.

In long-ago days, mutiny and sedition would probably result in a fate you really don't want to think about. These days, the chief casualties are the company's financial performance and its stock price. (Which is a good thing. How would it look if your disgruntled co-workers were made to walk the plank at work?)

Inconsistent Internal Communications from Management

So one day everyone in the company gets an e-mail saying that there will be an upcoming reorganization with everyone primarily assigned to a functional area rather than a geographical office and that details will follow. Weeks and months go by, and then everyone gets another e-mail describing another reorganization with everyone being assigned into some matrix structure and that details will follow.

So what happened to the first reorganization? Did it fall apart for some reason? Did it actually happen, but nobody actually knew it did? Is this new reorganization announcement for real, or just another "smoke screen"?

A hallmark of an outstanding management team is that it not only communicates frequently and openly with employees, but that when situations change — and they will — management immediately informs employees of the change and explains why and discusses what will come next.

Conversely, a manager issuing memos one right after another with little or no follow-through is a good early warning indicator that the company's leadership is somewhat lacking and that rough times are ahead.

A Sense of Panic

When a company is in some type of crisis — serious product recall, an extreme earnings shortfall, or whatever — then cool heads need to prevail. If, however, a sense of panic pervades all levels of the company from top to bottom, then recovery from the crisis may be in doubt, and your stock options may be in for a one-way, no-return trip to oblivion.

Chapter 22

Ten Things to Look for in Your Stock Option Agreement

In This Chapter

▶ Knowing what kind of options you are receiving

▶ Making sure dates are consistent and logical

▶ Looking for inconsistencies in details

▶ Understanding clawback provisions

▶ Reading about provisions for a change of company control

▶ Paying attention to expiration and cancellation details

▶ Knowing what happens if a stock split occurs

▶ Understanding if and when pre-IPO options can be exercised

▶ Noticing differences among your previous and new stock option agreements

*T*his chapter tells you what you need to watch out for in any stock option agreement. (See Chapter 5 for more information on the legal language of stock option agreements.) Make absolutely sure you read and understand every word in the stock option agreement before you sign it — and especially watch out for the items listed in this chapter. If you have any uncertainty or uneasiness about what you're reading in the agreement, you should seek advice from an attorney with experience in stock option plans before signing anything.

What Kind of Options Are You Receiving?

Even though the basic principles of Incentive Stock Options (ISOs) and Non-qualified Stock Options (NQSOs) are the same — you receive a contractually "locked in" price at which you can purchase the specified number of shares in the future, no matter what the market price is then — there are some significant differences between ISOs and NQSOs, particularly in how they're taxed at various stages.

Too often, stock option grantees just focus on the basics — the strike price, the number of shares, and the vesting schedule — and don't even know what kind of options they're being granted!

So take a look at your option agreement, most likely somewhere near the top of the first page, and find out what kind of option you're receiving. If you are receiving options on, say, 10,000 shares with 5,000 under an ISO grant and the remaining 5,000 under an NQSO grant, you will likely receive two different stock option agreements to sign. So check all of your paperwork so you can make intelligent choices when you exercise your options!

Are the Dates Consistent and Logical?

Your stock option agreement will be full of dates: grant date, expiration date, vesting dates, and so on. Make sure that all the dates are consistent (for example, make sure that the expiration date of ten years after the grant date is actually ten years after the grant date) and logical (for example, make sure that a vesting schedule doesn't incorrectly specify the third vesting date prior to the second vesting date).

Are There Inconsistencies in Details?

Make sure that all details in all sections are consistent — not just dates (see the preceding section). And make sure that the shares, places, the strike price are specified, and so on.

Is There a Clawback Provision?

Check out the discussion about clawback provisions in Chapter 18. Ideally, your stock option agreement won't have anything that even resembles the more onerous type of clawback that requires you to forfeit recent stock option profits if you leave the company and go to work for a competitor. However, if the stock option agreement does have such a clause of some variation thereof, make absolutely sure you fully understand all of the consequences, and start thinking about workarounds if you decide to take the job anyway.

Is There a Provision for a Change of Control?

The change of company control can affect your stock options. Make sure you understand what happens to your stock options if the company is sold or goes through some other type of change of control while you're an options-holding employee.

Are the Expiration and Cancellation Details Clear?

You probably won't spend the rest of your career at the same job. So you need to understand exactly what happens to your options if you leave (aside from any clawback provisions that I previously mention) or if your options have or will soon expire under certain circumstances. Understanding what happens to your stock options in the following situations is important:

- When you resign
- When you are fired
- When you are laid off
- When you retire
- When you become disabled and can no longer work
- When you die while still an employee

Are There References to the Company's Stock Option Plan?

Reading your stock option agreement usually isn't enough. As soon as you find a clause that reads something like "as specified in the Company's Stock Option Plan (The Plan)," then you need to demand to receive a copy of that document. The fate of your stock options — and your personal wealth (or lack thereof) — will be directly impacted by that plan.

What Is the Effect of a Stock Split?

Make sure that, if the company's stock splits, the shares that cover your stock options, as well as all applicable strike prices, are similarly adjusted. Otherwise, you're in for some very serious unfortunate consequences that can cause paper wealth to evaporate even if the company's stock price doesn't drop.

What Can You Do and Not Do with Pre-IPO Options?

You may want to exercise pre-IPO options as part of a tax minimization strategy (see Chapter 12), but are you allowed to? And if so, when? Your stock option grant may prohibit you from exercising options while a company is still privately held, or may require you to wait for years to do so. Make sure you know what you can and can't do with those pre-IPO options so you can accurately determine your short-term and long-term strategy for your options.

Are There Differences Among Stock Option Agreement Documents?

Every time you receive a new stock option grant, you receive a new stock option agreement document. Not only should you read that document, but you should compare it side-by-side with every other stock option agreement document you've received at that company, looking for sneaky little changes — or plain old mistakes — that could cause you big problems down the road.

If you find anything that causes you concern, then by all means, ask your boss or stock option plan administrator immediately. And don't sign anything until you do!

Index

• *Numbers & Symbols* •

10 percent Beneficial Owner, 58
1099 form, 99

• *A* •

acquisitions, 227–229, 230–235
  cash deals, 230
  dilutive, 229
  private-private, 234–235
  private-public, 234
  public-private, 235
  public-public, 233–234
  stock deals, 231–233
  stock options, effect on, 235–238
  stock price and, 228–229, 232–233
administrator, stock option plan,
    96, 97–101, 300
affiliate, 57–58
Allen, Paul, 46
Alternative Minimum Tax (AMT), 170
  basis, 209–210
  calculating, 208–209, 220
  credit, 211, 222–223
  deductions, 221
  exemptions, 220–221
  incentive stock options and,
    207–215, 219, 220, 222
  kick in, 208
  rates, 220
  regular tax compared, 221–222
  state tax considerations, 223
  wash sale rules, 214—215
AMT. *See* Alternative Minimum Tax
analysts, opinions of, 249–250
angel investor, 64
applicable law clause, stock option
    agreement, 91
Approved Share Option Schemes, 175
asset allocation, 149

attitude, job
  entrepreneurial, 44–46, 51
  investor, 47–48, 52
  working stiff, 48–49, 52
averaging down, 276–277
Ayco Company, The, 135

• *B* •

B2C companies. *See* business-to-consumer
    (B2C) dot-com companies
basis, 183, 184, 209–210
beta, 162
big guys
  blackout periods, 121, 122
  board members, 59
  convertible debt, 62
  employment contract, 258
  "friends and family" stock programs, 67–68
  insider trading, 57–58, 60, 243–244
  investment vehicles, 60–62
  loans for, 69
  ownership stake in the company, 63–66
  recognizing, 57–59
  restricted stock, 61
  turnover in, 242
  warrants, 62
Black, Fischer, 135
Black Monday, 40
blackout period, 88, 89, 255
  description of, 121–122
  occurrences of, 121
  repricing, 272
  resignation during, 272
  strategy for, 122–123
Black-Scholes Model, 127, 128, 135–136,
    138, 265
Board of Directors, 57–58
  active, 286
  disinterested friends and
    investors–dominated, 292
  types of, 59

bonuses, 114, 255

borrowing money to exercise options, 102

brokerage
 cashless exercise, 100–101
 IPOs and, 106–107
 margin loans, 102
 stock certificates, holding, 98–99
 stock plan, 96–101
 tax forms from, 99

Buffett, Warren, 24

business-to-consumer (B2C) dot-com
  companies, 152, 161–162
 as fad companies, 39
 stock price decline, 38–39

• *C* •

calculators, online, 125–128, 145

California Qualified Stock Option
  (CQSO), 173

calls, 13, 160

Cambridge Technology Partners, 123

Canada, 174–175

capital
 investment, 23, 54
 venture, 23, 64, 226, 230

capital gains
 basis, 183, 184
 in cashless exercise, 183
 distributions, 168
 long-term, 167, 169–170, 185–186, 207, 210
 losses, 184
 Section 83(b) and, 188
 short-term, 169, 185, 205
 state taxation of, 185

Carville, James, 246

cash diversion from salaries, 23–24

cashless exercise, 84–85, 99, 100–101
 of nonqualified stock options, 182–184
 reasons for, 182
 Schedule D reporting of, 192
 tax consequences of, 179–181, 182–184
 tax withholding, 190

cause, termination for, 87, 257–258

certificate, stock, 98–99

Certified Financial Planner (CFP), 150

change of control, 225–238
 acquisitions, 227–229, 230–235
 cash deals, 230
 clause, stock agreement, 75, 87–88,
   114–115, 299
 divestitures, 229–230
 lockups, post-acquisition, 236–237
 mergers, 229
 private company acquired by a private
   company, 234–235
 private company acquired by a public
   company, 234
 public company acquired by a private
   company, 235
 public company acquired by a public
   company, 233–234
 reasons for, 25–227
 stock deals, 231–233
 stock options, effect on, 235–238
 tax implications of, 238

change of control clause, 75, 87–88,
  114–115, 299

chat room, 250

clawback, 258–261, 298

cliff vesting, 14

Clinton, Bill, 246

CNET News.com, 265

Collins, Judy, 27

common stock, 78

communication from management,
  inconsistent internal, 295

company, evaluation of, 285–291–295
 board of directors, 286
 customers, returning, 288
 employee empowerment, 288
 employee turnover, 287
 growth, steady, 285–286
 internal systems and infrastructure, 288
 management, 286
 products or services, 287
 training programs, new-employee, 289

company, future of your, 239–250
 amateurs, opinions of, 250
 analyst, opinions of, 249–250
 cronyism, 245
 economic factors and, 246–247
 insider trading, 242–244

market conditions, adapting to, 247–248
outside influences on, 246–250
restructuring, 241
retention and turnover, 240–242
sales picture, analysis of, 242–243
company loyalty trap, 151
company stock
   buying shares, 151–157
   discount, purchase, 154
   Employee Stock Purchase Plan (ESPP), 153–157
   loyalty trap, 151
company-specific rules, 74
Compaq, 40
compensation. *See also* salary
   assessment of, 43
   from new employer, 261–262
   pre-IPO stock options as, 281
compliance officer, 58
Consider Your Options, 203
conspiracy theory of golden handcuffs, 35–36
contractor status, 263–264
convertible debt, 62
corporate change. *See* change of control
corporate governance, 59
cronyism, 245
currency
   conversion issues, 80
   stock option use as, 281–282
customer
   dissatisfaction, 294
   returning, 288

• D •

Data Warehousing For Dummies, 55
date of stock option agreement, 76–77
death and option expiration, 87, 253
debt, 226
   convertible, 62
deductions
   AMT, 221
   from ordinary income, 169
Dell Computer, 11
Digital Equipment Corporation, 40, 148, 248

directors, 57–58. *See also* Board of Directors
disability and option expiration, 87, 253
disposition of incentive stock option (ISO) shares
   disqualifying, 202–207
   nondisqualifying, 207–211
disqualifying disposition of an incentive stock option, 202–207
   lose money scenario, 206
   make money scenario, 203–206
diversification, 95, 149, 151, 161
divestitures, 229–230
Doonesbury, 283

• E •

early in/early out approach, 46
earnings and stock price, 141–144
economy, 53–55
EDGAR Online, 60, 129, 245
efficient stock market theory, 139–140
Ellison, Larry, 11, 66
employee
   empowerment, 288
   retention, 22–23, 240–242
   talk of leaving, open, 294
   training programs, 289
   turnover, 240–242, 287, 293
employee stock options. *See* stock options
Employee Stock Purchase Plan (ESPP), 153–157
   basics, 153–155
   dangers, 155
   Digital Equipment Corporation example, 40
   stock options and, 156–157
employment. *See also* employment situation; employment termination
   contractor status, 263–264
   leave of absence from, 264–265
   part-time, 263
employment agreement
   stock option grants and, 90–91
   termination provisions of, 257
Employment Rights clause, 89

employment situation
  best, determining, 52–56
  high-risk, high reward, 50, 51–53
  risk-managed situation, 50–51
  risk-reward balance, 52–53
employment termination, 251–266. See
    termination of employment
  during blackout period, 272
  for cause, 87, 257–258
  clawback provisions, 258–261
  employee agreement and, 257–258
  exercising stock options, 85–87
  incentive stock options (ISOs) and,
    252–253
  lawsuits, wrongful termination, 265–266
  new employer, compensation from,
    261–262
  nonqualified stock options (NQSOs)
    and, 253
  pre-IPO options and, 256
  reason for, importance of, 252
  repriced options and, 272
  termination agreements, 254
  underwater options and, 256–257
  vesting and, 85, 253–254
empowerment, employee, 288
England, 175
entrepreneur, management by serial,
    291–292
entrepreneurial approach to stock options,
    44–46
  attitude, 45
  early in/early out approach, 46
  focus, short-term, 45–46
  gains expected, 46
  salary, acceptance of lower, 44–45
  timing, 45
equity investments, 150. See also stock
ESPP. See Employee Stock Purchase Plan
exchange options, 274. See also reissued
    options
exchange ratio, 232
executives. See also big guys
  compensation packages, 245
  cronyism, 245
  golden parachutes, 228

insider trading, 243–244
  ownership stake, company, 63–66
  stable and highly qualified, 286
  turnover, 242, 292–293
exemptions, AMT, 220
exercisability clause, stock option
    agreement, 84
exercise price, 79. See also strike price
exercise-and-hold strategy, 102–103
  estimated tax, filing, 190
exercising stock options, 15–18, 93–103
  cashless, 84–85, 99, 100–101
  condition of employment and, 85–87
  to convert paper wealth to cash, 94
  for diversification, 95
  employment termination and, 252
  exercisability clause, stock option
    agreement, 84
  incentive stock options (ISOs), 201
  mechanics of, 97–99
  from multiple grants, 17–18
  nonqualified stock options (NQSOs),
    179–184, 187–190, 193–197
  paperwork, 96–97
  paying for, 101–103
  pre-IPO options, 99, 110
  procedure, 15–16
  reasons for, 93–95
  to salvage profits, 94–95
  stock certificates, 98–99
  for tax reasons, 95
  timing of, 193–195
  unvested shares, 188–190
expiration date, stock option, 15, 87, 253
expiration of grants
  date, 86
  reasons for, 86–87
  special clauses, 89
extrinsic value of stock options, 128, 136

• F •

fad company, 39–40
failure
  acceptance of, 45
  company, 40

fair market value, 134–135, 187
Federal Reserve, 142
financial planning, 147–162
  beta, 162
  company stock, 151–157
  Employee Stock Purchase Plan (ESPP),
    153–157
  equity investments, 150
  paper wealth, 157–160
  principles of, 149–150
  sector exposure, 161–162
  unvested stock profits, protecting,
    160–161
flipping shares, 107
focus, short-term, 45–46
Form 3, 58, 60
Form 4, 58, 60
Form 5, 58, 60
Form 144, 57, 60, 244
Form 1040, 191–192, 223
Fortune, 259
Fortune 500 ownership model, 66–67
founders, ownership percentage of, 63–65
France, 176
FreeEDGAR.com, 60, 129, 245
Friedman, Richard, 135
"friends and family" stock program,
    67–68, 106

• **G** •

gain in value, 134
Gates, Bill, 11, 46, 66
Geer, Carolyn T., 259
General Electric, 143, 287
Gibson, Mel, 35
Global Tax Guide, 174, 175
golden goodbye, 237–238
golden handcuffs, 34–36
  conspiracy theory, 35–36
  description of, 34–35
golden parachute, 228
governance, corporate, 59
grant, stock option. *See* stock option grant
Grateful Dead, the, 167
Greenspan, Alan, 142

• **H** •

hedging strategies, 161
high-risk, high reward employment
    situation, 50, 51–53

• **I** •

IBM, 40
icons, meaning of, 6–7
incentive stock options (ISOs), 199–216
  contractor status, switching to, 263–264
  conversion to nonqualified stock options
    (NQSOs), 178, 264
  definition, 199–200
  disqualifying disposition, 202–207
  employment termination and, 85, 252–253
  Internal Revenue Code (IRC)
    restrictions, 25
  nondisqualifying disposition, 207–211
  nonqualified stock options compared, 25
  stock option agreement, indication in,
    74–75
  surrender of, 85
  Titanic scenario, 211–214
incentive stock options (ISOs) tax
    consequences
  alternative minimum tax, 170, 207–215,
    219, 220, 222
  capital gains, 205
  disqualifying disposition of shares,
    202–207
  at exercise-time, 201
  at grant-time, 200
  nondisqualifying disposition of shares,
    207–211
  Section 83(b) election, 216
  selling ISO shares, 201–215
income tax. *See* tax
information resources, 125–129
infrastructure, company
  good, 288
  poor, 294

initial public offering (IPO). *See also*
    post-IPO stock options; pre-IPO
    stock options
  basics, 106–107
  canceled, 111, 113
  description of, 105–106
  first day pop, 107
  friends and family options, 106
  "friends and family" stock program, 67–68
  lockup period, 108, 119–121
  over-subscribed, 106–107
  ownership allocation after, 65–66
  price declines, post-IPO, 107
  sequence of events, 106–107
insider trading, 37, 242–243
  blackout periods, 121–123
  Securities Exchange Commission (SEC)
    rules, 57–58
  tracking with the Internet, 60
insider-dominated ownership model, 66
insiderscores.com, 60
institutional investors, 67
insurance policies, 160
Intel, 37, 38
Internal Revenue Code (IRC)
  AMT primer, 220
  Employee Stock Purchase Plan (ESPP), 153
  incentive stock options and, 25, 199–200
  Section 1036, 279, 281
  tax-deferred exchange, 279, 281
internal systems
  good, 288
  poor, 294
international tax considerations, 173–176
  Canada, 174–175
  England, 175
  France, 176
  Ireland, 175
Internet stocks, price decline of, 2, 37,
    38–39, 107, 159
intrinsic value of stock options, 128,
    134–135, 136, 198
Investing For Dummies, 142, 149
investment
  capital, 23, 54
  stock options as, 47–48

investor
  angel, 64
  employee, 64
  philosophy, 47–48, 52
  seed capital, 63–64
IPO. *See* initial public offering
Ireland, 175
ISO. *See* incentive stock options

• J •

Jordan, Michael, 171–172

• K •

Kawamoto, Dawn, 265
Krantz, Matt, *55*
Krieger, Ruderman, and Co., LLC, 127

• L •

Lardner, James, *24*
lawsuits, wrongful termination, 265–266
layoffs, 241, 251, 252, 253–254, 265–266.
    See also termination of employment
leave of absence, 264–265
legal considerations
  lawsuits, wrongful termination, 265–266
  stock option agreement, 73–92
loans
  to exercise options, 102
  for stock option purchase, 69
lockup period
  post-acquisition, 236–237
  post-IPO, 108, 119–121
long-term capital gains, 167, 169–170,
    185–186, 207, 210
loyalty trap, 151

• M •

management. *See also* change of control
  communication from, inconsistent
    internal, 295
  golden parachute, 228
  rose-colored glasses syndrome, 293–294
  serial-entrepreneur, 291–292
  stable and highly qualified, 286

margin loans, 102
market price, 101
maternity leave, 265
medical leave of absence, 264
Medicare tax, 181
mergers, 229
Microsoft, 11, 37, 38, 46, 66, 148
motivation, stock options as, 21–22
mutual funds, 150, 168
MyInternetOptions.com, 128, 136, 145
MyOptionValue.com, 126–127
myStockOptions.com, 59, 125–126, 135, 145, 174, 175

● *N* ●

National Center for Employee Ownership (NCEO), 127, 128
NCEO. *See* National Center for Employee Ownership
New York Times, The, 13
noncompete terms, 254
nondisqualifying disposition of incentive stock options (ISOs), 207–211
nonqualified stock options (NQSOs), 177–198
  definition, 177
  employment termination and, 253
  incentive stock options compared, 2525
  incentive stock options (ISOs) conversion to, 178, 264
  reload options, 280
  rules and guidelines, 25
  stock option agreement, indication in, 74–75
nonqualified stock options (NQSOs), exercising
  cashless, 182–184
  as late as possible, 194–195
  at regular intervals, 195
  as soon as possible, 193–194
  tax consequences of, 179–184
  timing, 193–195
  which to exercise, choosing, 195–197
nonqualified stock options (NQSOs) tax consequences
  capital gains, 184–186

  at exercise-time when holding shares, 179–182
  at exercise-time with cashless exercise, 182–184
  at grant-time, 178–179, 186–187
  Section 83(b) election, 187–190
  tax forms, 191–193
  timing of exercise and, 193–195
  withholding, 190
nonstatutory stock options, 137
notice clause, stock option agreement, 92
NQSO. *See* nonqualified stock options
number of shares, 77–78

● *O* ●

officers
  company, 58, 59
  compliance officer, 58
  ownership stake of, 63–66
online resources, 125–129
option price, 14, 79. *See also* strike price
options. *See* stock options
Oracle, 11, 37, 38, 66
ordinary income, tax on, 169, 179, 180–181, 182, 183–184, 185, 204–206
Orwell, George, 199
owners in waiting, 106
ownership, change in company. *See* change of control
ownership, stages of
  early startup, 63–64
  Fortune 500 stage, 66–67
  post-IPO, 65–66
  pre-IPO after investment, 64–65

● *p* ●

panic, sense of, 295
paper wealth, 157–160
part-time employment, 263
Pastore, Robert, 134, 187, 198, 203, 281
paternity leave, 265
Personal Finance For Dummies, 149
personal situation and stock options, 49, 51–52

philosophy
  entrepreneurial, 44–46, 51
  investor, 47–48, 52
  working stiff, 48–49, 52
portfolio management. *See* financial
      planning
portfolio volatility, 162
post-IPO stock options
  pre-IPO options compared, 114–115
  stock price fluctuation and, 115–116
  stock price runup, 116–117
pre-IPO stock options
  as compensation, 281
  employment termination and, 256
  exercising, 99, 109–111
  failure to go public, 111–114
  post-IPO options compared, 114–115
  pricing, 109
  stock option agreement provisions, 300
  vesting, automatic, 110–111
price-earnings ratio, 141–142
Priceline.com, 281, 282
price-sales ratio, 142
private companies
  acquisitions, 234–235
  failure to go public, 32, 111–114
  going public, 2, 29, 65–66, 110–111
  owners in waiting, 106
  ownership stages, 63–65
  valuation of shares, 108
publicly traded stock options, 13
"pump and dump" scheme, 250
puts, 13, 160

• R •

Raging Bull, 250
real companies *versus* fad companies, 39–40
recession, 246
reissued options, 274–277
  averaging down stock options, 276–277
  basics of, 274–275
  catches, 275–277
  vesting schedule, 274–275

reload options, 277–281
  basics of, 278–279
  benefits of, 279–280
  cautions, 280
  complication, 280–281
reorganization, 295
replacement clause, stock option
      agreement, 88
replacement options, 228. *See also* reload
      options
repricing, 89, 255, 270–273
  basics of, 270–271
  blackout period, 272
  conditions applied to, 271–272
  criticism of, 273
  vesting schedule, 271, 272
resignation, 85–86, 254. *See also*
      termination of employment
  during blackout period, 272
  golden handcuffs, 34–36
restoration options, 228. *See also* reload
      options
restricted stock
  description of, 61
  employee-held, 63
  loans for, 69
  tax implications, 61
restructuring, 241
retention, employee, 22–23, 240–242, 293
retirement, 253. *See also* termination of
      employment
reward, stock options as, 21–22
risk taking, 49, 51–52
risk tolerance, 43
risk-managed employment situation, 50–51

• S •

sabbatical, 265
salary. *See also* compensation
  acceptance of lower, 44, 47
  diverting cash from, 23–24
sales picture, analysis of company, 242–243
Schedule D, 192–193
Scholes, Myron, 136
SEC Rule 124, 120

SEC Rule 701, 120
Section 16 Reporting Persons, 58
Section 83(b) election, 187–190
  basics, 188–189
  deadline, 216
  incentive stock option (ISO) shares, 216
  mechanics, 189
  restricted stock, 61
  risks, 189
Securities Exchange Act of 1934, 58
Securities Exchange Commission (SEC)
  filing, company, 112
  Form 144, 57, 60
  insider trading, 57–58
  IPOs, 106
  post-IPO lockup period, 120
  Rule 124, 120
  Rule 701, 120
  Section 16 Reporting Persons, 58
seed capital investors, 63–64
selling out, 225–227
severance packages, 228, 237–238, 254, 258
shareholder rights, 20–21, 90
Shatner, William, 281–283
short-selling, 141
short-term capital gains, 169, 185, 205
signature, stock option agreement, 92
Silicon Investor, 250
social security taxes, maximum, 181
spin-off, 229
split adjustment clause, 82–83
startup company
  management, serial-entrepreneur, 291–292
  ownership stages, 63–64
state tax
  alternative minimum tax and, 223
  capital gains, 185
  equalization program, 172
  'Michael Jordan Law,' 171–172
  from nonqualified stock option
    exercise, 181
  nonresident taxation, 171–173
stock. *See also* stock price
  in acquisitions, 231–233
  certificate, 98–99
  common, 78
  diversification, 149, 151, 161

flipping, 107
  restricted, 61, 63, 69
  shareholder rights, 20–21
  split, 54, 82–83, 300
  stock options compared, 20–21
  tax-deferred exchange, 279, 280, 281
  unvested profits, protecting, 161–162
stock option agreement
  applicable law clause, 91
  blackout clause, 88, 89
  cancellation details, 299
  change of control clause, 75, 87–88,
    114–115, 299
  clauses, list of typical, 75
  clawback provisions, 258–261, 298
  company plan, references to, 91
  company-specific rules, 74
  conditions of employment and
    exercisability, 85–87
  date of agreement, 76–77
  dates, consistency and logic of, 298
  description of, 73–74
  employment condition and, 252, 255
  exercisability clause, 84
  expiration date, 86, 299
  inconsistencies in, 298
  ISO *versus* NQSO, 74–75
  kind of stock, 78
  notice clause, 92
  number of shares, 77–78
  part-time employment status and, 263
  post-IPO lockup period, 120
  pre-IPO provisions, 300
  replacement clause, 88
  repriced options and, 272
  signatures, 92
  split adjustment clause, 82–83
  stock option plan, references to
    company 299
  stock splits and, 300
  strike price, 76–77, 79–80
  "supersedes" verbal clause, 92
  termination provisions, 86–87
  things to look for in, 297–300
  type of option, specification of, 297–298
  vesting schedule, 80–81

stock option grant
  contents of, 13–15
  defined, 12
  expiration date, 15, 87
  number of shares, 14
  strike price, 13–14
  value at grant time, 136–137
  vesting schedule, 14–15
stock option plan, company, 115
  stock option agreement reference to, 299
stock option value, 27–41
  change in, reasons for, 37–38
  determination (valuation) of, 126–128,
      133–145
  failing companies, 40
  future, 38–41, 239–250, 285–289, 292–295
  golden handcuffs, 34–36
  real companies *versus* fad companies,
      39–40
  signs that they will be worth a lot, 285–289
  signs that they will be worthless, 291–295
  timing, influence of, 32–34
  underwater stock options, 31–32, 37–40
  upside, 28–30
stock options
  currency, use as, 281–282
  defined, 12
  as golden handcuffs, 34–36
  reasons for granting, 21–24
  as right *versus* obligation, 19
  stock shares compared, 20
  Titanic Scenario, 211–214
  types of, 13, 24
Stock Options: An Authoritative Guide to
    Incentive and Nonqualified Stock
    Options, 134, 187, 198, 203, 281
stock options, reasons for granting
  diverting cash from salaries, 23–24
  rewarding hard work, 21–22
  stable workforce, building, 22–23
stock price. *See also* strike price
  acquisitions and, 228–229, 232–233
  earnings and, 141–144
  economy and, 246–247
  efficient stock market theory, 139–140
  IPO, 106–107
  overvalued and undervalued, 140–142
  post-IPO, 108–109, 116–117

stock options, effect on, 115–116
  trading ranges, 116
  volatility point, 159
stock price change, reasons for, 37–38
  company-related financial, 37
  insider trading, 37
  marketplace, 37
  timing, 37–38
StockOptionsCentral.com, 127
stock-options.com, 127–128
strike price, 14
  below-market, 136–137
  currency conversion issues, 80
  date of stock option agreement, 76–77
  description of, 13–14
  stock option agreement, listing of, 79–80
"supersedes" verbal clause, 92

• *T* •

tax
  Alternative Minimum Tax (AMT), 170,
      207–215, 219–223
  brackets, 169, 181
  brokerage withholding of, 101
  on capital gains, long-term, 169–170
  on capital gains, short-term, 169
  change of control, implications of, 238
  deductions, 169
  estimated, 190–191
  exchange of stock, tax-deferred, 279,
      280, 281
  forms, 99, 191–193, 223
  incentive stock options (ISOs) and,
      199–216
  international, 173–176
  laws, changes in, 167
  Medicare, 181
  on ordinary income, 169, 179, 180–181,
      182, 183–184, 185, 204–206
  reasons for exercising stock options, 95
  reload options and, 279–281
  Section 83 (b) election, 61
  shelter, 219
  social security, 181
  state, 171–173
  strategy, 165–167
  withholding, 190

tax forms, 99
  estimated tax, 190–191
  Form 1040, 191–192, 223
  Schedule D, 192–193
  W-2, 191
tax strategy
  importance of, 165–166
  tax law change and, 167
tax-deferred exchange, 279, 280, 281
Taxes for Dummies, 193
technology stocks, price decline in, 2, 37
termination agreements, 254
termination of employment, 251–266
  during blackout period, 272
  for cause, 87, 257–258
  clawback provisions, 258–261
  employee agreement and, 257–258
  exercising stock options, 85–87
  incentive stock options (ISOs) and,
      252–253
  lawsuits, wrongful termination, 265–266
  new employer, compensation from,
      261–262
  nonqualified stock options (NQSOs)
      and, 253
  pre-IPO options and, 256
  reason for, importance of, 252
  repriced options and, 272
  termination agreements, 254
  underwater options and, 256–257
  vesting and, 85, 253–254
Thomas, Kaye, 203
timing
  employment, 115
  stock option value and, 32–34, 37–38, 78
total value, 134
trading range, stock price, 116
training programs, new-employee, 289
transfer rights, 90
Tribbles, 281
Trudeau, Gary, *283*
turnover
  employee, 240–242, 287, 293
  executives, 242, 292–293
Tyson, Eric, 142, 149, 193

• *U* •

underwater stock options
  description of, 31–32
  employment termination and, 256–257
  future potential of, 38–41
  nonqualified stock options (NQSOs), 179
  real companies *versus* fad companies,
      39–40
  reasons for, 37–38
  reissued options, 274–277
  repricing, 89, 270–273
uniqueness, value of, 55–56
United Kingdom, 175
US News & World Report, 24
U.S. Stell, 66
USA Today, 55

• *V* •

valuation of stock options, determining,
      126–128, 133–145
  Black-Scholes Model, 135–136, 265
  current worth, 138–139
  fair market value, 134–135
  future worth, 142–145
  gain in value, 134
  at grant time, 136–137
  importance of, 135
  Internet resources for, 145
  intrinsic value, 134–135, 136
  overvaluation and undervaluation,
      140–142
  total value, 134
valuation of stock shares. *See also* stock
      price
  in privately-held company, 108
value of stock options, 27–41
  change in, reasons for, 37–38
  failing companies, 40
  future, 38–41, 239–250, 285–289, 292–295
  golden handcuffs, 34–36
  real companies *versus* fad companies,
      39–40
  signs that they will be worth a lot, 285–289
  signs that they will be worthless, 291–295
  timing, influence of, 32–34
  underwater stock options, 31–32, 37–40
  upside, 28–30

value proposition, 64
venture capital, 23, 64, 226, 230
vesting
  accelerated, 236, 253–254
  cliff vesting, 14
  description of, 14–15
  employment termination and, 252, 255
  golden handcuffs, 34–36
  multiyear, 34
  pre-IPO options, 110–111
  restricted stock, 61
  termination of employment and, 85
  unvested shares, exercising, 188–190
vesting schedule, 14–15
  employee retention and, 22–23
  incentive stock options (ISOs), 200
  leave of absence, effect of, 264–265
  multiyear, 80–81
  reissued options, 274–275
  repricing, 271, 272
  staggered, 83
  stock option agreement specification
    of, 80–81
volatility point, 159
volatility, portfolio, 162

• W •

W-2, 191
Wall Street Journal, The, 13
warrants, 62

wash sale, 214–215
Web sites
  CNET News.com, 265
  EDGAR Online, 60, 129, 245
  fortune.com, 259
  FreeEDGAR.com, 60, 129, 245
  insiderscores.com, 60
  Internal Revenue Service, 220
  MyInternetOptions.com, 128, 136, 145
  MyOptionValue.com, 126–127
  myStockOptions.com, 59, 125–126, 135,
    145, 174, 175
  National Center for Employee Ownership
    (NCEO), 127, 128
  Raging Bull, 250
  Silicon Investor, 250
  StockOptionsCentral.com, 127
  stock-options.com, 127–128
Welch, Jack, 143, 287
Willis, Bruce, 239
workforce, building stable, 22–23, 287
working stiff philosophy for stock options,
  48–49
worth of stock options. *See* value of stock
  options
wrongful termination lawsuits, 265–266

• Y •

Yahoo!, 60, 245, 250

FOR DUMMIES®

The easy way to get more done and have more fun

PERSONAL FINANCE

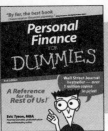

0-7645-5231-7

0-7645-2431-3

0-7645-5331-3

Also available:

Estate Planning For Dummies
(0-7645-5501-4)
401(k)s For Dummies
(0-7645-5468-9)
Frugal Living For Dummies
(0-7645-5403-4)
Microsoft Money "X" For Dummies
(0-7645-1689-2)
Mutual Funds For Dummies
(0-7645-5329-1)

Personal Bankruptcy For Dummies
(0-7645-5498-0)
Quicken "X" For Dummies
(0-7645-1666-3)
Stock Investing For Dummies
(0-7645-5411-5)
Taxes For Dummies 2003
(0-7645-5475-1)

BUSINESS & CAREERS

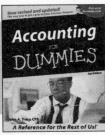

0-7645-5314-3

0-7645-5307-0

0-7645-5471-9

Also available:

Business Plans Kit For Dummies
(0-7645-5365-8)
Consulting For Dummies
(0-7645-5034-9)
Cool Careers For Dummies
(0-7645-5345-3)
Human Resources Kit For Dummies
(0-7645-5131-0)
Managing For Dummies
(1-5688-4858-7)

QuickBooks All-in-One Desk Reference For Dummies
(0-7645-1963-8)
Selling For Dummies
(0-7645-5363-1)
Small Business Kit For Dummies
(0-7645-5093-4)
Starting an eBay Business For Dummies
(0-7645-1547-0)

HEALTH, SPORTS & FITNESS

0-7645-5167-1

0-7645-5146-9

0-7645-5154-X

Also available:

Controlling Cholesterol For Dummies
(0-7645-5440-9)
Dieting For Dummies
(0-7645-5126-4)
High Blood Pressure For Dummies
(0-7645-5424-7)
Martial Arts For Dummies
(0-7645-5358-5)
Menopause For Dummies
(0-7645-5458-1)

Nutrition For Dummies
(0-7645-5180-9)
Power Yoga For Dummies
(0-7645-5342-9)
Thyroid For Dummies
(0-7645-5385-2)
Weight Training For Dummies
(0-7645-5168-X)
Yoga For Dummies
(0-7645-5117-5)

Available wherever books are sold.
Go to www.dummies.com or call 1-877-762-2974 to order direct.

FOR DUMMIES

A world of resources to help you grow

HOME, GARDEN & HOBBIES

Feng Shui FOR DUMMIES
A Reference for the Rest of Us!
0-7645-5295-3

Gardening FOR DUMMIES
A Reference for the Rest of Us!
0-7645-5130-2

Guitar FOR DUMMIES
A Reference for the Rest of Us!
0-7645-5106-X

Also available:

Auto Repair For Dummies
(0-7645-5089-6)

Chess For Dummies
(0-7645-5003-9)

Home Maintenance For Dummies
(0-7645-5215-5)

Organizing For Dummies
(0-7645-5300-3)

Piano For Dummies
(0-7645-5105-1)

Poker For Dummies
(0-7645-5232-5)

Quilting For Dummies
(0-7645-5118-3)

Rock Guitar For Dummies
(0-7645-5356-9)

Roses For Dummies
(0-7645-5202-3)

Sewing For Dummies
(0-7645-5137-X)

FOOD & WINE

Cooking FOR DUMMIES
A Reference for the Rest of Us!
0-7645-5250-3

Cookies FOR DUMMIES
A Reference for the Rest of Us!
0-7645-5390-9

Wine FOR DUMMIES
A Reference for the Rest of Us!
0-7645-5114-0

Also available:

Bartending For Dummies
(0-7645-5051-9)

Chinese Cooking For Dummies
(0-7645-5247-3)

Christmas Cooking For Dummies
(0-7645-5407-7)

Diabetes Cookbook For Dummies
(0-7645-5230-9)

Grilling For Dummies
(0-7645-5076-4)

Low-Fat Cooking For Dummies
(0-7645-5035-7)

Slow Cookers For Dummies
(0-7645-5240-6)

TRAVEL

Italy FOR DUMMIES
A Travel Guide for the Rest of Us!
0-7645-5453-0

Hawaii FOR DUMMIES
A Travel Guide for the Rest of Us!
0-7645-5438-7

Las Vegas FOR DUMMIES
A Travel Guide for the Rest of Us!
0-7645-5448-4

Also available:

America's National Parks For Dummies
(0-7645-6204-5)

Caribbean For Dummies
(0-7645-5445-X)

Cruise Vacations For Dummies 2003
(0-7645-5459-X)

Europe For Dummies
(0-7645-5456-5)

Ireland For Dummies
(0-7645-6199-5)

France For Dummies
(0-7645-6292-4)

London For Dummies
(0-7645-5416-6)

Mexico's Beach Resorts For Dummies
(0-7645-6262-2)

Paris For Dummies
(0-7645-5494-8)

RV Vacations For Dummies
(0-7645-5443-3)

Walt Disney World & Orlando For Dummies
(0-7645-5444-1)

Available wherever books are sold. Go to www.dummies.com or call 1-877-762-2974 to order direct.